T5-AQF-710

DISCARD

DISCARDED BY
Jim Dan Hill Library
U of Wis. – Superior
Superior, Wis. 54880

Teaching Children to Read

RICHARD J. SMITH
DALE D. JOHNSON
UNIVERSITY OF WISCONSIN—MADISON

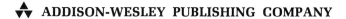 ADDISON-WESLEY PUBLISHING COMPANY

READING, MASSACHUSETTS · MENLO PARK, CALIFORNIA
LONDON · AMSTERDAM · DON MILLS, ONTARIO · SYDNEY

To our families:

Jeannine	Sandy
Karen	Lisa
Theresa	Julie
Suzanne	Kirk
Anthony	

and Joyce Griesbach, our secretary

Credits for extracts: **p. 17**—Reprinted by permission of the publisher from Frank G. Jennings, *This Is Reading,* New York: Teachers College Press, copyright 1965 by Teachers College, Columbia University. **p. 167**—"Reading as Reasoning: A Study of Mistakes in Paragraph Reading," *Journal of Educational Psychology* **8** (1917): 323–332. Copyright 1917 by the American Psychological Association. Reprinted by permission.

The photographs in this book were taken by W. Skot Widemann and Zane Williams.

Copyright © 1976 by Addison-Wesley Publishing Company, Inc. Philippines copyright 1976 by Addison-Wesley Publishing Company, Inc.

All rights reserved. No part of this publication may be reproduced, stored in a retrieval system, or transmitted, in any form or by any means, electronic, mechanical, photocopying, recording, or otherwise, without the prior written permission of the publisher. Printed in the United States of America. Published simultaneously in Canada. Library of Congress Catalog Card No. 75-9016.

ISBN 0-201-07077-4
BCDEFGHIJK-HA-79876

Preface

For a number of years we have been experimenting with content, materials, and activities for preparing teachers to teach reading in elementary schools. The content, materials, and activities that have been evaluated by the students in their reading-methods classes as being most helpful, most interesting, and most inspirational are included in this book. Each of the 14 chapters in the book focuses on an aspect of teaching children to read that we feel is important for elementary school teachers to study; taken as a whole, the book may be used as a complete initial course of study for preparing classroom teachers to teach reading.

The chapters are presented in a sequence that we have followed with our students, and there are references in some chapters to information in other chapters. However, the chapters may be studied in any order preferred by professors and their students, without interfering with the comprehensibility of the book.

Each chapter contains two unique features. The first is the "Suggested Activities for the Methods Class" section. In a sense these activities might be thought of as "laboratory" exercises. Most of them are designed to give teachers the kinds of learning experiences that they are advised to provide for their own students. Professors and their students may engage in all, some, or none of these activities. We have used all of the activities with students in methods classes or in workshops with experienced teachers, and the exercises have been revised according to the users' suggestions.

The second unique feature is the "Teaching Suggestions" section. The suggestions are specific enough to give teachers, especially beginning teachers, the direction they need. They have proved especially helpful to prospective teachers who have a student-teaching assignment either as part of their reading-methods course or shortly thereafter.

Another feature of *Teaching Children to Read* is that we have made clear our personal preferences or biases in regard to teaching children to read. The chapters contain points of view as well as information about how to teach skills, develop positive attitudes toward reading, and foster good reading habits. In addition to being informative, the chapters are intended to be thought provoking and to stimulate post-reading discussion and supplementary reading.

Madison, Wisconsin   R. J. S.
November 1975   D. D. J.

Contents

About the Authors

Richard J. Smith (Ph.D., University of Wisconsin, Madison) has been teaching on the high school and college levels for more than 20 years and is currently Professor of Curriculum and Instruction at the University of Wisconsin, Madison. He has written numerous published research and descriptive articles and several books—including *Teaching Reading in the Middle Grades* (Addison-Wesley, 1974, with Thomas C. Barrett). When he is not busy writing or conducting his classes, Dr. Smith serves as a reading consultant for various school districts in Wisconsin and surrounding states. He is also a member of a medical center learning disabilities team.

Dale D. Johnson (Ph.D., University of Wisconsin, Madison) served as Assistant Dean of the School of Education for three years and is now Associate Professor of Curriculum and Instruction at the University of Wisconsin, Madison. Also a prolific author, Dr. Johnson has many published research and descriptive articles to his credit. He plays an active role in several professional organizations, including the International Reading Association and the National Council of Teachers of English. Dr. Johnson is especially interested in developmental reading.

With the prodigious outpouring of techniques and
methods, gadgets and gimmicks of reading, it
is small wonder that having become so engrossed
with the nuts and bolts of our profession we
seldom lift our eyes to the horizon to see where
we are going.

WALTER PAUK

1 Teaching Reading as a Communication Process

The perception many students form of the reading process is, unfortunately, that reading is the act of saying words—to their teacher or to themselves—depending on whether they are reading orally or silently. They have not learned that reading is in essence an exchange of ideas between an author and themselves. The personal element in reading is often obscured in the mechanics of recognizing and pronouncing words.

In the second act of *Hamlet* Polonius asks, "What do you read, my lord?" and Hamlet replies, "Words, words, words." Hamlet's retort was meant to rebuke the scheming Lord Chamberlain and should not be interpreted as revealing Hamlet's misperception of the reading process. We trust that Hamlet was engaged in extracting ideas, not words, from his book.

A close look at the reading instruction many children receive reveals the cause of their frequent misperception of the nature of the reading process. Children learn what they are taught; unfortunately, they are often taught to read as if the phenomenon of written discourse exists to give children opportunities to mouth words to one another in small groups and under the direction of a teacher who can say them better than any student in the class can. Witty (1968, p. 249) comments:

Certainly pronunciation without understanding is not the aim of modern reading instruction. Nor is meaningless pronunciation thought of as reading. Reading is considered by some as a thinking process through which meaning is obtained from printed symbols. It is recognized that we do not get the meaning of a word—invariably or generally—from its spelling or from its pronunciation. To some of us, failure to obtain meaning is the most significant and unfortunate outcome of faulty or inadequate reading instruction.

Another characteristic of some instructional reading programs—one that in all likelihood detracts from, rather than adds to, students' conceptualization of reading as a communication process—is their emphasis on postreading exercises that require very little thinking about, and very little personal involvement with, the selections. A number of teacher educators have expressed their observations in this regard. Smith (1973, p. 42) says:

Observation of instructional reading programs indicates that the reading experiences that some, and perhaps many, students have in school are more mechanical than meaningful. They produce more correct responses to factual recall questions and multiple-choice tests than satisfaction from sharing ideas with an author. Short selections from basal readers or kits are read, the accompanying comprehension checks are done immediately and quickly, and the selection is promptly forgotten. Students are moved through a progression of short selections and related exercises that often only faintly resemble the communication process that reading should be.*

Jennings (1965, p. 61) is highly critical when he describes the effect of the materials and the reading-related activities many teachers "feed" to children:

The result is sometimes pretty horrible. A lesson or a collection of lessons that has proven effective for one teacher sometime, somewhere is not likely to be effective everywhere. One of the sources of its excellence is that it was originally tailor-made for a specific group of children living in a certain place at a certain time. When these lessons are immortalized . . . they become strait jackets for other teachers. When these lessons are shredded into bits called study helps or "questions" they often cause intellectual indigestion in the reader.†

The point that cannot be overemphasized is that in too many classrooms, the teaching of reading has deteriorated to the point that teachers have become dispensers of commercial reading materials consisting of short selections with coordinated "things to do" or "questions to answer," prescribed by someone other than the teacher. Dealing in a personal and relaxed atmosphere with ideas and feelings that an author wanted to share with readers has become a scarce item in too many elementary classrooms. It is not difficult to understand from observations of reading classes why students learn to value a score of 80 percent more than a relationship with Tom Sawyer through the imagination and via the pen of Mark Twain. They have been taught how to answer questions at the expense of being taught how to read. Bill Martin, Jr. (1967, p. 57) sums up the situation remarkably well:

Children come to first grade with the expectation that they can learn to read immediately. They have absorbed this vision of school from their culture. Imagine their disappointment when their early and impressionable reading experiences begin, not in storybooks filled with memorable language, but in tool books that rob language of its wholeness and reduce dreams to boredom. It is my opinion that many, many children never recover from this disappointment.

----

* Copyright 1973, National Association of Elementary School Principals. All rights reserved.

† Reprinted by permission of the publisher from Frank G. Jennings, *This Is Reading*. New York: Teachers College Press, copyright 1965 by Teachers College, Columbia University.

Perhaps Harper Lee's (1960, p. 37) literary character can help teachers and administrators get a feeling for many children's disappointment with the school program. In *To Kill a Mockingbird,* Scout says:

The remainder of my schooldays were no more auspicious than the first—indeed, they were an endless project that slowly evolved into a unit, in which miles of construction paper and wax crayon were expended by the State of Alabama in its well meaning but fruitless efforts to teach me group dynamics ...I knew nothing except what I gathered from Time Magazine and reading everything I could lay my hands on at home, but as I inched sluggishly along the treadmill of the Maycomb County school system, I could not help receiving the impression that I was being cheated out of something. Out of what I knew not, yet I did not believe that twelve years of unrelieved boredom was exactly what the state had in mind for me.*

Children do get bored with school. More specifically, they get bored with reading instruction. They don't, however, get bored with communicating. Healthy children have a natural inclination to communicate. If this were not so, they would never develop the language abilities they do before they even enter school. Unfortunately, they too often miss the connection between reading and communicating, perhaps because their teachers have themselves failed to see, or at least have failed to teach, the connection.

The word "communication" comes from the Latin *"communis,"* meaning "common." When people communicate, they attempt to establish a "commonness" with someone. Schramm (1973, p. 28) delineates the communication process as follows:

Communication always requires at least three elements—the source, the message, and the destination. A "source" may be an individual (speaking, writing, drawing, gesturing) or a communication organization (like a newspaper, publishing house, television station, or motion picture studio). The "message" may be in the form of ink on paper, sound waves in the air, impulses in an electric current, a wave of the hand, a flag in the air, or any other signal capable of being interpreted meaningfully. The "destination" may be an individual listening, watching, or reading, or a member of a group, such as a discussion group, a lecture audience, a football crowd, or a mob; or an individual member of the particular group we call the "mass audience," such as the reader of a newspaper or a viewer of television.†

---

* From *To Kill A Mockingbird* by Harper Lee. Copyright © 1960 by Harper Lee. Reprinted by permission of J. B. Lippincott Company.

† Wilbur Schramm. "How Communication Works," in *Basic Readings in Communication Theory,* ed. C. David Mortensen, New York: Harper & Row, 1973, p. 28. Reprinted by permission.

This concept of communication is one that should be understood by every teacher of reading and by every child learning to read. As early as kindergarten, children should be taught that their stories originated with authors who put their ideas and feelings in writing so that readers could learn what the authors knew about the world they share through the language they also share. If the stories were written to help the children learn how to read, so be it. They should be just as aware of that intent as the teacher is. Ideally, early in the reading program, students' instructional reading materials will be supplemented with materials written for other purposes, so that other motivations for writing can be recognized and appreciated.

When children discover or speculate about the author's motivation for writing a particular message, they become better receivers of that message. If they know that their story was written to help them learn several new words, they read for that purpose and see the relationship between their reading of the story and the workbook exercises that follow or precede their reading. If they know that they are reading to share with the author the feelings of a boy who lost his dog, they will be better able to verbalize those feelings and to speculate about the experiences and personality of an author who would write about such things. Ultimately, they will be better able to detect propaganda devices, irony, humor, anger, and other elements in written material that make the English language in print the remarkable phenomenon it is. In short, children should be taught to use print as language. In this regard, the definition of the term "logos" might help to clarify the point being made. According to Egan (1973, p. 202):

Logos, in the strict or restricted sense refers to man's ability to translate his real self into language. Logos is language filled with the person who is speaking, and therefore refers to his ability to use speech to express his identity. It also refers to the use man makes of speech in order to establish some kind of growthful interpersonal contact . . . Logos implies a respect for language as a form of communication and contact. It implies dialogue.*

People write and read to be in contact with other people. Teachers who do not keep this concept in the forefront of their awareness are likely not to teach it, and children who do not learn this concept are likely to miss the personally enriching experience of using reading as a communication process.

---

* Gerard Egan. "Logos: Man's Translation of Himself into Language," in *Language: Concepts and Processes,* Englewood Cliffs, N.J.: Prentice-Hall, 1973, p. 202. Reprinted by permission.

Teachers should recognize that for a variety of reasons, some students will attain a higher level of communication through reading than other students will. The intelligence, general language facility, and experiential background each person brings to a reading selection determines to a great extent what he or she is able to take from it. Certain students may never be able to interpret highly figurative language, subtle comparisons, reasoning by analogy, and other devices used by accomplished writers. Some writing is beyond the limitations of some students. But all writing is human communication. Students must be taught that the "source" of the message is another person, that the "message" is generated from an awareness of some part of life that can be shared with other persons, and that they, as the "destination" of the message, must become personally involved before the communication can be completed. The level of involvement varies, but without the involvement of the reader there is no message. The personal ingredients are as necessary for a letter to the editor as they are for a novel, a poem, or a history textbook.

Although the importance and logic of teaching reading as a communication process may seem obvious, it is not difficult to find teachers and instructional materials that are more skillful at pulling the reading process apart than they are at putting it together. Children can be found supplying the letters that have been deleted from words, e.g., c—t, circling an "a," "b," "c," or "d" in response to a question about a statement that was made in the context of a short reading selection, drawing a line under the initial letter of every word in a list that begins with the same sound, and doing other exercises with the reading process in a fractionated state. Although a certain amount of this type of work with reading "components" is necessary to meet most students' needs, the proof of the pudding lies in putting it all together.

To comprehend a written message, the reader must deal effectively not only with the bits and pieces, but also with the whole message. Otto, McMenemy, and Smith (1973, p. 141) say: "The concept of the whole as being equal to the sum of its parts is not true for reading as it is for mathematics. In reading, the whole is greater than the sum of its parts." Therefore, children must have a reading program that emphasizes the reading of wholes rather than the working with parts. Teachers must be careful not to take reading apart so regularly that "all the king's horses and all the king's men" cannot put reading together again —in the mind of the child.

One might ask why it is necessary to keep reminding teachers, or for them to keep reminding themselves, of the true nature of reading and the ultimate goals of the instructional reading program. The answer probably lies in several areas. First, many elementary teachers may not take the time from their busy lives to cultivate their own reading abilities and interests. Consequently, they may not be able to share enjoyable personal reading experiences with their students regularly. Thus, over a period of years, even teachers may lose some of their love for reading. Second, completed exercises from workbooks, kits, or dittoed sheets are more tangible products than are chuckles, frowns, or quiet times with books. (How does a teacher measure and report a child's desire to tell about a reading experience? How can a teacher "grade" a child's absorption in a book or a newspaper article so that parents will know how their children are doing in school?) Third, teachers and administrators have been deluged with a plethora of commercial materials designed to help teachers give their students the best reading instruction money can buy. But commercial kits, games, and books with questions written by someone who never saw the city, let alone the students who go to school there, cannot be as relevant or generate the same enthusiasm in children as can sensitive, creative teachers who are skillful at designing reading-related tasks that meet the needs of their students at a given time. Teachers are the greatest resource children have for bridging the gap between themselves and authors. Teachers can keep students aware of the "source," the "message," and the "destination" paradigm that helps them attain the proper conceptualization of the reading process.

Teachers, then, should themselves be readers, in the best sense of the word, and give evidence of the value of reading as a personally enriching experience. Teachers must also find ways and be willing to report some of the more subtle but convincing signs that their reading program is "working"—a good class discussion, children reading quietly for increasingly longer periods of time, students wondering about the human characteristics of an author who committed her or his ideas and feelings to print. Finally, teachers must resist the temptation to exchange places with commercially prepared materials as the primary instructional resource children have. If children are to perceive reading as a human enterprise, it must not be depersonalized. Interactions with a "scoring key" are not as beneficial to students' reading growth as are interactions with other human beings.

Suggested Activities for the Methods Class

Activity 1

Read the following article, "Developing Reading Maturity in the Elementary School," with the questions below in mind. Be prepared to share your answers with others in the class, either in small groups or as a total class.
Some things to think about while you read:

1. How would you characterize the tone of the article (e.g., angry, sincere, sarcastic, persuasive)?
2. What may have motivated the author to write the article?
3. Why did the author direct his message to the audience he did?
4. Pretend that the article is an address being made to a group of elementary school principals at a sectional meeting of a convention. When the chairman of the sectional asks for questions or comments, one principal rises and speaks. Describe the principal in as much detail as possible and quote the words that were spoken. (This question is more effective if it is answered by each student privately in writing and if the sharing of responses is done by reading the written creations orally.)

DEVELOPING READING MATURITY IN THE ELEMENTARY SCHOOL
RICHARD J. SMITH*

The ultimate objective of reading instruction is to provide students with skills and attitudes necessary for them to use print to enrich their lives. Reading instruction which falls short of this goal is a failure. Print is a symbol system and Moffett says the following about symbol systems: "Symbol systems are not primarily about themselves; they are about other subjects. When a student 'learns' one of these systems, he 'learns' to operate it. The main point is to think and talk about other things by means of this system."[1] As instructional leaders elementary school principals are in a good position to assess the teaching of reading in their buildings to discover whether their students are or are not being taught to use reading to think and talk about other things.
Observation of instructional reading programs indicates that the reading experiences some, perhaps many students have in school are more mechanical than meaningful, more productive of correct responses to factual recall questions and multiple-choice tests than productive of satisfaction from sharing ideas with an author. Short selections from basal readers or kits are read, the accompanying comprehension checks are done immediately and quickly and the selection is promptly forgotten. Students are moved through a progression of short selections and related exercises that often only faintly resemble the communication process that reading should be. However, the selections and exercises do resemble the tasks students are asked to per-

* Copyright 1973, National Association of Elementary School Principals. All rights reserved.

form on standardized reading achievement tests. Consequently, students may be evaluated as superior readers when in fact they are relatively immature readers in regard to their ability to use reading to solve problems, apply ideas read about in one content area to another, detect an author's bias, evaluate their own biases, see themselves in a literary character, or arrive at a new idea not directly expressed by the author. Otto and Smith say, "The student who brings the full range of his thinking and feeling powers to a reading act is a mature reader. He comprehends not only the stated but also the implied meanings of the author. He recognizes and responds to nuances of language and subtleties of meaning. As he reads, he learns, applies, analyzes, synthesizes and evaluates. He is satisfied, frustrated, delighted, disquieted. He is personally changed by a reading experience, and the change is reflected in his behavior." [2]

Principals and other instructional leaders need to employ some guidelines that go beyond the findings of standardized tests to ascertain whether or not reading maturity is being developed as part of the reading program. The content of the materials, the instructional practices of the teachers and the reading-related activities of the students must be carefully examined. Reading programs need balance, and one dimension of a balanced reading program is thinking that involves analytic, creative, critical and other higher-level cognitive behaviors relative to reading selections. The following questions are meant to be helpful to principals in purchasing materials, supervising teachers and evaluating the effects of the reading program in this regard.

1. *Is the content of the reading material well written and relevant to the students with whom it is used?*

There is no substitute for good material. Interesting characters, vivid descriptions, unified and coherent paragraphs permit students to empathize, visualize and think through an idea with an author. The procedure of some developmental materials have devised elaborate word attack cues, comprehension questions, work sheets and other instructional aids for material that is poorly written and/or not relevant to the experiences and interests of the students for whom it is intended. Attractive packaging sometimes hides dull, meaningless material that students can do little more with than repeat or answer simple questions about. The development of higher-level comprehension skills begins with good poetry, narrative and expository writing.

2. *Are teachers asking questions that require higher-level thinking?*

A number of classroom interaction studies have shown a striking avoidance of the kinds of questions that elicit thinking above the memory level. Questions asked before and after reading can direct students to make applications, see relationships and read beyond the lines of print. Principals might observe their teachers at work and note the frequency with which they ask questions that require more than simple memory-level thinking. They might also observe the behavior of the students and the quality of students' responses to questions.

One indication that a teacher is infrequently asking questions that require higher-level thinking are students with their hands raised before the teacher is finishing asking the question. Students who "jump the gun" have apparently learned to expect questions that can be answered without much thinking. Another indication that a teacher is not asking questions that evoke higher-level thought processes are student responses that rarely if ever go beyond three or four words. Students who are asked frequently to respond to higher-level questions are usually more verbal in their responses than students who become accustomed to answering factual questions that require little qualification or elaboration.

3. *Are teachers providing the thinking time necessary for students to answer questions above the cognitive level of memory?*

The classroom is a busy place with schedules to be maintained and work to be done. It is not uncommon to observe a teacher ask a thought-provoking question, become increasingly uncomfortable as precious seconds are filled with silence, interrupt the thinking going on with more cues to the desired response, and just as students are beginning to put things together in their minds answer the question for them. Teachers have been urged to encourage verbalization and overt activity in their classrooms. But the kind of thinking necessary for developing higher-level comprehension skills often demands quiet reflection which should not be perceived as wasteful.

Some elementary schools have become such "busy" places with students being shuffled from group to group, from special teacher to special teacher or from one subject to another that thinking has become increasingly difficult. The primary business of the school is to provide students with opportunities to think. And reading is one of the best stimulators of thinking available to teachers. A major challenge to elementary school principals in this age of accountability, behavioral objectives, individualization, and pervasive "go-go" atmosphere is to keep thinking in the reading curriculum. Reading maturity is not the kind of phenomenon that occurs automatically as students are rushed through a progression of increasingly difficult selections followed by mutiple-choice questions. Students must be given time to think, talk and write about their reading; teachers must maintain classroom conditions that minimize distractions and encourage thoughtfulness; and principals must resist attempts to overload the curriculum at the expense of the thinking, talking and writing time necessary to the development of reading maturity.

4. *What kinds of activities are teachers involving students in relative to their reading?*

Teachers can teach students to look for relationships, evaluate ideas, create new ideas or products and engage in other mature reading behaviors by getting them involved in activities relative to reading selections. A good story might give rise to a simulated author meets the critics interview, a mock trial of the main character or the creation of a new character or bit of dialogue to interject at some point in the story. An account of some historical happening read in a textbook might lead to a debate, writing a newspaper account of the same event, or designing posters advertising for soldiers for the Continental Army. Choral reading of certain poems or writing plays to dramatize a particular period in the life of a great scientist who was discussed in a reading selection are other ways of helping students see the possibilities for stretching their minds while reading. Teachers who cannot or who do not take the time and expend the energy to get students responding to reading in interesting, meaningful activities are missing opportunities to teach higher-level comprehension skills.

Unfortunately, certain instructional materials that were produced to aid in the individualization of instruction have been extremely effective in taking higher-level thinking out of reading. Students have become conditioned to reading short selections and answering five or ten multiple-choice questions as the only reading-related activity. The questions are constructed to permit students to evaluate their answers as either ·correct or incorrect by referring to an answer key, thereby eliminating any question that requires more than a direct statement or a response of several words to be answered. In the name of "objective measurement" and "individualization" these materials with their post-reading exercises ultimately take the personality out of the highly personal enterprise of reading. There is no substitute for personal interaction relative to reading selections if the development of reading maturity is the goal of reading instruction.

5. *Are teachers providing the experiential background necessary for gaining a full understanding of reading selections?*

What a reader takes away from a reading selection depends to a large extent upon what he brings to it. Seeing implications, detecting subtleties, irony, or cynicism in a reading selection all require some experiential commonalities between the author and the reader. A major cause of poor comprehension is that the author and the reader are playing in different ballparks. As Professor Harold Hill proved in *The Music Man,* "You gotta know the territory."

Teachers must get students "ready" for reading selections if those selections contain unfamiliar vocabulary, difficult concepts or language devices such as figurative language that may be obstacles to experiencing the full impact of an author's message. Perhaps an analogy will make clear the role of the teacher in providing readiness for reading selections that require mature reading. Holidays are usually prepared for by people who want to enjoy them fully. If they are traveling or staying at home they make plans, discuss the meaning of the celebrated day with the children and purchase or make the ingredients that are needed to enhance the holiday. As the day or season nears, their preparations heighten their motivation; and when the anticipated date arrives, their preparations enrich their activities. Too much preparation can cause fatigue and boredom that interfere with the celebration. However, the right amount of preparation results in a more meaningful experience.

One especially important aspect of reading readiness for a particular selection is setting purposes for reading. Helping students read for purpose requires teachers to read the selection before their students read it to discover the opportunities to make applications, to evaluate and to do some thinking within the context of the ideas that are presented. Students can be given a set for reading that directs them to see relationships, pass judgment upon or create additions to the ideational content of a poem, story or piece of expository writing. Telling students to look for certain things or to respond in certain ways to a written message is a powerful technique for getting them to employ higher-level comprehension skills.

6. *Are teachers "readers" in the best sense of the word?*

Wendell Johnson says, "Reading is something we do, not so much with our eyes, as with our knowledge and interests and enthusiasm, our hatred and fondnesses and fears, our evaluations in all their forms and aspects. Because this is so, a fondness for reading is something that a child acquires in much the same way as he catches a cold—by being effectively exposed to someone who already has it." [3] Teachers who are themselves infrequent or superficial readers may pass their limited concept of reading on to their students. Gans says, "When I go into a group, I realize first of all that I carry something in. I reflect what I think reading means." [4] Principals who want their students to develop and use higher-level comprehension skills should hire teachers who are themselves mature readers and who use reading for getting information and for recreation. One aspect of a good interview or conference would be to ask prospective or practicing teachers to discuss something they are currently reading or have read recently.

Principals have a responsibility in regard to teachers' reading habits. They need to encourage the reading of professional *and* non-professional reading just as strongly as they encourage teachers to use innovative grouping plans, behavioral objectives, and skill development assessment exercises. It is difficult to believe that all of the innovations in organizational plans, physical facilities, the writing of objectives and the measurement of skill development are going to have as strong an impact on children's reading growth as their close association with teachers who love to read and who share their reading experiences with their students.

7. *Are students given opportunities to read self-selected material and converse with other students about it?*

Higher-level comprehension skills are more likely to be employed when students are reading material that interests them. Free reading time should be allocated at all grade levels as a major dimension of the school reading program. Unless school time is provided, the students who need reading practice most will get the least. Practice reading is essential for interpretative, critical, creative and other higher-level thinking behaviors to become an integral part of a student's reading performance. Opportunities to converse about reading experiences with other students in small groups without a lot of structure or focus is also important. During these informal discussions students learn what other students get from their reading and by verbalizing their own reactions to a reading selection become more keenly aware of the mental processes one employs while reading.

8. *Are students using reading to satisfy their informational and recreational needs?*

Students who are not learning to use higher-level comprehension skills are likely to find severe limitations in the power of reading to satisfy their personal needs. Students who cannot comprehend beyond the level of literal interpretation will probably turn to sources other than reading to solve their problems. Signs of a well-balanced reading program include students reading books, magazines and newspapers, students asking for books, students using the library and students talking about what they are reading. Students who read only when they are receiving reading instruction are manifestations of a reading program going nowhere.

References

1. James Moffett. "A Structural Curriculum in English," *Harvard Educational Review* **36** Winter 1966): 21. Copyright 1966 by President and Fellows of Harvard College.

2. Wayne Otto and Richard J. Smith. *Administering the School Reading Program,* Boston: Houghton Mifflin, 1970, p. 72.

3. Wendell Johnson. *Your Most Enchanted Listener,* New York: Harper & Row, 1956, p. 123.

4. Roma Gans. "Meeting the Challenges of the Middle Grades," in *What is Reading Doing to the Child?* Highlights from the Sixteenth Annual Reading Conference of Lehigh University, Danville, Ill.: Interstate Printers and Publishers, 1967, p. 65.

Activity 2

Try to recall a reading experience in which you became highly intellectually and/or emotionally involved with the content of the selection. As best you can remember them, tell about the circumstances surrounding the experience (e.g., the material you were reading, the place where you were reading, the time of day or night, your age, your interests or aspirations at the time, and any other conditions that may have been factors in your involvement). After all volunteers have shared their remembrances, make a list of suggestions for teachers who would like their students to have at least one highly absorbing and personal reading experience each year during their elementary school experience.

Activity 3

Make a class list of as many teaching practices and school conditions as you can think of that might actually work against a child's learning to be a mature reader. As a teacher, how might you eliminate or at least decrease some of these practices and conditions?

Teaching Suggestions

Suggestion 1

Plan an instructional session that is intended to achieve the following objectives:

1. The pupil will demonstrate ability to state the probable purpose and motivation of the author. (E.g., the author wanted to show that people can't always do what they would like to do. Maybe once the author got blamed for not doing something someone thought he or she should do.)

2. The pupil will verbalize the effect the author's message had. (E.g., "It made me sad." "I hated reading it." "I would like to read or hear more about this character or this subject.")

3. The pupil will demonstrate willingness to listen and perhaps react to the responses other readers had to the selection.

When identifying the selection, note that some selections lend themselves better to the attainment of the specified objectives than other selections do. Note also the importance of matching the selection to the interest and ability of the pupil. Some commercially prepared materials in kits, workbooks, and basal readers may be used effectively to attain the desired objectives. If the questions that accompany these materials are not suitable, new ones can be constructed by the teacher.

Materials that have in the past been used effectively to attain the desired objectives are letters to the editor, short poems, short plays, advertisements, short stories, and editorials. The stories in the students' readers can be used effectively for primary grade students if the teacher asks the kinds of questions that elicit the desired responses to the stories.

Suggestion 2

Identify a reading selection of the appropriate length and level of difficulty for the pupil(s) with whom you are working or with whom you intend to work. Construct questions that will cause the pupil to attend to:

1. the content of the message
2. the source of the message
3. his or her personal cognitive and affective reactions to the message.

A sample plan that might work well is outlined briefly as follows.

Pupils: Five fourth graders with no intellectual or achievement deficiencies.

Materials: The following poem:

"Sympathy"
by
Richard J. Smith

A truck rolled by, its load piled high.
"My tires hurt," it pouted,
I limped along, my own song gone,
"You're not alone!" I shouted.

Instructional procedures: Before the students read the poem, point out that the quotation marks around the words in the second line indicate that these are the words of the truck. Point out also that the words in quotation marks in the last lines are the words of the person who wrote the poem.

After the students have read the poem, ask the following questions:

1. What do the car and the person in the poem have in common?
2. What words tell you something about how the poet felt when he saw the truck? What words tell you how he felt when he started his journey?
3. Pretend that you or one of your classmates has just asked the poet where he was coming from and where he was going when he saw the truck. Use your imagination and write a response you think he might give. Be ready to share your response with the other students.

REFERENCES

Egan, Gerard. "Logos: Man's Translation of Himself into Language," *Language: Concepts and Processes*, Englewood Cliffs, N.J.: Prentice-Hall, 1973, pp. 197–208.

Jennings, Frank. *This Is Reading*, New York: Bureau of Publications, Teachers College, Columbia University, 1965.

Lee, Harper. *To Kill a Mockingbird*, New York: Popular Library, 1960, p. 37.

Martin, Bill, Jr. "The Impact of Current Reading Practices on Beginning Readers," *What Is Reading Doing to the Child?* Danville, Ill.: The Interstate Printers and Publishers, 1967, pp. 57–63.

Otto, Wayne, Richard McMenemy, and Richard J. Smith. *Corrective and Remedial Teaching,* Boston: Houghton Mifflin, 1973, p. 141.

Pauk, Walter. "Beyond Nuts and Bolts," *Journal of Reading* **11,** 7 (April 1968): 507–508.

Schramm, Wilbur. "How Communication Works," *Basic Readings in Communication Theory,* ed. C. David Mortensen, New York: Harper & Row, 1973.

Smith, Richard J. "Developing Reading Maturity in the Elementary School," *The National Elementary Principal* **LIII,** 1 (Nov./Dec. 1973): 41–45.

Witty, Paul. "Reading Instruction—A Forward Look," *Readings in the Language Arts,* 2d ed., ed. Verna P. Anderson, Paul S. Anderson, Francis Ballantine, and Virgil M. Howes, New York: Macmillan, 1968, pp. 247–266.

A distinction has to be made between the different kinds and levels of reading. For mere survival, functional literacy is needed by everyone in our society. High reading efficiency is required by every specialist in his or her own field ... Some people will rarely use reading for anything beyond the simplest source of information. Some may never use it for entertainment ... We want the schools to make more people in our image. We will never be satisfied with the schools' success. But we can never afford to believe that the difference between us and all those who do not share our interests is a difference of quality. It is required of us that we respect the differences.

FRANK JENNINGS

2 The Nature and Causes of Differences in Reading Growth: Providing for the Differences

The goal of individualized reading instruction is *not* to eliminate individual differences. Among students of any given chronological age, there are wide differences in such characteristics as height, physical strength, health, background experience, oral-language development, ability to solve problems, ability to calculate numbers, and ability to read. The goal of individualized reading instruction is to provide learning tasks for students at or slightly above their present level of development and at a pace commensurate with their individual learning rates.

Materials and reading-related tasks which are so difficult that children perform poorly with them have a retarding rather than a beneficial effect on the students' reading growth. The stumbling, bumbling, tumbling kind of performance that can be observed too frequently in the reading activities of some students is deplorable. No football coach would sharpen the performance of his high school team by sending it against the Green Bay Packers. Nor would he expect all of his players to play like the Packers when they become adults, even if they held double practices and employed a remedial coach. However, to grow in reading ability, children must deal with increasingly sophisticated material and coordinated tasks. The high school football team that would be crushed by the Green Bay Packers would suffer differently, but would nonetheless never realize its potential if it were matched only with elementary school teams. The key to reading growth, then, is instruction with materials and coordinated tasks (e.g., skill-development exercises, conversation, writing activities) that become increasingly difficult or sophisticated in accordance with the individual child's increasing ability to complete such activities successfully.

Teachers at all academic levels must be prepared to provide instruction for students whose differing reading abilities may range from severely retarded to highly accelerated in comparison with the reading level of the majority of students at their chronological age. This is not to imply that the majority of students at any age or grade level are alike. Substantial differences exist within any group of children, regardless of attempts to achieve a homogeneous grouping. Nonetheless, a large percentage of the students in elementary schools throughout the nation do seem to develop in reading ability according to a similar, predictable, and satisfactory growth pattern. Perhaps this pattern is at least in part the result of the curriculum they receive and their teachers' expectations rather than of some innate normal developmental process. We suspect this to be the case and that as schools become more responsive to individual learning differences, the similarity in reading-growth patterns for the "majority" of students will become less apparent. However, for the foreseeable future, teachers can expect many of their students to develop in reading ability at a rate that is slower than that of some of their classmates, faster than that of others, and generally satisfactory to their parents, their teachers, and themselves.

Very often, students' development in reading is referred to in terms of grade-level achievement as determined by their scores on norm-referenced standardized achievement tests. Teachers should understand precisely what grade-level achievement means so that they can correctly interpret a child's placement in reading achievement at any particular grade level. Harris (1970, p. 154) explains how "grade-level achievement" is determined:

In computing the table of "reading grades" that is found in any reading test manual, the test author first classifies his results according to the grade. He then finds the median score for each grade. If the median score of all children in the first month of the fifth grade was 46, any child obtaining a score of 46 is said to have a reading grade of five years and one month, or 5.1.*

By definition, therefore, "grade level" is the point at which one-half of the children tested would be expected to score above and one-half below, assuming that the sample of students used by the test developers was representative of children in the grades sampled. Because reading-achievement tests are at best gross measures of reading ability and because of the difficulty in obtaining truly representative samples for establishing test norms, teachers must be advised to look at children in ways other than their grade-level placements when monitoring their reading growth and evaluating their instructional reading programs. Teachers, administrators, and parents must learn that because of the way in which grade level is determined, the goal of having every child reading at or above grade level is impossible.

Because they serve a population comprised mostly of educationally disadvantaged children, some schools will understandably find that the scores their students make on achievement tests distributed on a curve skewed to the left; that is, with more than half of the students scoring below grade level. Although individual students in these schools may give evidence of excellent reading achievement, most students in these schools will compare unfavorably to students in schools that serve a more advantaged population. Certainly, the goal is to teach every child as much as she or he is able to learn about reading. However, the instructional program is only one factor in a child's reading development. Environmental and personal factors, such as motivation and in-

---

* Albert Harris. *How to Increase Reading Ability,* 5th ed., New York: David McKay, 1970, p. 154. Reprinted by permission.

telligence, are also involved. Therefore, although the majority of the nation's children may cluster around the median score of a representative sample, the majority of the children enrolled in a particular school may cluster substantially above or below the national median.

The point to be made is that teachers, administrators, and parents must learn to accept and to respect individual differences in children's reading development, just as they accept and respect individual differences in other human characteristics and endeavors. Certainly, reading programs should be evaluated frequently and adjustments made to give students the kind of instruction that will enable them to achieve their greatest potential. However, continual explicit or implicit manifestations of frustration, guilt, or anger from people important in a child's life will not speed up that child's reading development. Students who are giving evidence of continuous progress in their reading development should be praised for their accomplishments, regardless of how their progress compares with that of other children in their age group. Although it is important to look at the development of a child in comparison to that of other children, it is more important to look at development in terms of the advantages the child, as an individual, has for learning. When children lack advantages that the educational system *can* provide, the educational system *should* provide those advantages. But individuals and institutions do have limitations, and these limitations must be acknowledged so as to avoid the damage caused to the persons and to the institutions from always being found unsatisfactory in spite of their major, and perhaps best, efforts.

FACTORS AFFECTING READING DEVELOPMENT

The answer to what causes some children to learn to read rapidly and easily whereas other children learn slowly and with great difficulty is in some cases quite obvious and in others obscured in an array of speculation. The emotional characteristics, home environment, and instructional programs that appear to cause some children to prosper seem to have a negative effect on other children's reading growth. In addition, the instruments and procedures available for measuring such phenomena as intelligence, self-concept, emotional stability, minimal neurological abnormalities, attitudes, teacher competence, and reading itself are of questionable validity and reliability. Nevertheless, formal and informal observations of superior, average, and retarded readers, as well as careful study of the nature of the reading process, do permit the identification of factors that apparently figure strongly in the learning-to-read process. These factors are highly interdependent; therefore, it is rarely, if ever, possible to isolate one of the factors and to say with reasonable certainty that "it" is responsible for a child's success or lack of success in learning to read.

Intelligence

Considerable controversy surrounds the definition and the measurement of intelligence. Some people are clearly better able to perform certain kinds of intellectual tasks than are other people. Yet how much their performance is due to training or lack of it and how much can be attributed to innate intellectual ability is a legitimate question in many cases. Although reading achievement (as measured by reading-achievement tests) and intelligence (as measured by intelligence tests) are highly and positively correlated, the validity and reliability of both measures are always questionable. Group-administered instruments are especially untrustworthy.

In spite of their questionable cultural biases and unreliability, individually administered I.Q. tests do apparently tap or assess some of the same aptitudes that are needed for success in learning to read. No one who has observed educable mentally retarded children or even children of low normal intelligence struggle to change money, remember colors, and perform other tasks that are easy for normal children can fail to take intellectual potential, whatever that phenomenon may be, into consideration when accounting for differences in reading development among children of the same chronological age and with similar environmental conditions. Teachers should be cautioned, however, against making unwarranted assumptions, based on I.Q. scores, about a student's development in reading. With good, properly paced instruction, personal support, and encouragement, children with intelligence test scores in the low 80s can be taught many words to serve as a "minimum essential vocabulary" and even to read simple materials. The key is to understand that some children, for no fault of their own and regardless of the instruction they receive, will lag behind most other children in reading development because of low intellectual ability. They need most of all a slower-paced program, realistic expectancies in terms of their ultimate ability to use reading for information and recreation, and patient, understanding teachers. We believe that many students with general behavior problems have been pushed beyond their capabilities. In attempting to keep these children progressing academically with their more intelligent peers, teachers and parents have made them anxious, hostile, and understandably disruptive. Unfortunately, because of unrealistic demands that have been made on them, these students probably never realize the potential for reading they would have realized if their instructional programs had made better provision for their intellectual limitations.

Maturation and Readiness Skills

Unfortunately for some, perhaps many, children, formal reading instruction is given to them before they are ready to profit from it. Consequently, they become confused about the nature and benefits of reading and are subjected to some personally unrewarding and even humiliating experiences. They are crushed by the burden of a task they never should have been given in the first place; by the time they are ready to profit from formal instruction, they are so fearful, antagonistic, and confused, they cannot learn or will no longer try to learn.

Beginning formal reading instruction with children who have poor aural/oral language development is a case in point. Writing is a secondary system. It represents oral language. Therefore, children cannot deal with print until they are able to process oral language. Too many children are asked to decode words before they can discriminate and remember differences in the shapes of the letters or words and in the sounds they represent. Or, they are asked to interpret sentences containing words or concepts they have not encountered in their preschool experiences.

Sometimes, children lack the social and/or emotional maturity to attend to the instructional tasks that are necessary for learning to read, or they lack the motor skills necessary to complete them. These children simply are not able to pay attention to their teachers' instructions or to concentrate on the practice exercises necessary to build reading skills. They shift their attention from one distraction to another, fail to complete assigned activities, or guess at answers. Much of their school time is spent seeking the attention of their teachers and peers. Consequently, they learn few if any reading skills and more poor habits than good ones. What these children need more than formal reading instruction is time to mature and a reading-readiness program that prepares them for formal reading instruction.

Schools are becoming increasingly aware of the need to postpone reading instruction for children who are immature and who lack important readiness skills. Information including readiness test scores and data collected from kindergarten teachers is examined carefully to avoid starting children who are not ready for it in a reading program. Readiness activities are provided for these children either in addition to or instead of formal reading instruction. Postponing reading instruc-

he implied meanings of the author. He recognizes and responds to nuances
•f language and subtleties of meaning. As he reads, he learns, applies, ana-
yzes, synthesizes, and evaluates. He is satisfied, frustrated, delighted, dis-
rusted. He is personally changed by a reading experience, and the change is
eflected in his behavior.*

However, many children require extrinsic rewards to keep them
notivated. They need much verbal praise, charts showing their achieve-
nents, constant or frequent urging, and penalties for failure to com-
)lete assignments or pay attention; in some cases, nothing short of cash
)ayment or tokens that can be redeemed for prizes seems to work (Co-
1en, 1965). Obviously, intrinsic motivation is more powerful in produc-
ng readers in the fullest sense of the term, but teachers and parents
nust be prepared to provide extrinsic rewards for students who require them, because motivation is a powerful factor affecting reading
development.

Physical Condition

Children who are in good physical health are much better able to learn
to read than are children who have aching teeth, runny noses, head-
aches, sore eyes, or other physical ailments. In addition, children who
have poor health are absent from school more frequently than are
healthy children. Mumps, measles, chicken pox, and other childhood
communicable diseases do not in and of themselves cause reading retardation, but they do interrupt the child's instructional program. In
checking the attendance records of students referred for remedial reading instruction, we have become keenly aware of how little time some
of these poor readers spend in school. Furthermore, in teaching such
children, we have been impressed by their lack of energy because of
poor diets, substandard housing, inadequate medical care, and other
factors that contribute to a generally debilitated physical state.

The term "dyslexia" is frequently used in reference to a severe
reading disability that is physiologically based. The condition supposedly results from the abnormal development or some kind of minimal dysfunction of the central nervous system. Some medical and educational specialists believe that the condition is genetic in origin and
that it is transmitted mostly from fathers to their sons. Other specialists
are highly suspect of cerebral developmental lag, minimal cerebral dysfunction, and genetic transmission as causative agents of reading disability. We add our suspicions to those of the latter group. Almost

---

* Wayne Otto and Richard J. Smith. *Administering the School Reading Program,* Boston: Houghton Mifflin, 1970, p. 72. Reprinted by permission.

tion for children who are not ready for it is preferabl
them for failure by trying to teach them to read at
as their more able classmates. When readiness skills
struction can be taught simultaneously, certainly that :
and some publishing companies have developed progra:
that purpose (see Chapter 5).

Of course, some children are ready for actual readir
kindergarten or earlier. Their powers of auditory and vi:
tion are well developed, they can deal with abstraction
make symbol-sound relationships with relative ease. Ir
can attend to tasks for long enough periods of time to le
Children who are likely to profit from reading instruct:
most of their peers usually manifest their readiness b
tions, learning words, and displaying good memory po
words, and stories. Therefore, these children should be
tools of reading; when they manifest readiness, they sh(
aged and helped to learn as much as they can at their o
is a mistake to assume that because *some* three-year-ol
read, *all* three-year-olds can or *should* learn to read. *F*
preschool children is to let the *child* lead the way. The]
early readers report that their children practically tau,
how to read. On the other hand, the child who has to v
to "catch on" and remember probably isn't ready for forr

Motivation

For many reasons, some children are much more eager t
than are others. Children who have learned to value r
respond positively to materials and activities designed to
toward a desire to read are much more likely to becom(
than are children who don't put much effort or enthusi
learning.

Motivation to read may be either intrinsic or extrin
hope that students would come to value reading as a sou:
enrichment. We would like to have them empathize witl
acters, be delighted with the exposition of some historic;
entific enterprise, chuckle or weep inwardly with a poe
in other personally satisfying ways to printed material. T
motivation. Children who develop that kind of motivatior
ers in the fullest sense of the term. Otto and Smith (197(

The student who brings the full range of his thinking and fe(
a reading act is a mature reader. He comprehends not only the

always there are more likely reasons for poor reading growth than minimal cerebral abnormalities that are diagnosed by noting specific reading disabilities such as word and letter reversals and poor visual memory for words. At any rate, the number of "dyslexics" we have encountered in many years of classroom and remedial teaching are too few to convince us that dyslexia, as most specialists define it, is a prevalent condition in elementary schools. Other factors must be highlighted in a consideration of the many factors that affect reading development.

Emotional Condition

Although "riting" and "rithmetic" are important curriculum areas, "reading" is clearly the first "R" in the total elementary school curriculum. Therefore, the pressure placed on children to learn to read by parents, teachers, and administrators is considerable. Some children react well to these pressures and excel. On other children, these pressures appear to have a deleterious effect. The pressures both in and out of school to succeed in reading can create enough anxiety within certain children to interfere with the learning process. These children in effect try too hard to please those who are fearful that they may not learn to read well.

Some children come to school anxious about people or conditions in their lives that have nothing to do with reading. Frequent family quarrels, a death, a divorce, or a serious illness in the family—all elicit worry, fearfulness, defensiveness, hostility, or other strong feelings that interfere with the concentration necessary to learn to read. Children with a great deal of emotional anxiety from one source or another are likely to experience much more difficulty learning to read than are children who are in good emotional health while they are receiving instruction.

Environmental Conditions

A child's environment, both in and out of school, may or may not promote the development of good reading ability. In some homes, families use reading a great deal, and the children in those families learn to regard reading as a valuable and normal daily activity. They come to school already knowing what reading is all about and how to use it for personal enrichment. In other homes, quite the opposite is true. Children never see family members reading, never hear talk about what someone has read, and are infrequently, if ever, read to and talked with about stories and pictures. The only pictures that hold their attention are on television, and the life-style of their families appears to place much greater value on that machine than on books, magazines, and newspapers. We believe that these children are at a great disadvantage in regard to learning to read.

The school environment also exerts a great influence on children's reading growth. Some schools are in a continual state of flux, changing from one organizational plan to another or one reading program to another. Some teachers are warm and supportive in their relationships with children; others are cold and insensitive. Some classrooms are well organized, under control, and conducive to concentration and learning; others are disorganized and at times almost chaotic. In some schools children have easy access to library books and instructional materials, as well as having opportunities and encouragement to use them. In other schools these resources are not utilized as effectively. Some school programs are organized to account for differing attention spans among children, the fatigue factor in learning, and other factors that contribute to learning. Other schools appear to be organized not so much to contribute to learning as for the convenience of administrators, teachers, or the "special" teachers who often serve more than one school.

The Instructional Program

Reading specialists generally agree that probably the major factor in most children's reading development is the instructional program—not only the particular approach to initial instruction and the materials used, but also the degree of individualization, the pacing, grouping plans, diagnostic services, and all other aspects of the reading program. In total, these various aspects determine to a great extent the reading skills, attitudes, and habits that children develop.

Within the parameters of the instructional reading program, broad as they may be, the teacher is in all likelihood the one factor that makes the greatest difference in students' achievements. The critical factor is the ability of the teacher to diagnose students' needs, plan suitable activities, select proper materials, monitor progress, and perform the many necessary teaching tasks skillfully while at the same time motivating students to learn and giving them the right amount and kind of personal support. Although the job is difficult and is both an art and a science, many teachers do it well—not perfectly, but well.

Summary

How maturely, how quickly, and with what expenditure of effort children learn to read, then, depends on many factors. These factors are characterized more by their interrelatedness and overlapping than by their existence in isolation. The question as to what causes some children to learn to read easily whereas others struggle painfully with the task is seldom, if ever, answered simply or with surety. The following scheme highlights some of the major factors operating on and within a child's learning to read:

Intelligence
    Verbal intelligence
    Nonverbal intelligence

Maturation and readiness skills
    Attention span
    Social skills
    Auditory discrimination
    Visual discrimination
    Eye-hand coordination
    Oral-language development

Motivation to read
    Values formed out of school
    Values formed in school

Physical condition
    Auditory acuity
    Visual acuity
    General health
    Neurological development and function

Emotional condition
    Out-of-school pressures
    In-school pressures

Environmental conditions
    Opportunities to use language
    Opportunities to investigate the environment
    Distractions

The instructional program
    The teacher
    Quality of instruction
    Quantity of instruction
    Time of initiation of instruction
    Pacing of program

CHILDREN WITHOUT READING PROBLEMS

Because most children have the intelligence, motivation, emotional stability, and physical health necessary to learn to read and to enjoy reading and because most schools have good teachers, good instructional materials, and good conditions for learning, most children in our country learn to read with relatively little difficulty. So much attention is focused on the children who have trouble learning to read that teachers sometimes receive and give the impression that schools have more failures than successes in teaching children to read. Such is not the case. A day spent visiting classrooms in almost any elementary school will provide ample evidence that most children are learning to read and are enjoying their achievement.

Superior Readers

Educators are becoming increasingly aware of and attentive to children who come to school already knowing how to read. In a study of 2265 children entering kindergarten in the Madison, Wisconsin, public school district, Harty (1975) discovered that 687 were able to name at least 20 letters of the alphabet and that 130 recognized at least four out of five words selected from a basic word list and were able to read at least one out of two 5-word sentences that were shown to them. Admittedly, Madison, Wisconsin, is not representative of the majority of school districts in the country. Nonetheless, some children can and do learn to read before they enter school. Durkin's (1966) longitudinal study of early achievers in reading showed that children who learned to read early and easily tended to retain their accelerated reading development throughout their educational experience.

Teachers must not assume that fast learners who apparently rely heavily on their own resources to learn to read do not need or profit from the resources of a teacher and a good instructional program to aid them in their reading growth. They do indeed need and profit from reading instruction, but a special kind of instruction that takes into consideration their superior ability to learn on their own. In other words, these students' progress should be monitored, guided, and assisted when the need for assistance is indicated. They should not be required to complete the same number or kind of learning tasks that less able students require in order to master the reading process.

Because superior readers learn a great deal about how to read while they are reading, the principal responsibility of their teachers is to keep them reading. This means permitting superior readers to bypass instruction and exercises which may be interesting and challenging for less able students but which amount to drudgery for them. They must have ready access to a variety of reading materials and opportunities to read them without distraction. These fast learners have a voracious appetite for library books, magazines, and other kinds of reading material. Generally, they enjoy selecting their own materials, and usually they select material that they can read with little or no difficulty. If they select a book that is highly interesting but difficult for their level of skill development, they frequently persist in their reading and get what they can from the material, probably learning new vocabulary words, discovering how to interpret difficult sentence structures, and generally improving their reading ability in the process. If the material they select proves to be uninteresting or simply too difficult for their level of skill development, they should be helped to select something different.

If superior readers are left too much on their own, they may either develop some poor reading habits or lose the interest they once had in reading. It follows that if they stop reading, their reading-skills development will also stop. In some respects it is more difficult to "recharge" a one-time reading enthusiast and fast learner than it is to foster gradually the skill development and appreciations of slower learners. Having lost their reading "high," fast learners may reject reading altogether. Their interest in reading will obviously be greater at some times than it is at others, but teachers must guard against the complete "turn-off" that some fast learners have experienced because they have been left too much on their own. The key to the continued progress of these students is to give them the right amount and the right kind of attention. Teachers should be alert for signs that a fast learner needs more attention. Such signs include disruptive behavior, unwillingness to talk about reading selections, showing off, feigning difficulty with reading, and substituting "browsing" for actual reading. Responding to these danger signals immediately may prevent a lifetime, or at least a school life, of unhappiness and poor achievement.

A list of good practices for teachers to follow in regard to their superior readers follows:

1. Meet with them individually—at least twice a week if they are in the primary grades and once a week if they are in the upper grades —to ask them questions and to talk with them about their reading.

2. Monitor their skills development with periodic diagnostic and achievement tests and with exercises from developmental materials (workbooks, kits, selections from basal series).

3. Suggest books or other materials you think they would enjoy reading. If they appear interested, help them find the material you suggest.

4. Let them know you are keeping a record of their reading achieve-

ments, and be explicit about your pleasure with their reading
growth.

5. Arrange for them to share reading experiences with their peers (see
Chapter 3).

6. When you detect or suspect weaknesses in certain skills, give them
the materials and instruction necessary to strengthen the skills. For
example, you might have them work for a period of time with a
group of less able students who are learning those same skills.

7. Don't pressure them into reading "more difficult" material. Their
skills development may be years ahead of most of their peers, but
their interests and life experiences may be very similar to those of
the majority of their fellow students. Assigning or even urging a
fourth grader to read the books assigned in the eighth-grade English class is poor practice, even if that student has scored at the
eighth-grade level on a reading-achievement test.

Developmental Readers

Before selecting "Developmental Readers" as the heading for this subsection, we considered "The Average Reader," "The Student at Grade
Level," and "The Majority of Students." Regardless of how we refer to
them, a large percentage of the students in our nation's elementary
schools do, as we stated earlier, develop in reading ability in a similar,
predictable, and satisfactory growth pattern. Perhaps, as we also said
earlier, this is more the result of the curriculum they receive and of
educators' expectations than of some "innate, normal developmental
process" characteristic of child growth. We will not argue about the
reason for the phenomenon, but for various reasons teachers find a
large number of students who can learn comfortably with materials
and activities designed for the majority of children in a particular age
group. Certainly, teachers should adjust the curriculum for these students as need for a faster or slower pace is indicated; but by and large,
these students can be expected to become mature readers because of
the systematic instruction they receive from year to year in a curriculum designed to meet the needs of a large percentage of students. Their
reading development is not comparable to that of the "fast learners"
described in the preceding subsection, but they don't have any particular difficulty learning to read the materials most school children their
age are able to read. To attempt to make these developmental readers
fast learners is unrealistic, unfair, and unnecessary.

Teachers and administrators should not, as we indicated earlier, expect that the majority of students in their particular school or school district will be developing at a rate that results in specific grade-level scores on achievement tests or in satisfactory performance with materials designed for the grades they are in. The normal curve of distribution is applicable to reading development, but many, perhaps most, schools find that their children's achievement scores are distributed on a curve skewed to either the left or right, depending on the population served by the school or the school district. The achievement of the majority of the students in any school is influenced by the advantages and disadvantages the children bring to school, as well as by the advantages and disadvantages they are given in school. For example, the majority of students in private and suburban schools tend to score higher than the national average on reading-achievement tests; the majority of students in urban, and especially inner-city, areas tend to score lower than the national average. In other words, some schools have more developmental readers than other schools do, and some have fewer.

The point we wish to make is that students who are giving evidence of continuous progress in their reading development should be praised for their accomplishments and should have their instructional program continued at a comfortable pace for them. These students usually do well with basal series (i.e., a series of books at progressive levels of difficulty constructed to serve as the major or basic materials resource for teaching children to read—see Chapter 5 for a thorough discussion) and supplementary materials that are designed to challenge students with increasingly difficult tasks according to the estimated capabilities and pacing needs of a large percentage of children at specific grade or age levels.

Although students developing at a normal rate usually do well with materials that are sequenced according to the grade-level expectancies for most children, teachers should not lock students into these sequences by requiring them to experience all of the materials in the series. Instead, the progress of these students should be monitored by means of periodic informal and formal assessments of skill strengths and weaknesses, and the emphasis and pacing of their instructional program should be adjusted according to their needs. The teacher's responsibility is to modify the sequence of a program to meet the needs of students who, although making good progress, may nonetheless profit from some program individualization.

A list of good practices for teachers to follow in regard to their students whose reading ability is developing at a normal rate follows.

1. Continue the sequence and pacing of the basic program that is apparently working well for them. Shifting to different basic approaches may be confusing to the students and may interrupt the developmental process for them.

2. Supplement the basic program, but only with materials and activities that are coordinated and consistent with the basic program. Programed reading, for example, is not a good supplement for a basic language-experience approach. Nor is a fast-paced synthetic phonics program a good supplement for an approach that provides for the gradual introduction of phonics according to a carefully thought-out developmental program. The difficulty of the material in a third reader in basal series "A" may be very different from that in basal series "B." Supplements should be "supplements," not different basic approaches applied simultaneously. Teaching certain skills out of the context of the basic program may work at cross-purposes to the systematic plan of reading strategies being taught in the basic program.

3. Provide practice exercises in the different skills to the degree that they are needed to give students a reasonable level of competence with those skills. Developmental readers often need to be taught a skill and to practice it with developmental materials before they can apply it in their reading of informational and recreational materials. However, too much practice becomes drudgery. When students demonstrate their ability to perform well with developmental materials, they should spend their time reading for information-getting and for recreational purposes.

4. Keep the students aware of the value of reading as a source of information and pleasure. Developmental readers, because of their success with developmental materials, may lose sight of the reasons for learning how to read. Consequently, when the exercises are no longer necessary or the students tire of the developmental materials, they may avoid reading as much as possible. Teachers should remember that a child who can read but does not is no better served by print than is a child who cannot read. Teachers should strive from the beginning of their reading instruction to balance the program for developmental readers so that it includes skill-building instruction and other kinds of reading activities.

5. Acquaint students with the wide variety of reading materials available to them in our society. Developmental readers may make more use of newspapers, magazines, brochures from service agencies, almanacs, atlases, road maps and materials that are shorter, easier to read, and more functional than novels, biographies and literary classics. Therefore, those materials should be regularly available to them and in

fact an important dimension of their reading program from the time they are able to read and enjoy them.

6. Praise developmental readers for their progress in reading and for the good reading habits they develop. Understandably, teachers are sometimes so impressed with the progress of their superior readers and so concerned about praising poor readers for any progress they make that they neglect to give positive reinforcement to their students who are neither brilliant nor slow in their achievement. Too often we neglect the students who are more strikingly similar to most of their peers than strikingly different.

CHILDREN WITH READING PROBLEMS

Children who are unable to meet their parents' or teachers' expectations in reading have a reading problem. Parents and teachers who accept individual differences in other human characteristics and endeavors often have difficulty looking on individual differences in reading as a natural and expectable human phenomenon. Because reading ability has become equated with success in school and ultimately with economic and social prosperity, persons directly concerned with children's well-being cannot envision anything for students who read poorly except a life filled with failure. Therefore, accepting a child's slower development in reading in comparison to his or her more able peers seems tantamount to irresponsible and unprofessional behavior.

The fact is that individual differences in reading do exist, and some children in our society will never, given our present resources and state of knowledge, read as well as other children. Indeed, some children are so handicapped by low intelligence, emotional instability, poor health, or other conditions that are major obstacles to reading development that the likelihood of their developing the skills and attitudes necessary for them to turn to reading when they need information or want recreation is slight. We certainly would not say that the future will never bring the kind of social technology, genetical engineering, psychological therapy, educational methodology, and curriculum innovation necessary to eradicate reading problems. In the past generation, we have put men on the moon, practically eliminated poliomyelitis, and achieved other feats that were considered forever out of reach. However, at least for the foreseeable years, teachers will need to educate children whose reading retardation ranges from mild to severe. Teachers will need to: (1) help them achieve as much reading ability as they are capable of achieving; (2) give them the information they need with media other than print; (3) teach them to utilize nonprinted media to get information and recreation; and (4) protect their self-esteem from people and forces in a society that assumes that everyone—given the proper determination and schooling—can be a good reader.

Parents, teachers, and even children have often been unrealistic in their expectations of the instructional reading program. They set a standard, which is typically "grade-level" achievement, and then feel angry or guilty (if they are parents), or frustrated (if they are teachers), or worthless (if they are poor readers) when that standard is not met by their offspring, their students, or themselves. By definition, 50 percent of a heterogeneous sample of children at any grade level would score below grade level if the normative sample used by the test developers were a representative sample of children in that grade, and 50 percent would score above.

Our point is not that teachers, parents, and children should placidly accept and do nothing about reading retardation. Rather, the reading potential of children who are slow in learning to read is often reduced by giving them formal reading instruction before they are ready for it and/or by the anxiety within and around themselves that almost surely occurs when they don't perform with reading tasks the way the top 50 percent of the children in their grade perform. We emphasize this point because we feel that this is a basic issue that has been ignored too long, often at the expense of the poor reader's realization of the potential she or he has.

Corrective Readers

We are not unmindful of the dangers of categorizing students on the basis of their performance with a behavior as complex and as strongly characterized by individual differences as reading. However, helping teachers to recognize and respond to different patterns of reading growth is necessary. You should be aware that we are offering you only one way of perceiving and discussing growth patterns among students. The labels that are used are unimportant, and the individual differences within each category soon become obvious to teachers. Nonetheless, patterns can be discerned and described. We hope that our discussion will be seen as a way of helping teachers alter their perceptions from the gross categorizations we provide toward a sharper focus on each student.

Corrective readers might be characterized as follows. (1) They are making progress in their reading development, but their reading skills are not sufficient to allow them to perform the tasks designed or prescribed for students at their grade level. (2) They require slower, more careful instruction, and more repetition and practice. (3) Their skill weaknesses are obvious or at least comparatively easy to diagnose. (4) They give evidence that more help at the classroom level will enable them to narrow the achievement gap between themselves and developmental readers.

These four characteristics suggest that the greatest instructional need of these students is more of their teachers' time. We want to stress that it is their teachers' skillful teaching that is needed, not the administrations of an untrained or semitrained aide or other kind of paraprofessional. Corrective readers need the best instruction and motivation that can be given, because of the special difficulties they have in learning to read. The instruction given them should be carefully focused on the development of specific skills, with a careful eye to the development of positive attitudes toward reading and good self-concepts. Extra worksheets and extra doses of oral reading will not suffice. Unless these children are given extra personal contacts with a well-trained, skillful teacher, they will become increasingly disabled in both skill development and attitudinal development. If teacher aides are available (and we would like all teachers who work with corrective readers to have assistants), they should be given tasks related to the instruction of students without reading problems, thereby giving the best-trained person, the teacher, more opportunities to work with the students who require the most skillful teaching.

The first step in working with corrective readers is to diagnose their skill strengths and weaknesses (diagnostic instruments and procedures are discussed in Chapter 9). The next step is to find instructional materials and to plan activities that permit the students to use successfully their strongest skills. At the same time, new skills are introduced and taught slowly and carefully until they become functional with material at the independent level of difficulty, i.e., material which students can read orally with no more than one or two errors per 100 words and silently with approximately 90 percent accuracy on factual recall items. In our experience, most corrective readers do not suddenly blossom into developmental or superior readers. They require special attention and materials at a lower level of difficulty than those designed for grade-level peers throughout all or most of their elementary-school experience.

Corrective readers need to be shown—through progress charts, grades, the completion of praiseworthy reading-related projects, and other devices and procedures—that they are indeed becoming good readers. Praise for these students for whom learning to read is difficult should be sincere and frequent. This requires assigning them tasks at which they can be successful, given the help of the teacher.

Corrective readers have definite skill weaknesses, and they need specific skills instruction. But they also need recreational reading and information-getting reading experiences. Teachers must guard against developing a program that lacks balance. The teaching of reading as a communication process is a concept that must be kept clearly in mind when teaching corrective readers, so that the reading program for them does not become a progression of skill-development exercises that are never or infrequently used to get information or for pleasure.

Remedial Readers

According to the classification scheme we are using, remedial readers are characterized primarily by the severity of their reading disability in contrast with their other intellectual abilities. Their difficulty in developing reading skills is so great that they make no or very little progress in spite of the best efforts of their classroom teachers. Furthermore, they give no evidence of general intellectual retardation. Their oral-language development, their ability to process ideas they hear, their ability to calculate with numbers, solve problems, and perform other nonreading tasks is normal or sometimes even better than average. Their disability is severe, and it is specific to reading.

The sooner in their schooling that these children are identified and referred to a remedial-reading specialist, the better are the chances for helping them to overcome their reading problem. If their program is not adjusted to permit them to have successful reading experiences, they become frustrated, angry, sometimes disruptive, fearful, and progressively more difficult to teach. Therefore, classroom teachers should be on the alert for generally bright students whose ability to learn to read seems far inferior to their ability to learn in other curriculum areas. When such children are identified, they should be referred to a remedial-reading specialist for diagnosis and therapy.

Often, administrators, teachers, and parents who have not specialized in remedial-reading instruction either overestimate or underestimate the ability of remedial teachers to help children overcome reading problems. Essentially, remedial-reading specialists may be better able than classroom teachers to help remedial readers, for four reasons: (1) remedial teachers may have a larger repertoire of diagnostic instruments, procedures, and techniques to call upon; (2) remedial teachers may have a larger repertoire of instructional approaches, materials, and strategies to experiment with; (3) remedial teachers may be better able to structure the learning environment, e.g., eliminate typical classroom distractions, provide one-to-one or small-group contacts; and (4) remedial teachers are especially committed to focusing their efforts on children who are bright, but who can't learn to read and who almost always present emotional problems that must be attended to concurrently with the reading instruction they receive.

Remedial-reading teachers can guarantee no sure cures. There is much trial and error in what they do. Since the problems they deal with are complex, remedial teachers are not always successful. Sometimes, their lack of success may be attributed to human error, sometimes to their ineptness, sometimes to their working conditions (e.g., unrealistic student load, poor referral system, lack of materials), and sometimes to the complexity of the problem they are trying to overcome.

For remedial-reading instruction to be maximally beneficial, it must be carefully coordinated with the rest of the remedial student's school program. This requires good working relationships and frequent consultations between classroom teachers and remedial teachers. The following guidelines are intended to help classroom teachers increase the likelihood of a successful school experience for remedial readers:

1. Be prepared for the remedial teacher's recommendation that remedial instruction be given in place of, not in addition to, classroom instruction. Remedial readers sometimes require a period of time when they are receiving instruction from only one person, using a particular approach, in a particular setting, under specially designed conditions. For some, perhaps most, remedial readers, the best approach is careful coordination with the classroom program from the outset of remedial instruction. The remedial teacher and the classroom teacher should make these decisions cooperatively.

2. Do not expect noticeable gains in the first year or two of remedial instruction. Severely disabled readers often require four or five years of remedial instruction before their performance is noticeably improved.

3. Follow the remedial teacher's recommendations about giving reading assignments to children receiving remedial instruction. For some remedial readers, short assignments using certain classroom materials are beneficial. For other remedial readers, reading assignments other than those provided by the remedial teacher should be avoided.

4. Give remedial readers opportunities to work with better readers on tasks and projects that don't require much or any reading, e.g., viewing and discussing films and film strips, art projects, listening to and discussing audio tapes and phonograph records, science projects and experiments.

5. Develop a library of audio tapes, filmstrips, and pictures that allow remedial readers to get the information they need without reading.

Senior high school drama and forensic groups and community organizations are often willing and eager to put chapters from textbooks, stories, articles, and other printed material on audio tape for the benefit of remedial readers.

6. Develop a proper perspective about a reading disability. There are many handicaps that interfere with good citizenship and successful living far more than poor reading ability does.

Slow Learners

In the United States all children have a right to expect an education that provides the opportunity to learn as much as they are able to learn. Consequently, children with limited intellectual ability, but who are not so retarded that they qualify for special education, must be provided for in the regular classroom setting. Since reading is an intellectual activity, children with poor visual and auditory memory, decreased awareness of details, and other intellectual abnormalities never develop much proficiency at recognizing words and comprehending printed material.

Children with limited intellectual ability require a later start with formal reading instruction and a slower-paced program than that given to their more able peers. Some publishers have produced programs that include more readiness activities in the initial stages of instruction and reading selections that become progressively more difficult at a much slower rate than that found in programs for more able children. In effect, these programs postpone actual reading tasks while providing more readiness activities and move children more slowly through the developmental reading process. We think that most slow learners profit greatly from these programs that match their developmental growth pattern more closely than other programs do.

Slow learners can learn enough vocabulary, word-attack skills, and comprehension skills to give them considerable facility with simple materials if their interest in reading and learning to read is kept alive. Therefore, teachers should be as concerned about motivation, attitudes, and reading habits for slow learners as they are for the rest of their students.

Recently, we have become aware of programs designed to give slow learners "compensatory" reading skills. The objective seems to be to teach students with poor basic-skill development to skim materials, to summarize selections, and to use atlases, encyclopedias, and other reference materials. We take a dim view of such programs. The abilities that are being termed "compensatory" are more difficult to master than are the basic reading skills and, in our judgment, are most unlikely to be learned to any level of proficiency until the basic skills have been mastered. There are no short cuts to reading maturity, and if there were, slow learners would be the least likely candidates to profit from them.

A CONCLUDING STATEMENT

Perhaps the most difficult task confronting elementary teachers is that of providing for the wide range of individual differences among the children they teach. Perhaps this is also their greatest responsibility.

In Chapter 3 we offer some specific suggestions for individualizing reading instruction, given the existing conditions and available resources in most elementary schools. Although teachers are not tutors and cannot be expected to perform as such, they can be expected to attain a degree of individualization in their teaching. The suggestions and guidelines in Chapters 2 and 3 are intended to impress teachers with their responsibilities in this regard and to give direction toward the achievement of that goal.

Suggested Activities for the Methods Class

Activity 1

Each student in the class should respond to the following questionnaire anonymously. The responses should be shuffled and the class divided into groups of five or six. The sheets with the responses should be divided randomly among the groups for tabulation, study, and interpretation. The interpretations should be presented to the whole class by spokespersons from each group. (Just the answers for each item may be written on a sheet of paper for distribution among the groups.)

Reading-Perception Inventory

1. Rank-order the language arts listed below from 1 to 4, with "1" representing the art with which you feel most proficient and "4" the least.

    _____ Reading   _____ Speaking
    _____ Writing   _____ Listening

2. Check the language art which for you deteriorates most under emotional pressure, e.g., listening to directions when lost, reading after a trying day or after receiving some important news, speaking before an audience, writing an important essay exam.

    _____ Reading   _____ Speaking
    _____ Writing   _____ Listening

3. As best you can remember, how would you now evaluate yourself as a reader when you were:

   a) in the primary grades (K–3)?

   _____ superior   _____ corrective

   _____ developmental   _____ remedial

                       _____ no recollection

   b) in the intermediate grades (4–6)?

   _____ superior   _____ corrective

   _____ developmental   _____ remedial

                       _____ no recollection

   c) in junior high school?

   _____ superior   _____ corrective

   _____ developmental   _____ remedial

                       _____ no recollection

   d) in senior high school?

   _____ superior   _____ corrective

   _____ developmental   _____ remedial

                       _____ no recollection

4. How do you presently perceive yourself as a reader?

   _____ superior   _____ below average

   _____ average   _____ poor

5. Do you remember ever getting any *special* reading instruction, e.g., summer remedial program, reading efficiency course, tutor? Respond below. Was the program designed mostly for:

   _____ students with serious problems?

   _____ students with minor problems?

   _____ students who were basically good readers?

   _____ never received special instruction

6. At the time, was your attitude or feeling about the special instruction you received:

   _____ more positive than negative?

   _____ more negative than positive?

   _____ don't remember

   _____ never received special instruction

7. Would you have liked to talk with a reading specialist about your reading when you were a child?

   _____ yes   _____ no

8. Would you like to talk with a reading specialist about your reading now?

   _____ yes   _____ no

9. Would you like to talk with a reading specialist about the reading of someone you know other than yourself?

_____ yes _____ no

Activity 2

After dividing into groups of three or four, each group or each individual should use the following form to create a hypothetical, logical reading evaluation and should share the finished products for discussion purposes.

1. Name of student: _____

2. Chronological age: _____

3. Present grade: _____

4. Verbal IQ (from Wechsler Intelligence Scale for Children): _____

5. Nonverbal IQ (from Wechsler Intelligence Scale for Children): _____

6. Grade-level placements on latest reading achievement test:

_____ vocabulary

_____ comprehension

_____ rate of comprehension

7. Informal observations of student's reading skills, attitudes and habits:

8. Suspected causes of present reading status:

9. Specific suggestions for instructional program:

Teaching Suggestions

Suggestion 1

Fill in the evaluation form for Activity 2 for an actual student.

Suggestion 2

Identify a corrective reader and a superior reader. For five consecutive days, give them both a 15- to 30-minute silent reading period with books at a reasonably easy level of difficulty. After each reading period, ask them several or all of the following 13 questions suggested by Hunt (1970). Compare their responses.

1. Did you have a good reading period today? Did you read well? Did you get a lot done?
2. Did you read better today than you did yesterday?
3. Were you able to concentrate today on your silent reading?
4. Did the ideas in the book hold your attention? Did you have the feeling of moving right along with them?
5. Did you have the feeling of wanting to go ahead faster to find out what happened? Were you constantly moving ahead to get to the next good part?
6. Was it hard for you to keep your mind on what you were reading today?
7. Were you bothered by others or by outside noises?
8. Could you keep the ideas in your book straight in your mind?
9. Did you get mixed up in any place? Did you have to go back and straighten yourself out?
10. Were there words you did not know? How did you figure them out?
11. What did you do when you got to the good parts? Did you read faster or slower?
12. Were you always counting to see how many pages you had to go? Were you wondering how long it would take you to finish?
13. Were you kind of hoping that the book would go on and on—that it would not really end? *

Suggestion 3

Have one or several private conferences with a remedial reader. After establishing a good rapport, discuss the following questions with him or her in any order that seems most appropriate and comfortable.

1. Would you like school better if you didn't have to do any reading at all?
2. How does your body feel when you have to read in school (tight, scared, eyes hurt, stomach feels funny, sweaty, cold)?
3. Do you think you have more trouble with reading than most other students do? If you think you do, why do you think reading is hard for you?
4. If reading were very easy for you, what kinds of things would you most like to read or to read about?
5. Do you think you will like to read some day more than you do now?

Suggestion 4

Collect four or five 100-word selections at different levels of difficulty, e.g., from second-, third-, fourth-, fifth-, or sixth-grade readers. Identify a corrective reader and a superior reader in the third or fourth grade. In private, have each read the selections orally into a tape recorder, beginning with the easiest selection and progressing to the hardest. When they hesitate on a word for more than five seconds, tell them the word and urge them to continue.

---

* Lyman C. Hunt. "The Effect of Self-Selection, Interest and Motivation upon Independent, Instructional, and Frustrational Levels," *The Reading Teacher* **24,** 2 (November 1970):148. Reprinted with permission of Lyman C. Hunt and the International Reading Association.

Stop the process when you are no longer obtaining insights into their reading strengths and weaknesses. As they are reading, observe the following:

1. General body posture, e.g., slumped, erect, rigid, relaxed
2. Position and movement of feet
3. Hand posture
4. Head movements
5. Characteristics of voice, e.g., high-pitched, frequent swallowing, soft, frequent throat clearing.

After they finish reading, listen to the tape and record the following information for the most difficult selection read.

Characteristics	Superior reader	Corrective reader
Number of five-second hesitations		
Number of omitted words		
Number of substituted words		
Number of added words		
Number of mispronounced words		

	Strength	Weakness
Vocal expression		
Ability to sound words out		
Ability to figure out words from context clues		
General attitude		
Experiential background		
General fluency		

REFERENCES

Cohen, H. L. "Project CASE: Contingencies Applicable for Special Education," Silver Spring, Maryland: Institute for Behavioral Research, 1965.

Durkin, Dolores. *Children Who Read Early,* New York: Teachers College Press, Columbia University, 1966.

Harris, Albert. *How to Increase Reading Ability,* 5th ed., New York: David McKay, 1970.

Harty, Kathleen. "Factors Affecting Preschool Reading Ability," Ph.D. diss., Madison: University of Wisconsin, 1975.

Hunt, Lyman C. "The Effect of Self-Selection, Interest and Motivation upon Independent, Instructional, and Frustration Levels," *The Reading Teacher* **24,** 2 (Nov. 1970): 148.

Jennings, Frank. *This Is Reading,* New York: Bureau of Publications, Teachers College, Columbia University, 1965, p. 194.

Otto, Wayne, and Richard J. Smith. *Administering the School Reading Program,* Boston: Houghton Mifflin, 1970.

The similarities among students are important in planning the curriculum because they are, to a large extent, instructed in groups. Understanding the likenesses among them aids in the formation of these aspects of the curriculum that may be considered suitable for many students at a particular age or grade level. For planning the curriculum and for teaching, an understanding of each learner's uniqueness is also a necessary guideline, since learning success often is determined by differences.

GLENN HASS, KIMBALL WILES,
and JOSEPH BONDI

3 Individual-izing and Grouping for Reading Instruction

Ms. Thompson arrived at Emerson Thoreau Elementary School on the corner of Hubbard Avenue and Monroe Street at 8:12 A.M. When she entered her classroom, two of her eight third graders were already there, busy at work on a word puzzle that Ms. Thompson had constructed to help them learn to use context clues. They wanted to have the puzzle completed for their private conference with Ms. Thompson at 9 A.M. They knew she would have another interesting assignment ready for them to do after their conference. In all likelihood, each child would receive a project planned according to the student's individual needs and interests.

The other six students in Ms. Thompson's third-grade class arrived before 8:30. Each had an individually planned reading assignment to work on in preparation for a private conference with Ms. Thompson that day. Each child knew that sometime that day, all eight in the class would gather together to hear a story, tell about their self-selected reading, and perhaps rehearse their class play. They would probably also work in pairs or play some reading games in pairs or in groups of three while the private conferences were going on. (And the drinking fountain gave students a choice of strawberry soda or ginger ale, and the windows were made of translucent taffy, and there were piles of gumdrops and licorice whips in every corner of the room.)

The fairy tale in the two preceding paragraphs could come true if the Mr. and Ms. Thompsons of the teaching profession had to teach only eight students to read. However, most elementary teachers are responsible for the reading instruction of 25 or more students. Although this teacher-pupil ratio does not preclude the individualization of instruction, it does present some obstacles to that goal. Planning meaningful assignments, holding individual conferences, identifying and selecting materials, and keeping records on an individual basis for 25 or more students is more than many teachers can manage, given the demands on their time and the resources made available by the schools.

The arguments for individualization of reading instruction cannot be denied. No two children are exactly alike in the many variables that influence reading growth. Children vary greatly in such important factors as intelligence, motivation, oral-language development, interests, and attention span. Therefore, we think that each teacher should individualize instruction as much as is possible for any group or class of students. But just as children differ, so do teachers and schools. Consequently, some teachers are more able than others to achieve a high degree of individualization in their reading programs without becoming disorganized and without running short of materials, time, and other resources that are needed to instruct a group of students on a highly individualized basis. We do not want to imply that ideally, all reading instruction would be given on a one-to-one basis. The ideal instructional plan includes opportunities for children to be taught on a one-to-one basis and in groups. Children need to have the reading teacher's individual attention periodically, and they also need to use reading in personal interactions with their peers in group situations. Therefore, elementary teachers should arrange for children to have both kinds of experiences throughout their instruction at each grade or with each teacher if they are in a nongraded school or being taught by a team of teachers. Every reading teacher should spend some time with the child on a one-to-one basis and should arrange for the student to develop her or his reading skills in small-group situations. Individualization and group instruction, then, are not mutually exclusive methods. The object is to strike a balance between the two that best meets the needs of the particular group of students being taught.

THE HIGHLY INDIVIDUALIZED PROGRAM

As we mentioned earlier, the percentage of the total reading curriculum allotted for one-to-one instruction varies considerably from teacher to teacher and frequently from class to class. Some teachers find that they do much more one-to-one work with a particular class than they did with the class they taught the previous year. The needs and abilities of students taken as classes or groups do differ, and teachers who are sensitive to these differences adjust their instructional programs to accommodate them.

We know no teachers or administrators who would *never* arrange for students to work together in small groups or as a total class on a reading or reading-related activity. Nor are we acquainted with teachers who would *never* work with a child individually in a reading program. Therefore, when we describe the highly individualized program, we are describing a program in which one-to-one contacts form the basis of the skill-development program, and private conferences are the primary vehicle for sharing perceptions and attitudes toward reading done on an individual basis.

There are two approaches to a highly individualized program. In one approach, the more prescriptive, the teacher identifies the library books and the skill-development materials that will probably be the most beneficial for each student's reading development. The student is given specific assignments to complete between individual conferences with the teacher. In the other, less prescriptive approach, students select their own reading materials, read them at their own pace, and discuss them with the teacher during their individual conferences. Obviously, the second approach is more suitable for highly motivated students who learn to read mostly by reading and who require little formal instruction or guidance. The first approach is probably more suitable for most students in the earlier grades and for some students throughout their elementary school experience.

To conduct a highly individualized reading program, teachers need an efficient record-keeping system and a large selection of materials to provide for the variety of interests and skill needs within any group of students. In addition, teachers need to have considerable expertise in the following: (1) conducting personal conferences; (2) diagnosing skill strengths and weaknesses; (3) selecting and sequencing materials and activities focused on the development of specific skills, and (4) planning productive activities for the rest of the class while individual conferences are in progress. All in all, the greater the degree of individualization, the more knowledgeable the teacher must be about the nature of the reading process and reading pedagogy.

It is possible for first-grade teachers to initiate reading instruction with their students on a highly individualized basis. For example, each student could be helped to write a personal language-experience story to read (one or two sentences) as a beginning point. Or, each child could be met with individually to begin learning how to read in the preprimer of a basal series. However, many teachers prefer to move to a highly individualized approach only after all, most, or at least some of their students have attained a degree of independence in reading from group instruction. We think that this is sensible, because students who cannot engage in some reading without the direct assistance of the teacher are difficult to keep productively busy while they are waiting for their turn with the teacher.

Record-Keeping

Keeping records of specific skills development, attitudes toward reading, and materials successfully read is a major task in a highly individualized reading program. If teachers use detailed record forms, they may spend more time recording than teaching. If they use abbreviated forms, they run the risk of overlooking important aspects of a student's growth in reading. Therefore, it is important to use a procedure that strikes a good balance between overkill and superficiality.

We recommend that the form used in the first two illustrations that follow be appropriately marked after each pupil-teacher conference and referred to when planning for the next conference. The third illustration is intended to show how a teacher might record a conference with a very able student who is keeping a log of her or his reading experiences and who meets for relatively unstructured conferences with the teacher.

Illustration 1

Name: Tony Smith

Date and time of conference: Wednesday, February 6, 9:15–9:30

Material evaluated: (1) sight words on flash cards ("American," "between," "flag"); (2) language-experience story and Tony's picture; (3) audio tape of "Bruce the Moose."

Results of evaluation: (1) called "between" "because"; (2) no errors in oral reading, but poor expression—picture indicates good understanding of the story; (3) recalled "Bruce the Moose" story accurately and with good detail.

Instruction given: (1) had Tony trace and say the word "between" and then read it in the sentence, "I sit between Terry and Karen."; (2) had Tony reread his story after I read it; (3) Tony dictated another story (two sentences). The words "camper" and "highway" from his new story were added to his flash-card pack.

Assignment: (1) review flash cards and practice reading language-experience stories with Terry and Karen; (2) put all of the words on Tony's flash cards that begin with the same sound "Tony" begins with in one pile; (3) listen to audio tape "Rabbits, Rabbits, and More Rabbits"; (4) draw picture for new story; (5) continue reading the stories in the primer *Friends.*

Illustration 2

Name: Sandra Johnson

Date and time of conference: Wednesday, February 6, 9:30–9:45

Material evaluated: (1) pages 6–8 in *Getting Meaning from Context;* (2) *The Mystery of Hammer Hill.*

Results of evaluation: (1) 90%, 90%, and 80% correct on pages 6, 7, 8, respectively; (2) discussed Chapters 3 and 4 with good general understanding of the plot, but poor recall of details.

Instruction given: (1) helped Sandra find the right answers for incorrect responses on pages 6, 7, 8 and had Sandra predict what would happen in Chapter 5, including specific details (who will do what, when, for what reasons).

Assignment: (1) pages 9, 10, 11 in *Getting Meaning from Context;* (2)

pages 1, 2, 3 in *Find the Answer;* (3) continue *The Mystery of Hammer Hill;* (4) discuss her reading with Marsha, Pete, and Bob.

Illustration 3

Name: Maria Sando

Date and time of conference: Wednesday, February 6, 9:45–9:55

Evaluation: Maria finished her book, *People, Places and Penguins,* and also read two stories in the January issue of *Ebony Jr.* She apparently enjoyed all of her reading and told what she had learned about penguins with enthusiasm and excellent recall. I thumbed through the materials and asked several factual questions, which she answered with complete accuracy. She has recorded the book and the stories in her notebook and has written a short paragraph summarizing each and indicating her enjoyment of them. She is now searching for a new book and will show it to me when she selects it. I wrote a note of praise in Maria's notebook regarding how well she understood what she read and how well she was summarizing her reading experiences in her log. Before parent conferences, Maria should be given a standardized achievement test to get some objective evidence to support my observations that her reading growth is progressing well.

Teachers may want to modify these sample forms for keeping records, or they may want to create their own. We believe that the forms we have used as models permit the efficient recording of the most important aspects of a child's progress in an instructional reading program. Teachers who require extensive checklists to keep them aware of what needs to be taught or who don't have time to do more than check off on a list of skills those that have been "mastered" are, in our judgment, probably not ready to implement a highly individualized reading program.

Some teachers have discovered that able students, such as Maria in Illustration 3, can be taught to keep their own records or logs of their reading experiences. These students record the number of pages read or the exercises completed and make notations of questions they want to ask or comments they want to make during their individual conferences. At the conclusion of each conference, they and the teacher can together compose a short evaluation of the conference for the students' logs.

Instructional Materials

Ready access to a wide variety of instructional materials with a wide range of difficulty levels is vital to the success of a highly individualized reading program. Teachers who wish to teach reading in this way usually want several complete sets of basal series in their rooms, as well as skill-development books, games, flash cards, audio tapes, ditto masters, and multilevel skill-development kits. A central library or instructional materials center with a good supply of library books, magazines, and newspapers is a major asset because of the emphasis in a highly individualized program on reading library books and other non-text materials. Teachers in schools without an ample supply of reading materials are likely to be frustrated in their attempts to maintain a highly individualized reading program. However, some enterprising teachers have tapped the attics, basements, and libraries of friends, students, and students' parents to supplement the materials provided by the school, and with these additional materials they have been able to conduct a highly individualized program.

Other Considerations

Record keeping and the availability of instructional materials are only two major considerations in the conduct of a highly individualized reading program. The ability to plan activities for students to do independently between their conferences is an important part of such a program and requires considerable knowledge of students' motivations and the process of learning to read. Furthermore, the conferences themselves must be carefully planned and efficiently conducted. Because of their personal insecurity or the problems they are having, some students need more conferences and/or more time per conference than other students do. Generally, teachers like to allot at least 15 minutes for each student conference, but variation and flexibility must be more the rule than the exception. Finally, teachers must be thoroughly familiar with the instructional materials they use and be skillful diagnosticians of children's reading strengths and weaknesses.

Basic to the conduct of a highly individualized reading program are the concepts expressed succinctly by Johnson and Kress (1969): "A reader is one who reads" and "One learns to read by reading." Teachers of highly individualized programs must believe that children who are sitting and reading is one mark of a good program. If they feel that they "must instruct" every child every day, they will be uncomfortable with a plan that emphasizes one-to-one rather than group contacts. Many books have been written about individualized or, as it is sometimes called, "personalized" reading instruction (Veatch, 1969; Jacobs, 1970). We would urge teachers who plan to implement a highly individualized reading program to read more extensively on the subject. Our brief discussion here is no more than a starting point.

INDIVIDUALIZING WITHIN A GROUPING PLAN

Many, perhaps most, teachers feel or discover that they can teach reading better by grouping children for instruction than they can by using a one-to-one approach as the basic plan. Using groups as the basic instructional unit does not preclude one-to-one contacts with children, both as part of the group experience and as children are working independently on some learning activity. Again, the decision is not "either-or," but rather "how much of each?"

The number of groups and the number of students who should be in each group cannot be specified for all teaching situations. Typically, elementary teachers have been able to achieve a fair amount of individualization with children grouped as poor, average, or superior readers in terms of their skills development. However, there is nothing magic about the number "3." Furthermore, teachers who do not vary the number and composition of their groups throughout the school year must be held suspect of holding their students captive in their originally assigned groups. In other words, any groups that are formed should be formed for specific purposes and should remain flexible in that children may be shifted from group to group as they show significant improvement, show a need for more instruction on a specific skill, or show a need for a slower-paced program.

Ability groups are relative. The "top" group in one school may be comparable with the middle or even the low group in a school that serves a different population. Some schools may have very few students who qualify for the label "poor readers," and some schools may find very few "superior readers." The objective, then, is not to label children as "superior," "average," or "poor," but rather to teach as a unit within a larger unit (the class) children who have similar needs in skill development and pacing.

Some schools have instituted organizational plans that go beyond the scope of the kind of grouping done by a teacher who teaches a heterogeneous class of students. For example, in some schools students from different grades but of similar overall reading ability leave their various homerooms and meet together at a specified time and place each day for reading instruction given by a teacher assigned to teach reading to that group. This procedure is known as the Joplin Plan. A modification of the Joplin Plan consists of having one teacher teach reading to the least able group of students in a particular grade, another teacher teach a middle-ability group from that same grade, and a third teacher teach the most able students. Similarly, some schools, in what they refer to as team-teaching, do little more than group students homogeneously for reading instruction and assign different teachers to the different groups—the Joplin Plan under a misnomer.

At the risk of being called "old-fashioned," we admit to a preference for instructional groups being formed within a heterogeneous class, thereby permitting students to move from group to group without changing teachers. We also prefer to see elementary teachers teaching science, social studies, language arts, and arithmetic to the same students to whom they teach reading. We believe that the likelihood of adjusting the curriculum of these content areas to meet the reading needs of the students is greater when the same teacher is responsible for all areas.

The plan we recommend for achieving a high degree of individualization in a framework based on groups is most effective in heterogeneous classes. However, the plan can also be used effectively in classes that are homogeneously grouped for reading instruction. In our plan, each student, after having attained some ability to read independently, participates in more than one group. In the skill-development group, the child receives instruction with students of similar reading ability. But in the information-getting and the recreational-reading groups, the child reads and participates in reading-related activities with students of various reading abilities.

Skill-Development Groups

Skill-development groups are formed for the purpose of developing the basic word-identification and comprehension skills we discuss in Chapters 7 and 8, respectively. Therefore, insofar as possible, students who have similar skill-development needs should meet together for skills instruction.

Elaborate assessment systems and other diagnostic instruments and procedures (discussed in Chapter 9) have been developed for the purpose of helping teachers group students for skill development on the basis of highly specific skill deficiencies. The assumption appears to be that a student who has difficulty analyzing certain phonic elements, e.g., consonant blends, may not have trouble with other phonic elements, such as short vowels, or with using context clues. Similarly, a student who can recall events in the sequence in which they occurred in a narrative may be unable to find a central thought in the passage. The assessment systems and other diagnostic procedures and instruments have thus been designed to break reading into its smallest components so that students with the same needs can be grouped in a highly specific way.

We think that such an approach to the diagnosis of specific skills is unnecessary if the objective is to collect data for grouping purposes. In our experience, most students who have difficulty learning several basic skills also have difficulty with many other skills, and most students who master several basic skills quickly, master most of the others quickly, too. In other words, there are "slow" learners and "fast" learners, and somewhere in between are students who are neither noticeably slow nor fast. The need, then, from our point of view is for pacing instruction as much as for focusing on specific skills. The highly integrated nature of reading skills and the integrated manner in which these skills are learned suggests to us that teachers need not tear reading into *all* of the components that can be identified to group students for skills instruction.

Teachers should spend several weeks at the beginning of each school year making informal observations about their students' reading. Teachers should listen to their students read orally, observe their ability to answer questions about material they have read silently, and observe how they interact socially. Teachers should discover the difficulty level of material their students can read with no help, that of material they can read with good comprehension if they have assistance, and that of material that is frustrating for them to read even with assistance. First-grade teachers should discover which students know the letters of the alphabet, each student's listening ability, each student's ability with oral expression, his or her attention span, the ability of each to interpret pictures, and other abilities that suggest readiness for formal reading instruction. Reading-readiness test scores and scores on other formal assessment instruments may be helpful, but we believe that they should be given much less weight than the teacher's observations of how children perform with the actual materials that will be used for instructional purposes. For example, teachers should discover how well their students read orally and silently in the basal readers that will be used for instructional purposes. They should also discover basic word-recognition and comprehension strengths and weaknesses by having their students do some exercises in workbooks, kits, and other skill-development materials that are used to supplement the reading program.

After several weeks of informal observations, teachers who have a good knowledge of the vocabulary development and comprehension skills that are discussed in Chapters 7 and 8 will be able to form three, four, or more groups of students with similar skill-development needs. As instruction proceeds, teachers will periodically need to change the composition of the groups to reflect the changing needs of individual students. However, a continual shuffling of students from one group to another or from one teacher to another is, in our opinion, both unnecessary and unwise. Teachers can accommodate many individual differences within the context of a skills group by differentiating the assignments students are given to complete between the times they meet with the teacher, by asking different students different kinds of questions while they are meeting as a group, and by responding in other ways to individual differences. On occasion, students will be held back, exposed to material, or involved in activities that are not advancing their skills development. This lack of efficiency and productivity can, and probably does, occur even when instruction is given on a one-to-one basis. However, there is no excuse for placing students in a group and keeping them there for an entire school year. The need for frequent assessment of each child's growth in ability and in comparison with other students in the child's group is essential and a reasonable expectation of a competent teacher.

After students have been tentatively grouped, teachers may want to conduct additional informal or standardized diagnostic testing with certain students in order to focus more sharply on their specific skill weaknesses. We discuss instruments and procedures for these kinds of diagnoses in Chapter 9, and at the end of that chapter is an informal diagnostic test that has been helpful to many beginning and experienced teachers.

We think that a basal series is a valuable resource for a teacher to use with students in a skill-development group. After determining the difficulty level of material that is appropriate for a particular group and the specific skills that need to be taught, teachers can select the book, story, or other selection from the series that is designed to help do the job. There is no need to push, jam, and drag students through every selection in the series. Instead, the books and other materials should be used selectively so that students continue to have successful experiences with materials and related activities that are helping to build their reading skills. Worksheets, skill-development books, kits, games, and other materials may be used to supplement the basic material provided by the series. While one group is working with the teacher, other groups can be preparing for their instruction, completing skill-development exercises to practice and reinforce their group instruction, or reading self-selected materials.

Whether or not each group should be learning from a different basal series is not easily answered. There may indeed be some stigma attached to a child's belonging to a group that is working at a slower pace in a series than classmates working in the same series at a faster pace. Also such a child has probably heard a faster group read and discuss several weeks earlier the stories she or he is presently reading. On the other hand, it is much better for a teacher to be very familiar with one set of materials than to have a superficial knowledge of several. Teachers should be aware that the vocabulary, sequencing of skills, and general approach to developing skills differ from series to series. They should not assume that they can be used interchangeably. If a series is to be used selectively for teaching specific skills, teachers must know exactly where to go in that series for the kind of material that is needed. Rather than dodge the issue, we will take a long-range view and recommend that teachers use one series until they are very familiar with it and then add another series to their repertoire. In three years they should be able to use three different series expertly. Of course, this recommendation argues against the frequent changing of series that occurs in some schools.

When they are working in their skill-development groups, the children and the teachers should be aware that their job is to improve the students' reading ability, not to enthuse over stories or hold psychotherapy sessions. Obviously, the task will be accomplished more pleasantly and perhaps more effectively if the material is attractive and interesting. However, basal series and other developmental materials do not need to be, and in fact ought not to be, the student's entire reading experience. The materials used in skill-development groups are and should be perceived as means to an end, not the end in themselves. We wish to make this point because some teachers have overused developmental materials and have on more than one occasion been more impressed by the packaging of developmental materials than by the quality of the materials and the soundness of the pedagogical approaches.

Recreational-Reading Groups

Students who have developed their reading skills to a level that permits them to read material of any kind for a period of time without requiring continual assistance are ready to participate in recreational-reading groups. For social reasons or to impress on them that reading can be fun, teachers may wish to include children in the recreational groups who are not yet able to read independently. Picture books should be available for them to "read," show, and talk about. The major objective of grouping students for recreational reading is to provide them with a pleasant reading experience that permits them to practice and strengthen their reading skills as well as to develop positive attitudes toward reading. In the recreational-reading groups, students read self-selected material for a period of time and then, at a signal from the teacher, tell one another in an unstructured way what they have been reading about.

Recreational-reading groups are formed by the teacher with the following guidelines in mind: (1) the students should have mixed reading ability, so that good readers will be nearby to help less able readers with a word now and then and so that poor readers can learn from good readers how to think and talk about a reading selection; (2) the students should be grouped so as to avoid serious behavior or group interaction problems; and (3) the students should be reading different materials, so that each can read at his or her own rate and tell about the selection without stealing a slower reader's thunder.

As is true of most educational activities, students need to be introduced gradually to the rules of the game before recreational groups function with maximum benefits. Teachers have found that they can begin to give students the training they need for these groups by being good models themselves. They begin by sharing with the whole class some of their own recreational reading. They may keep their class posted on the progress of a certain character in a novel they are reading, or they may tell about their reactions to a magazine article they read the day before. The point is to show students the many different ways to think about and share a self-selected reading experience. Some teachers have advised that students be given whole-class experiences with silent reading and conversation before they are given small-group experiences, as a transition between the modeling done by the teacher and the group experience that deemphasizes the leadership provided by the teacher. To accomplish this, teachers merely give the entire class some time for silent reading and then elicit comments about their reading from various class members. All recreational reading appears to be most productive if teachers are active participants. That is, teachers should read recreational materials while their students are doing likewise and join in the postreading conversations.

When students appear ready to engage in some silent reading and some conversation in a small group with peers (we have had our best results when each group has been arranged in a small circle), their teachers should give them an opportunity to select a newspaper, magazine, picture book, novel, comic book, or other selection for silent reading. Some students may need help with the selection process, but as much as possible, students should be free to select what they want to read, so long as the material does not violate school or community taboos. Teachers should not be unduly concerned about the difficulty level of the material that is chosen. For this group activity, it is better for students to comprehend only 20 percent of something they want to read than 90 or 100 percent of something that is unappealing to them. They are not required to give a strict accounting of their comprehension, and 20 percent or even less is sufficient for some conversation with fellow students. Obviously, the second grader who chooses *War and Peace* should be steered to something more suitable or to the psychologist for an IQ test.

Teachers report that some of their first graders are ready to participate as readers in recreational-reading groups near the middle of the school year. If picture books are readily available, teachers may wish to include students whose reading skills are not sufficiently developed to allow them to read independently. By the middle of the second grade, many more students will be able to participate as independent readers. Students who by the end of the second grade cannot participate in recreational-reading groups as actual readers need some diagnostic work with a reading specialist and perhaps a remedial program. The length of time allotted to the silent-reading period and to the conversation period varies from grade to grade and from day to day. Trial and error seems to be the best way to find the length of time that is most suitable for a particular class of students.

Teachers who have reported the results of their efforts to give students productive recreational-reading experiences as part of the reading curriculum find that their students read more than they did before time was allotted for this kind of small-group activity. They think that they may have started a habit in their students that will persist and that they surely have set the stage for mature reading experiences in later grades. Interestingly, the books that have been told about in a group often become those most sought after by other members of the group. Finally, teachers have found that recreational-reading groups function best when they are comprised of four or five students. The composition of the groups can be changed at any time. The length of time a particular set of groupings remains intact is best left to the judgment of the teacher, based on her or his observations of the social and academic progress of the groups.

Information-Getting Groups

Students are assigned to information-getting reading groups on the basis of their expressed interests. The objective is to let students with similar interests read together to gather information about a topic that interests them and then as a group present their findings to the whole class. The materials they might read range from newspaper and magazine articles to content-area textbooks and encyclopedias. Their presentations may be panel discussions, creative dramatizations, illustrated lectures, mock interviews, puppet shows, or other kinds of presentations that permit the members of an information-getting group to transmit their knowledge about a particular subject to their classmates.

When students are grouped according to their interests, they are likely to vary greatly in their skill development. Therefore, one of the teacher's major tasks is to identify and make available reading material about interest topics at various difficulty levels, and thus the assistance of a librarian or other resource person is very desirable when materials are being gathered. Another major task of the teacher is to act as a resource person to the various information-getting groups while they are reading, discussing their material, and planning their presentations. In effect, the teacher must move from group to group, helping students with words, stimulating discussion, giving ideas for presentations, and coordinating the progress of the groups in terms of time. Although it is not necessary for the groups to give their presentations at the same time, it is important to see that no group bogs down and has interest replaced with boredom.

Information-getting groups are usually not formed before the end of the third grade, although there may, and indeed should, be exceptions for children who develop good reading ability before most other children do. Teachers have found these groups to be more difficult for themselves and for students to manage than either the skill-development groups or the recreational-reading groups. Nonetheless, they are important to the total reading development of students, largely because they permit good and poor readers to work together on tasks that develop the study skills that are vital to their success in content-area curriculums. These groups differ from groups that might be formed within the content-area curriculums, because they arise from students' interests rather than from a curriculum with prescribed topics of study. Students interested in horses, for example, might never have an opportunity to pursue that interest unless it is provided as part of the reading curriculum.

Teachers have found that the newspaper is an excellent starting point for the formation of information-getting groups. For several days or more they bring a daily newspaper to class with them. They read an article or two from it and perhaps tell about some other article that has caught their interest. Students are encouraged to add their comments and tell about any articles or features they may have read. In time, a number of students begin to look more closely at their local newspaper than they previously had. The teacher then makes a conversational survey of who is reading what in the daily newspaper. Eventually, students begin to identify common interests in the class. At that point, the time is ripe for asking students to identify a topic they would like to read more about, and a list of topics (e.g., jets, pollution, horses, baseball players, cooking, television) is put on the chalkboard. Teachers then must take some time to divide the class into interest groups. The groups may range from two to five members. Generally, groups larger than five are difficult to manage. Occasionally, a student will have no one else in the class who shares his or her interest. That student should be permitted to work alone, and an effort should be made to get the child together with other students the next time information-getting groups are formed. Students who are unable or unwilling to identify a topic to read about should be either given a choice of several groups to join or simply assigned to a group. Most students are willing and able to identify five or six different topics they would like to read about with fellow students during a school year.

The length of time an information-getting group can work together on one topic varies with the age and academic ability of the students. Generally, four or five 30-minute meetings over a period of two weeks is sufficient for intermediate-grade students to collect enough information to give a good presentation. Teachers report that after about two weeks of reading and talking about the same topic, students are tired of it and want to select new topics.

Collecting enough materials to satisfy the needs of various information-getting groups comprised of students with different reading abilities has presented problems. However, teachers find that after three or four years, they and their librarians can amass an adequate supply of material relevant to the interests students express. For one thing, some of the interests appear to be classics, in that they are expressed year after year. Space travel, pollution, horses, automobiles, and professional sports figures are examples of these "classics." In addition to newspapers, magazines, content-area textbooks, library references, filmstrips, and other obvious sources of informational materials, certain materials packaged for use as comprehension skill builders have proved valuable. Kits, workbooks, classroom newspapers, series of books designed to improve comprehension skills, and basal readers (minus the accompanying questions and activities) can all be tapped for printed matter relevant to a particular topic at different difficulty levels.

Many teachers have students in their classes who are nonreaders or almost nonreaders. These students need not be deprived of participating in information-getting groups because of their reading disability. Movies, audio tapes, picture books, and filmstrips permit these students to join in the presentation. Elementary schools can enlist the aid of the senior high schools, universities, and community groups in their area to begin a collection of audio tapes geared to the interests of elementary students. Advanced English classes, drama groups, forensic teams, and service clubs are all excellent sources for good readers to record information on audio tape. In one elementary school, the teachers themselves made a small library of tapes so that their poor readers would not be deprived of the information and social interactions they need as much as good readers do.

Coordinating the Three Groups

A shift in emphasis from skill-building to recreational and informa-tion-getting reading activities is evidence of an effective instructional program. In the early grades more attention needs to be given to the development of basic reading skills; consequently, skill-development groups are more active than recreational and information-getting groups throughout the first and perhaps the second grades. However, teachers should always be mindful of the importance of transferring skills from developmental materials to informational and recreational materials. If the transfer is not actively taught, it may not occur. In addition, the importance of putting reading into a social context and impressing students with the utilitarian and aesthetic dimensions of reading cannot be overstressed.

All of the specifics of the grouping plan whereby each student be-longs to three different groups cannot be prescribed. Each teacher must assess the ever-changing needs of her or his students and decide how much of each school week or month will be devoted to skill develop-ment, recreational, and information-getting reading. Furthermore, the decision as to when to introduce students to the latter two groups must be made by teachers on an individual basis. The critical factor is to include, on a systematic basis, all three dimensions in every child's ele-mentary school instructional reading program.

By the time students reach the fourth grade, they should have learned how to conduct themselves in each of the three groups. Teach-ers are then able to shift them smoothly from one group to the other. It is best if the operation of the plan is kept flexible. That is, on any given day, teachers should be spontaneous in moving students from information-getting groups to recreational-reading groups if and when the information-getting groups are obviously not being productive. Or, recreational groups might not meet one or two weeks while students concentrate on skill building or plan and give information-getting group presentations. In other words, Friday should not be set aside for recre-ational reading. Students should not be implicitly taught that recre-ational reading is a prize for working hard for four days. Recreational reading should be perceived as a daily as much as an end-of-week ac-tivity. The same perception should hold for using reading to get infor-mation. The three-group plan is maximally beneficial when teachers avoid routinizing the manner in which the plan functions.

Smith and Barrett (1974) have chosen the fifth grade to illustrate schematically precisely how the three-group plan might function over a three-week period. Their introductory paragraph, their illustrative scheme, and their concluding paragraph follow.

The following schedule for a hypothetical heterogeneous class of 30 fifth graders illustrates how the three different phases might be coordinated throughout a three-week period. The schedule assumes a 50-minute time block for reading instruction five days a week and represents a period of time during which four different skills groups are meeting regularly for developmental instruction—at times combined and at other times broken up.

A FIRST WEEK

Monday	Developmental	Information-Getting	Recreational
9:00–9:15	10 students[1]		20 students
9:15–9:40	5 students[2]		25 students
9:40–9:50			30 students
Tuesday			
9:00–9:20	8 students[3]		22 students
9:20–9:30			30 students
9:30–9:50		30 students	
Wednesday			
9:00–9:10	7 students[4]	6 students[5]	17 students
9:10–9:20	5 students	6 students	19 students
9:20–9:50		30 students	
Thursday			
9:00–9:15	10 students	4 students[6]	16 students
9:15–9:30	5 students	10 students[7]	15 students
9:30–9:50			30 students[8]
Friday			
9:00–9:10	8 students	22 students	
9:10–9:50		30 students[9]	

1. Middle-ability group.
2. Low-ability group.
3. Another middle-ability group.
4. High-ability group.
5. An information-getting group that defined a project well enough the previous day to get started on it.
6. The same information-getting group that worked on Wednesday, with two students removed for developmental instruction.
7. Students representing several information-getting groups working independently on their parts of the group projects.
8. Ten minutes of conversation in recreational groups.
9. All information-getting groups meeting, with teacher available for consultation.

A SECOND WEEK

Monday	Developmental	Information-Getting	Recreational
9:00–9:30	15 students[10]		15 students
9:30–9:50			30 students
Tuesday			
9:00–9:20	5 students	17 students	8 students
9:20–9:50	15 students[11]		15 students
Wednesday			
9:00–9:50	30 students[12]		
Thursday			
9:00–9:15	30 students[13]		
9:15–9:50			30 students
Friday			
9:00–9:50		30 students	

A THIRD WEEK

Monday	Developmental	Information-Getting	Recreational
9:00–9:15	2 students[14]	28 students	
9:15–9:30	10 students	20 students	
9:30–9:50	5 students	25 students	
Tuesday			
9:00–9:15	2 students[15]		28 students
9:15–9:30	7 students		23 students
9:30–9:50	8 students		22 students
Wednesday			
9:00–9:50			30 students[16]
Thursday			
9:00–9:50		30 students[17]	

10. One middle- and low-ability groups combined.
11. Two middle groups combined.
12. Whole-class instruction in some skill.
13. Whole-class review of skill taught Wednesday.
14. Intensive work with two students having trouble with a particular skill.
15. Same two students who received special help on Monday.
16. Recreational groups completing this round of reading and conversing together.
17. Two information-getting reading-group project presentations.

Friday	Developmental	Information-Getting	Recreational
9:00–9:10	2 students[18]	20 students	8 students
9:10–9:50	15 students[19]	7 students	8 students

18. Teacher conference with students who need help finding additional reading material to read before new recreational groups are formed.
19. Two middle groups working together on a troublesome skill.

In the illustrative schedule, students received specific skills instruction in flexible groups, worked independently and in small groups on interesting reading-related projects, read and discussed material of their own choosing, and formally presented some projects to their classmates. At the conclusion of this particular three-week period the class appears ready to wrap up the unit. The next several class periods would probably be spent completing unfinished group work and having the remaining information-getting reading-group project presentations. Students who were finished with their group responsibilities might do some additional free reading, work in supplementary materials or under the direction of the teacher, tutor some students needing special help. The teacher would probably be busy prodding the procrastinators so that the unit could be completed before enthusiasm waned. After all groups had completed their project presentations and their recreational group conversations, several days would be spent setting up new information-getting and recreational groups and doing some whole-class activities such as listening to a recorded story or discussing interesting characters the students had met in their reading.*

SUMMARY

Individualization of reading instruction is necessary because of the highly individual way in which students learn to read. Some teachers are able to teach reading using a one-to-one approach as the basic instructional plan. However, a degree of individualization can also be attained when students are grouped for reading instruction. A plan whereby each student belongs to a skill-development group, a recreational-reading group, and an information-getting reading group affords opportunities for individualization, even though grouping is the basic instructional plan.

* Richard J. Smith and Thomas C. Barrett. *Teaching Reading in the Middle Grades,* Reading, Mass.: Addison-Wesley, 1974, pp. 18–21. Reprinted by permission.

Suggested Activities for the Methods Class

Activity 1

For some future class period, each student should have some recreational reading material, e.g., a novel, short story, magazine, newspaper. The instructor will arbitrarily divide the class into small recreational-reading groups in small, circular arrangements, with four or five students in each group. After approximately 25 minutes of silent reading, the instructor—who has also been reading recreational material—will signal the class to stop reading and begin talking. Within their groups, the students should converse about what each has been reading, giving some notion of the nature of the content, why that particular material was chosen, and any personal responses to the story, article, novel, or whatever.

Following the conversation, students should discuss the following:

1. Was the reading period pleasant or a strain? Why?
2. Was the conversation free, comfortable and interesting? Why or why not?
3. If this exercise were repeated with the same groups, would "1" and "2" probably be answered in the same way? What if the composition of the groups were changed?
4. What are the implications in the answers to "1," "2," and "3" for involving elementary students in recreational-reading groups?

Activity 2

Have a volunteer or appointed student ascertain the interests of the class in terms of topics each would like to have an opportunity to read about and discuss with fellow classmates who share that interest. What compromises would have to be made to arrange for every student to read with at least one other student? Make a list of formats that might be used to present the findings of an information-getting group to the rest of the class.

Activity 3

Read the following selection, "Readers and Reading" by Johnson and Kress. Then as an entire class or in small groups, evaluate your own elementary and secondary school reading program as best you can remember it.

"READERS AND READING"
MARJORIE S. JOHNSON AND ROY KRESS*

Two oft neglected common-sense ideas in the field of reading are these:

1. A reader is one who reads.
2. One learns to read by reading.

---

* Marjorie S. Johnson and Roy Kress. "Readers and Reading," *The Reading Teacher* **22** (April 1969):594. Reprinted with permission of the International Reading Association and Marjorie S. Johnson and Roy Kress.

Each individually and the two in combination have profound implications for reading instruction and, in fact, for the total school curriculum and for home life.

It certainly is a strong desire of most teachers and parents that children read widely. However, these same adults seem to work actively, as well as passively, *against* the actualization of this goal. Considerable attention has been given to the passive discouragement—that which arises out of the fact that children do not ordinarily see adults who are important in their lives devoting time to reading because they want to read. Much in the way of recognition of the importance of reading could be gained by the child's seeing his teachers and parents absorbed in reading which had nothing to do with school work, father's business, or the running of the house. Having to wait occasionally for the next lesson to begin because the teacher was stealing a few minutes to read (not that lesson) might be a fine experience for many children. Less attention has been focused on the active discouragement of truly independent reading.

A child's school day normally runs from lesson to lesson, exercise to exercise, assignment to assignment, with no time available for reading beyond that which these structured activities demand. Oh, there may be five minutes between this and that— but who wants to get involved in self-motivated reading only to be wrenched away from it almost before the involvement can become complete. At home things often run much the same way. Furthermore, both at home and at school the impression is often created that reading of this type is at the bottom of the activity ladder in value. "Put your book away, now. You can read if you have some time *after* you've . . ." After what? To the child it must seem after everything—after spelling class, math work, doing the dishes, finishing a book report, trumpet lesson—even after recess. How can an activity over which everything else takes precedence really amount to much?

Unavailability of time for reading and relegation of it to the bottom of the barrel are further compounded by inaccessibility of materials. Locating something he really wants to read is often quite a project for the child. In some schools the central library is the only real possibility and getting a library pass is too complex a process to make it worth the effort. These and many other factors combine to discourage reading. If adults are concerned about children's being readers, they should keep in mind that no one can really be called a reader unless he reads. High scores on achievement tests do not give evidence that an individual is a good reader. The fact that he *reads,* and does it well, gives the evidence.

Finally, re-examination of reading instructional programs *per se* is certainly indicated. For how much actual reading do they provide? Only by reading extensively will the child become a facile reader. Learning about reading or learning how to read may not be either learning to read or the path to becoming a reader.

Activity 4

Discuss the logistics, furniture, floor plan, and other practical matters inherent in the illustrative schema designed by Smith and Barrett and presented on pp. 62–64.

Activity 5

Draw a picture of the classroom as it might be viewed from the ceiling during the 9:00–9:10 block of time on Friday of the third week in the schema designed by Smith and Barrett.

Teaching Suggestions

Suggestion 1

Organize a group of four or five elementary students into an information-get-ting reading group. Help them specify the topic they would like to read about. Help them find materials to match their different ability levels. If they need assistance with more than five of 100 words read orally, the material is too difficult. Give them opportunities to read their different materials in a small circle. Help them plan a presentation of the information they have read about and shared within their group. Finally, arrange for an audience to view their presentation.

Suggestion 2

Organize a group of four or five elementary students into a recreational-reading group. Help each student who needs it, to find material he or she thinks will be fun to read. Select something for yourself to read, and read with the small group in a small circle for an appropriate period of time. Then converse with the students about what each has been reading. Repeat the activity with the same students on another day.

REFERENCES

Hass, Glen, Kimbell Wiles, and Joseph Bondi. *Readings in Curriculum*, 2d ed., Boston: Allyn & Bacon, 1970, p. 136.

Jacobs, Leland B. *One-to-One—A Practical Individualized Reading Program*, Englewood Cliffs, N.J.: Prentice-Hall, 1970.

Johnson, Marjorie S., and Roy Kress. "Readers and Reading," *The Reading Teacher* **22** (April 1969): 594.

Smith, Richard J., and Thomas C. Barrett. *Teaching Reading in the Middle Grades*, Reading, Mass.: Addison-Wesley, 1974.

Veatch, Jeannette. *Individualizing Your Reading Program*, New York: G. P. Putnam's Sons, 1969.

Readiness for reading should not be viewed as comprising a single collection of abilities which will be the same for all children. Actually, what makes one child ready might be quite different from what makes another ready...

DOLORES DURKIN

4 Developing Reading Readiness

"Beginning reading" has never been clearly defined. Past and present practices have suggested that *getting ready* to learn to read and *beginning* to learn to read are two discrete stages. This belief has led to the situation found in many schools whereby a readiness program occurs at one point—in kindergarten or first grade—and a reading program begins at some later date. Yet no one knows precisely when a child achieves a necessary plateau of reading readiness and suddenly becomes a beginning reader.

Like most reading-methods textbooks, this book contains separate chapters on reading readiness and beginning reading. In this chapter we discuss the factors usually associated with preparing children for reading instruction. In Chapter 5 we examine a number of widely used approaches to beginning-reading instruction. Chapter 6 is devoted entirely to the beginning-reading approach we find most desirable—the language-experience approach.

We urge you to consider these three chapters as a "miniunit" on reading readiness/beginning reading. Many of the activities described in the three chapters will certainly be of a prereading nature for some children, but will just as certainly constitute beginning reading for other children.

In summarizing her view on reading readiness/beginning-reading activity, which she calls "opportunities," Durkin (1970, pp. 534, 564) comments:

What a child is able to learn as a result of these opportunities offers very specific information about his readiness. With some children, a particular opportunity will result in reading ability, and so, quite obviously, these children were ready. With others, however, the same opportunity will not "take," and as for them it is a type of readiness instruction. That the same teaching procedures can be reading instruction for some children and readiness instruction for others suggests serious flaws in school practices which seem to go out of their way to create an artificial separation between a readiness program and a reading program. A much more defensible way of working is to view readiness instruction as reading instruction in its early stages.*

We present separate chapters on reading readiness and beginning reading to give you a sharper focus on the distinct features of each. One could question the need for separate textbooks on reading, spelling, or grammar, when all are aspects of the language-arts curriculum. Similarly, one could question the existence of separate chapters on readiness, beginning-reading approaches, or word identification, when

---

* Dolores Durkin. "Reading Readiness," *The Reading Teacher* **23,** 6 (March 1970): 534. Reprinted by permission.

all are parts of reading instruction. The answer, of course, is simply that books are arranged into chapters for clarity of organization and presentation of ideas and activities that tend to cluster together in the perceptions of the authors. We invite you, then, to consider each of these three short chapters as parts of a greater whole, and we hope that this division will enhance your understanding and make for easier reading.

ASPECTS OF READING READINESS

Children need to have certain abilities if they are to become fluent readers. Some educators view readiness as a maturational stage and implicitly suggest that schools delay reading instruction until children mature to that stage. Other educators view readiness as a state of preparedness for learning a task which results from *both* native capacity and previous learning, which suggests that desirable learning opportunities can be provided. It is our view that many facets of readiness for reading *can* and should be developed and, although varying in kind and degree, should be an integral part of beginning-reading instruction.

In short, there are certain abilities that the school can influence and others that it cannot. Consider the following 20 factors, which *might* be called reading-readiness skills. Many of the factors are widely agreed upon by educators as being essential to learning to read. On the other hand, some of the factors have very few proponents who view them as essential to reading. As you read down the list (which is purposely arranged in no order of significance), check the factors which *you* think teachers can or should try to influence. Underline the factors you feel are important but cannot really be affected by schooling. Cross out those you feel are not really essential to reading acquisition.

1. Good normal or corrected vision
2. The knowledge of left-to-right sequence
3. The ability to discriminate sounds
4. "Sufficient" intellectual capacity
5. "Adequate" general health and vitality
6. Good balance
7. The ability to listen to and understand oral language
8. The ability to use oral language
9. A speaking/listening vocabulary
10. Good normal or corrected hearing

11. An absence of daily hunger
12. The capability of recognizing printed words
13. An interest in books and reading
14. A rich background of experiences
15. Freedom from aphasia (language disability due to brain damage)
16. The ability to read and comprehend printed sentences and larger units of discourse
17. Good eye–hand coordination
18. Emotional security and a sense of self-worth
19. Knowledge of the names of the letters of the alphabet
20. Knowledge of the colors.

There is no *one* correct way of responding to the exercise above, but there can be some consensus. Many educators would agree that children can learn to read without knowing letter names or the colors of the rainbow. Although good health, a full stomach, emotional stability, interest, and poise are indisputedly desirable, some children can learn to read despite poor health, hunger, emotional stress, low interest, or clumsiness. As important as vision, hearing, and native intelligence are to reading growth, there is little the instructional program in and of itself can do to change these aptitudes. On the other hand, the ability to read printed words, sentences, and larger units probably should not be viewed as aspects of reading readiness, but rather as reading itself.

The remaining factors on the list *are,* for most children, prerequisite to reading and, furthermore, are those that the teacher can affect. Clustered, they comprise the following five categories:

1. Oral language, both speaking and listening
2. Experiential background
3. Auditory discrimination
4. Visual discrimination
5. Perceptual-motor skill.

Stated differently, to read a child must: (1) be able to use and understand language; (2) have experience to which to relate language; (3) be able to note fine differences in speech sound; (4) be able to discern minute differences in graphic shapes; and (5) know up from down, left from right, and be able to turn pages. Some children enter school rich in these experiences and abilities, whereas others need a good deal of help.

ACTIVITIES FOR DEVELOPING ORAL LANGUAGE

Children talk and listen before they learn to read. Print is a secondary language system which, in beginning reading, must be related to oral language. Thus, a well-developed oral-language system is very important for learning to read. The more children talk, the broader their vocabulary becomes and the greater their familiarity with different sentence structures becomes. Each thing talked about is another possible topic for a written story. Teachers often find that the stories or words dictated in language-experience stories stem from oral-language activities. The following suggestions comprise a variety of ways the teacher can provide opportunities for oral-language growth:

1. *Introductions.* Early in their first week of school, children can be asked to introduce themselves or each other. Before the introductions begin, the teacher may discuss with the group the kinds of things they would be interested in knowing about one another: name, hobbies, pets, favorite food, favorite music, movie or T.V. show, family members, or vacation activities. Some children are shy when talking about themselves. In some classrooms children are asked to interview a classmate and then introduce that child; in that way, no one need tell about him- or herself.

2. *Show and tell.* Each day, some time may be set aside for a few children to tell about an object they have brought from home. Since this is done on a voluntary basis, the teacher will need to be alert to the children who never bring anything to tell about. Such children will need extra suggestions and encouragement.

3. *Topic days.* Two or three times a week, discussions of particular topics can be held. The topics may be selected from the children's interests as expressed during the introduction speeches or may be selected to dovetail with class activities. Topics such as pets, holidays, T.V. shows, surprises, and funny events may be interesting.

4. *Retelling stories.* After the teacher has read or told a story, children can be asked to retell it.

5. *Story endings.* The pupils are asked to gather around as the teacher tells or reads a story. The story is stopped at an exciting or suspenseful part, and pupils are asked to provide an ending for the story.

6. *Episodic pictures.* Once a week, a sequence of pictures or cartoon strips can be displayed and children asked to tell a story about them. A similar activity can be done with filmstrips, slides, or motion pictures with the sound turned off.

7. *Descriptions.* One at a time, children may be asked to describe an object in the classroom, school, playground, or neighborhood. The rest of the class guesses what it is.

8. *Mystery bag.* If an object is placed in a paper bag, individual pupils can feel inside and describe its size, shape, texture, and other features. From these descriptions, the rest of the class guesses what the object is. Pupils can also be asked to bring objects of their own and to keep them hidden as they describe them to the class.

9. *Imitations.* Individuals are asked to volunteer to imitate familiar sounds, such as a chicken, fire engine, cement mixer, train, jet plane.

10. *Voice changes.* After the teacher says a sentence, children repeat it, but in an altered voice, e.g., slowly, quickly, angrily, cheerfully, sadly, high voice, deep voice, tiny voice.

11. *Noting sequence.* The teacher performs a short sequence of acts, such as getting up, buttoning coat, walking to window, looking out, looking at watch, and returning to desk. Class members are asked to recite the exact sequence of events.

12. *Story additions.* Children are seated in a circle. One child is told to say, "I'm going to Milwaukee, and I'm taking a shovel" or "John went to the store to get pickles" or "Mary went downtown and saw a stoplight." The second child repeats the first child's sentence and adds an item. For example, "John went to the store to get pickles and some weiners." This continues all around the circle.

13. *Riddles and songs.* The children are helped to learn and recite rhymes, riddles, and songs.

14. *Puppet shows.* Many shy children "open up" when acting and speaking through a puppet. A box full of assorted scraps can be creatively used as each child makes a puppet. The puppets may be used informally during free time or in a puppet show.

15. *Role-playing.* In creative dramatics or role-playing, the teacher describes the different roles or situations, which children then volunteer to enact. A few sample situations are: a sportscaster at a ball game, asking or giving directions, talking with a sales clerk, making introductions, and answering a phone.

16. *Choral speaking.* Pupils are taught and memorize different parts of a story or poem, which they then recite in unison. Again, this is helpful to the shy child because of the security provided by the group.

17. *Class discussions.* After a field trip, movie, slide presentation, re-cording, or visitor, the class can be engaged in a discussion of the event by being asked the "who-what-when-where-why" questions, as well as things they liked or did not like or things they were re-minded of.

18. *Story telling.* Occasionally, time may be set aside for children to tell their favorite stories or relate events of interest in their lives.

19. *Conversations.* Many teachers try to engage, as frequently as pos-sible, in personal, one-to-one conversations with their pupils, par-ticularly those more reticent to speak in groups.

ACTIVITIES FOR DEVELOPING EXPERIENTIAL BACKGROUND

In beginning-reading programs that utilize a language-experience ap-proach, children read about what they have experienced and have either written themselves or have had written for them. A few children enter school as world travelers with rich experiential backgrounds. Many children enter school having traveled little or having done little besides watch television programs. As their reading ability increases and their interests broaden, humans learn vicariously. In the initial stages of many reading programs, however, children develop expe-rience charts and read about what they have done or seen. It is im-perative in these programs that teachers devise ways of enriching the backgrounds of their pupils by widening their experience. The follow-ing are ways in which students' experiential backgrounds can be en-riched.

1. *Field trips.* To experience means to do. Many field trips can be taken at no expense to anyone. Trips through the school to meet the principal, the cooks, the secretaries and custodians, and to see the music room, the instructional materials center (IMC), and the fifth-grade class can be enriching. Walks on the playground, in the neighborhood, and to the nearby stores, as well as visits to fire stations, factories, and parks are rewarding. Occasionally, trips by bus to points of interest in more distant areas can be arranged. Each trip provides background for discussions and group-experience stories.

2. *Resource people.* In every school and community there are many valuable people who can be invited to school to share their ex-pertise or interests. Parents can describe their occupations, retired people and older students can demonstrate their hobbies, repre-

sentatives of public and private agencies, such as hospitals or the humane society or the telephone company, can describe their activities. With little effort, it is usually possible to discover many people who can enrich the experiences of the pupils.

3. *Classroom pets.* Children can learn a great deal by observing and caring for fish and pets.

4. *Experiments.* The teacher and class members can conduct experiments with seeds and plants and observe how they grow. Melting snow, evaporating water, and similar aspects of life are of interest to many young children, and they also enjoy experimenting with batteries, levers, magnets, clocks, and other mechanical devices.

5. *Construction.* Opportunities to build things with assorted materials, as well as activities involving finger painting, clay modeling, soap sculpturing, macrame, and bead work will increase children's experiential backgrounds.

6. *Classroom stores.* Simulated stores of any kind can provide experience with marketing, display, counting, ordering, sampling, and buying and selling.

7. *Reading to children.* Nearly all children love to be read to. Unfortunately, some children are never read to at home by parents or older siblings. In many of the families in which parents *do* read to their children, this activity stops when the child learns how to read. We encourage teachers at any elementary school grade level to read to their classes every day. This practice does wonders for increasing students' interest in reading, and it enriches their backgrounds as well.

A PLEA TO TEACHERS: TEN REASONS FOR READING ALOUD *

Carroll Heideman, *Reading Teacher*
Odana School, Madison, Wisconsin

INTRODUCTION

I have special reasons for feeling strongly about reading aloud. I love books, was read to a great deal, and have read constantly ever since I learned to read in the first grade—through Row, Peterson's Alice and Jerry. But beyond that, I have read to my own children for years—from babyhood to mid-high school. I have seen what my reading did to their vocabularies, their language

---

* Reprinted by permission of Carroll Heideman.

patterns, their ideas, their reading habits. My "reading" child was opened to things he would never have cared to read on his own. My "not-much-of-a-reader" developed language patterns which showed up in her writing years later, surprising me with their style and balance. Incidentally, she has become much more of a reader recently.

Can we do any less for the children we teach? In some ways we have even more of a mandate, for we have these children with us only a year— nine months, to be exact. I believe we cannot fulfill our obligations as teachers unless we spend a part of *every day* reading aloud—reading books of style, feeling, and excitement.

1. *All language has oral beginnings.* There can be no more basic way to build and learn varied language patterns than to hear them. I believe this so strongly that reading aloud to my class is the last thing I would eliminate in a curriculum if I were to strip it to a skeleton. I simply *never* skip reading aloud. After all, story-telling is probably the first and most ancient of language-arts experiences.

2. *Reading aloud is a way of reaching the nonreader in a special way.* He will perhaps never read much nor enjoy it. But he can listen to you and love it. You are short-changing him if you don't read to him. How else can he ever enjoy beautifully worked language? How else can he ever come close to crying when a favorite character dies? How else can he get caught up in the excitement of a thrilling plot? You might even give him a desire to read by himself. I've seen it happen.

3. *Reading aloud is a way of expanding even good readers' horizons.* There are few readers, even among adults, who can be called "omnivorous" readers. Most tend to read within a narrow spectrum of subjects. A teacher can offer a veritable smorgasbord of exciting experiences which may stimulate one child or another to try something new. I rarely read two books by the same author—there are so many books and authors waiting.

4. *Many people are impoverished in their language experiences.* Ours is not a culture with a strong oral tradition; our source of language traditions has been the written word. However, since our staple of entertainment—T.V.—is beginning to usurp that position, children (and adults) have been offered a meager language diet indeed. Not only does TV usually offer a closed experience, leaving little space for expanding and deepening the imagination, but it rarely offers a model of rich and varied expression. How could we expect people fed a diet of cartoon shows, of sit-coms, of police-detective shows to be patient enough or even able to read Dickens, for example, the way our parents or grandparents could?

If you are not convinced, pick up a book like *Treasure Island* with its somewhat stylized language patterns. Read it to a 4th or 5th grade class. You'll find yourself doing a certain amount of "translating." This isn't entirely because Stevenson wrote 100 years ago; it is also because he has an elegance of style, a rhythm of phrasing that is lacking in the common language experiences of today. But now that you have picked it up, don't put it down. Read it. Translate. Your children will be the richer for it, and so will you.

5. *We can significantly improve children's writing ability.* We are told that high school and college students write poorly, judged in terms of usage, vocabulary, and language patterns. As teachers we feel an obligation to prepare our pupils better by practicing various aspects of *writing.* We ask them to produce types of sentences and paragraphs, to correct their usage and grammar, to do exercises in vocabulary-building. Some of this is certainly necessary but I believe that we have put the wrong thing first. We should be *reading* to children. There is just no better way to learn new vocabulary than a contextual experience that carries the listener along and fills a word with meaning. There is no better way to sense the balance of phrasing, the patterns of sentence structure, the beauty of figurative language than to *hear* it.

There are studies which show that high school students who make the most improvement in writing are not those who do the most writing but those who do the most reading and don't even practice writing skills. I make a leap of faith and conviction that those who are read to the most will also write better—simply because they have internalized language patterns of richness and variety.

Let me make it stronger. I believe the poor writers in high school and college are directly our responsibility as elementary teachers. I believe it is through our neglect—of mechanics and writing skills, perhaps—but certainly of reading aloud that they do no better than they do. Much of the blame must be ours.

6. *There is no other way to teach poetry.* I believe a very good case could be made that even in reading poetry silently, one must at the least subvocalize in order to appreciate it fully, for the "melody of language" that poetry embodies needs the spoken word to bring it to life. Listening to poetry read aloud can sensitize children to the beauty of poetic expression that brings exciting spinoffs. Choral reading, spontaneous poetry writing, rereading, even memorizing, all can come about naturally once given the stimulus of hearing poetry of all kinds. Through wise choices you can begin to break the stereotype of sentimentalized, rhymed jingles that so many children associate with poetry—all without that didactic, expository kind of teaching that can so quickly kill any budding delight in poetic images and phrasing.

7. *Oral reading is a wonderful way to help children step outside themselves,* to visit another culture, to experience what someone else may be feeling, to go back in time to a period where ways of thinking and expression may be quite different from our own. I must give credit here to some well-done movies and television shows which do this quite admirably, but their number is limited. There is a wealth of ideas, personalities, cultures which the visual media have not touched and perhaps never will.

8. *Reading aloud is the best way in the world of taking a break* in the middle of a frenetic school day. I personally have such a sense of relaxation and enjoyment when I sit down with a book and the children gather around, eager to pick up where we left off last time. There is no sense of having to "get something done," "finishing up work," etc. Some years it is the only time when the "discipline problems" sit, excited and enthralled, released from being "discipline problems" for a short time.

9. *Reading aloud is a wonderful way to get close to people.* How often we feel ourselves unable to express our deep and private emotions to others, including children. I find that when I read aloud, the books I choose do it for me. Feelings of love, of intense dislike, of fear, of elation all can flow from me as I read the words of an author like Felix Salton, J. R. R. Tolkien, R. L. Stevenson. And an added bonus are the feelings and insights that come right back to me—for example, the child who said to me after I had finished *The Bully of Barkham Street,* "I never knew a mean person could have feelings like that."

You might even offer a little unexpected therapy. I knew the youngest child in a large family who obtained the greatest satisfaction, even glee, from listening to the Elephant's Child finally having a chance to turn the tables upon his spanking-prone relatives.

10. Last but by no means least—*careful, critical listening is a skill needed perhaps more than any other in this civilization.* Certainly we do a great deal of listening as adults—possibly more than we realize. Think of the constant barrage of commercials and newscasts that come our way via radio and TV. Think of political campaigns and government pronouncements, to say nothing of sales pitches and just ordinary conversations and arguments—all of which need careful sorting out in terms of values and hidden messages. Surely we as teachers have a greater obligation than maybe ever before to lay the groundwork for critical thinking in the children we teach. I can think of no better way to begin than to read aloud selections worthy of being considered and discussed in a variety of ways.

EXTRA SUGGESTIONS THAT WORK FOR ME

Let the children sit close to you—on the floor, in a chair beside you, etc. There is a more intimate feeling established. Besides, they can see the pictures better.

Look at the children a lot while you read. You may have to mark your place with your finger as you read along, but so what! You have a perfectly legitimate reason to do so.

Stop and talk briefly about a new word, an unusual phrase, figurative language, a provocative idea. Ask about motives, about possible outcomes. This is one of the best ways to encourage critical listening. And you'll be surprised how perceptive your children are.

After reading a good solid book, try one that takes perhaps ten minutes to read. It's fun.

Don't read a book a child asks you to read unless you have read it first and really enjoy it. I have read sight unseen from time to time and always regretted it. Unless I truly enjoy a book, I can't communicate my pleasure particularly well.

As I mentioned before, I generally read only one sampling of an author or even genre. There just isn't time to try all the exciting kinds of books if you don't. (I don't think this rule applies to parents at all. There you have time —years—to read in depth.)

I always allow children to read along with me if there are extra copies of a book. It's good practice for them. They often get involved and motivated enough to reread the book. And if you make mistakes, it doesn't matter. Isn't that a good human model to set?

Don't stop reading to children because they can read to themselves. I believe this is the common mistake parents and teachers make. You can always expand horizons either outward or upward. I find that I can successfully read aloud a book that is 1–2 "grade levels" beyond the reading ability of most of a classroom of children.

A FINAL WORD

If, besides reading to children yourself, you can convince parents to read to their children, you will be doing more to create a literate, thinking population than you even dream.

ACTIVITIES FOR DEVELOPING AUDITORY DISCRIMINATION

An important aspect of reading is relating printed symbols to oral sounds. Basic to learning to read are good hearing, listening, and auditory discrimination. If a child does not correctly perceive aural impressions, confusion in auditory discrimination can result. Auditory discrimination is the ability to discern likenesses and differences in sounds. Without this ability, a child may be unable to distinguish between *pin* and *pen, pat* and *bat, cut* and *cud.* Many children enter school able to discriminate the full range of speech sounds and are ready to learn the graphic representations of the sounds. But some pupils need practice in hearing and differentiating between the very similar or less familiar phonemes of English. A child who doesn't hear the difference between m and n, for example, may interchange them when learning letter-sound relationships and therefore read *met* as *net* or *tan* as *tam*. The potential loss of meaning is obvious. Some children's inability to discriminate auditorially may be so great that they will need work with gross sound discriminations before they can tackle the fine discrimination between speech sounds. Many children will require auditory-discrimination activities. Of the kinds described below, some require finer powers of discrimination than others do.

1. *Guessing the speaker.* Each child may be asked to take a new seat. Then, all the children put their heads down on the desk and blind their eyes. The teacher walks about the room and taps someone on the shoulder. This person must speak until identified by someone else. When they become good at recognizing the voices of their classmates, the teacher might ask each speaker to disguise his or her voice.

2. *Listen to the room.* Here, the children are asked to sit as quietly as possible and to listen to the sounds inside and outside the room. Afterwards, they discuss the different sounds they heard.

3. *Comparing sounds.* Opportunities are provided for children to listen to and compare similar sounds: the ticking of a watch and a clock, a small bell and a large bell, the hand-clapping of a teacher and a child, a door closed and a door slammed, a tap on the table and a tap on a desk, a child walking and a child hopping.

4. *Guessing the sound.* One child hides behind a curtain or table and makes sounds with different objects. The rest of the class is to guess the objects. Some sounds are: a baby rattle, paper crumbling, water being shaken in a bottle, a pencil sharpener, an egg beater, a chain in a paper bag. Later, some of the sounds can be tried in combination.

5. *Echo.* The class is divided in two, one group on each side of the room. In unison, one side calls out sounds, words, or sentences. The other side repeats them, softer, like an echo.

6. *Story repetition.* The children listen to such stories as *The Three Bears* or *Little Red Riding Hood* and repeat phrases in the voice of the father, mother, baby, the wolf, etc.

7. *Word pairs.* Pairs of words are read to the class, and the pupils are asked to determine if the words start with the same sound *(cat-coat)* or end with the same sound *(pop-pot)*. Later, the number of words is increased, and the children decide which word in a group does not belong, e.g., *candy, car, dog, cottage.*

8. *Rhyming words.* The pupils are asked to listen to nursery rhymes and other poems and tell which of the words rhyme:

> "Jack and Jill
> Went up the hill . . ."

After they are proficient at this, they are asked to supply rhyming words of their own.

9. *Picture pairs.* Class members are shown pairs of pictures of words that sound alike: house and horse, pig and pin, turtle and turkey, lamp and stamp, whistle and window. One of the objects is named, and individuals are asked to point to the picture of that object.

10. *Making words.* The teacher makes a speech sound, repeats it two or three times, and asks the group to think of a word which begins with that sound. Some teachers begin by using the sounds of class members' names, e.g., "*s s s - Sam; p p p - Peggy.*"

ACTIVITIES FOR DEVELOPING VISUAL DISCRIMINATION

Visual discrimination is the ability to see likenesses and differences among graphic shapes, symbols, letters, and words. In order to read, a child must be able to differentiate the meaningless squiggles of print. The printed forms of many lower-case letters are very similar: *d b; f t; c o; c e; g q.* Likewise, many printed words differ only in one or two features: *these, those; them, then; dump, bump.* Young children often find it easier to remember "odd-shaped" or infrequently seen words, like *elephant* or *umbrella,* because they are visually unique. An important part of early reading is learning letter-sound relationships. Just as it is necessary for young readers to discriminate fine differences in sound, it is also essential that the minute differences in printed letters be discriminated.

A number of children come to school "knowing" the alphabet, although this may only mean that they have memorized the alphabet song. In any case, we know that it is not necessary for children to know the *names* of the letters to be able to read. But they must be able to differentiate the shapes and to recognize them; otherwise, a page would, to them, resemble a jumble of geometric forms or a graphic blur.

Again, some children will require practice making gross discriminations; most will not need such activities, but will be ready for practice with letters; and some children enter school with fully developed visual discrimination as it pertains to letters and words. The following activities have been found useful by some teachers with pupils who need help with visual discrimination. Again, some of the activities require finer discriminatory powers than others do.

1. *Picture matching.* For children greatly lacking in visual discrimination, picture matching can be useful. Small and large pictures of one object can be used, as can pairs of pictures of similar size. The child's task is to locate matching pictures.

2. *Content similarities.* The teacher shows the child two pictures similar in content. The child is asked how the pictures are alike (e.g., they may both contain a cat) and how they are different (e.g., sunny on one and raining on the other).

3. *Puzzles.* Putting together picture puzzles and later "pictureless" puzzles provides practice in noticing shapes.

4. *Dominoes.* In preparation, the teacher cuts tag board to a suitable size and on each half draws simple figures, symbols, and letters of the alphabet. Pupils play a game following the same rules as with regular Dominoes.

5. *Name game.* The names of all the children are written on the blackboard or on poster paper. Individuals are asked to find names that are similar in appearance to their own or to others (e.g., *Ron-Roy, Jill-Bill*). They then point out the similarities or the differences.

6. *Tracing.* Practice in tracing and copying different geometric shapes and letters contributes to visual discrimination.

7. *Word sorting.* On tag board or the chalkboard, the teacher writes three words, two of which are the same, on a line. The child's task is to find the two words that are the same. Some teachers begin with words that are obviously different and then use words that are more similar. Exercises can be reproduced on duplicating paper for independent, seat-work activities.

8. *Letter sorting.* This activity is similar to the one above, except that letters (or geometric shapes) are used. The number of letters and shapes can be increased so that the child is asked to find the two out of five, for example, that are alike.

9. *Letter matching.* Children are given two sets of the alphabet in cut-outs. The letters should be jumbled. The children are to find the letters that match and place one on top of the other.

ACTIVITIES FOR DEVELOPING PERCEPTUAL-MOTOR SKILLS

There has been considerable controversy about whether or not perceptual-motor coordination is integral to reading. Convincing research is needed to ascertain the effect of muscular coordination, balance, spatial awareness, and other perceptual-motor skills on reading. Two things are certain, however. Directionality—left to right and top to bottom—is vital to reading the English language, as is the motor ability needed to pick up a book and turn its pages. Although most children entering school can handle a book, many children need help with directionality. Moving the eye from left to right and from the top of the page to the bottom is a learned skill; children do not do it instinctively. An important concern of the teacher of beginning reading will be to help children develop left-right, top-bottom orientation to the printed page and reading. The following activities may be used to meet these goals:

1. *Simon Says.* Directionality can be taught through games like "Follow the Leader" and "Simon Says": "Put out your left hand; put your right hand on your left knee. Hop on your right foot three times."

2. *Follow the dots.* Activity sheets on which children are to create a picture by connecting dots can be useful if the dot numbers follow a general left-right, top-bottom sequence.

3. *Chalkboard.* Most children enjoy writing on the chalkboard, even before they can read and write. Nine permanent squares can be drawn on the board in three rows of three. Children take turns writing or drawing whatever they wish in the squares, as long as they follow the left-right, top-bottom sequence. Independent-activity sheets based on this same design can be distributed to the pupils for seat work.

4. *Read stories.* As often as possible, teachers should read to individuals, small groups, and the whole class. From time to time, the teacher turns the book toward the group and moves her hand from left to right beneath the line of print.

5. *Experience stories.* Language-experience stories (discussed in detail in Chapter 6) provide opportunities for the teacher and the pupils to demonstrate and practice left-right sequence.

SUMMARY

These five vital aspects of reading readiness—oral language, experiential background, auditory and visual discrimination, and directionality—are abilities the primary teacher can do something about. Another crucial aspect of reading readiness that the teacher can do something about is *interest*. Interest is important in reading, as in anything else, because it facilitates learning. Furthermore, children who have interest in reading have a virtually limitless source of pleasure available to them.

In the reading-readiness program and throughout initial reading instruction, teachers are especially encouraged to select activities of potentially high interest to the pupils. If, from the outset, reading is seen as an enjoyable activity, the seeds of a lifelong reading habit will begin to take strong root. Activities in such readiness areas as auditory and visual discrimination and directionality could easily become repetitious and dull, however. We therefore hope that some of the activities described in this chapter and in others, as well as those that the sensitive teacher will create or discover, will stimulate a strong interest in learning to read while building a firm platform of reading readiness.

Suggested Activities for the Methods Class

Activity 1

Using materials available from the IMC, college library, or nearby schools, select teachers manuals and reading-readiness workbooks from one or two published reading programs. Classify the teaching activities according to the five categories described in this chapter. Which types of activities seem to receive the most emphasis?

Activity 2

Return to the list of 20 factors at the beginning of this chapter. Do you agree with our treatment of these factors? Are there some you would describe differently? For example, do you think that a knowledge of colors is essential to reading? Or, is visual-discrimination ability something children possess when they come to school? Discuss each factor in terms of both its importance in reading readiness and the school's role in developing it.

Activity 3

Prepare a class booklet called "Specific Suggestions for Developing Reading Readiness." Each member of the class should review one or two articles in such journals as *The Reading Teacher, Elementary English, Early Childhood, Learning, The Instructor,* and *Grade Teacher.* Bring to class three or four specific suggestions, ideas, or activities that can be duplicated, stapled, and used later as a resource by everyone in the class.

Activity 4

Invite a kindergarten teacher and a first-grade teacher to class to discuss their views about reading readiness and its relation to beginning-reading instruction.

Activity 5

Research has shown that knowledge of the letters of the alphabet is generally a good *predictor* of later reading success. Note the word *predictor*, not *cause*. In other words, children who enter school knowing the alphabet often turn out to be better readers at the end of the year than do those who did not know the alphabet. In small groups, discuss this and try to think of four or five reasons why alphabet knowledge might be a good *predictor* of later reading success.

Activity 6

Examine any of the commercially available readiness tests. What aspects of readiness does each test seem to value?

Teaching Suggestions

Suggestion 1

Bring two sets of cut-out alphabet letters. Sit down with a child who has been identified as a nonreader. Ask the child to sort out the letters and find matching pairs. Do you detect any problems of visual discrimination?

Suggestion 2

Devise a short questionnaire (five or ten questions) which you can use with your group or class to determine the kinds of out-of-school experiences they have had. Compile the results of the survey and analyze them in terms of: (1) needed background development and (2) related instructional activities.

Suggestion 3

Select a reading-readiness teaching activity from each of the five categories described in this chapter. Use them with a group of prereading pupils. Evaluate each activity in terms of its interest to the children and its effectiveness.

Suggestion 4

Survey the kindergarten teachers in your building by asking them the following questions:

1. What percentage of their pupils enter school already reading?

2. What percentage of their pupils enter school ready to learn to read?
3. What percentage of their pupils enter school needing reading-readiness instruction?
4. How do they accommodate these three groups of children?

If time permits, repeat the survey with first-grade teachers.

Suggestion 5

Read to your pupils every day!

REFERENCES

Durkin, Dolores. "Reading Readiness," *The Reading Teacher* **23,** 6 (March 1970): 534, 564.

Heideman, Carroll. "A Plea to Teachers: Ten Reasons for Reading Aloud," Madison, Wisconsin, 1975.

Words which attain the printed form do not become gospel merely because they are published. There are as many fallacies between the covers of books as there are truths...

HUBERT BERMONT

5 Selecting Reading Materials and Approaches

INTRODUCTION

In many ways it is difficult, if not impossible, to separate reading materials from reading approaches. Most approaches to reading instruction depend on certain types of materials, and most materials lend themselves better to one approach than to another. Reading approaches stem, inevitably, from their underlying philosophy or definition of the reading process. In addition, it is certainly known that reading is a very complex process, a process not easily defined.

A few decades ago, Leonard Bloomfield, a noted American linguist, referred to reading as the greatest intellectual feat of anyone's lifetime. Indeed, it is difficult to imagine any more astounding intellectual accomplishment. Nearly 70 years ago, Huey (1908, p. 6), a respected psychologist interested in teaching and learning to read, said:

And so to completely analyze what we do when we read would almost be the acme of a psychologist's achievements, for it would be to describe very many of the most intricate workings of the human mind, as well as to unravel the tangled story of the most remarkable specific performance that civilization has learned in all its history.

It is no wonder that there is no simple definition of reading. Reading involves a peculiar intermingling of at least the following elements:

1. *People*

   A. The *reader's*

      1) Intelligence
      2) Language development
      3) Interest
      4) Experiential background
      5) Learning style
      6) Purpose:

         a) Skill acquisition
         b) Information
         c) Pleasure
         d) Others

   B. The *writer's*

      1) Intent

         a) To instruct
         b) To persuade
         c) To inform

        d) To entertain

        e) Others

    2) Literary style

    3) Writing ability

    4) Experiental background

2. *Language*

    A. Grapheme-phoneme (letter-sound) relationships

    B. Morphemic (meaning-bearing) units

    C. Syntactic structures

    D. Semantic nuances (idiomatic expressions, literary devices, etc.)

3. *Printed matter*

    A. Type size, variety, and legibility

    B. Quantity and quality of illustrations

    C. Graphic repetition

    D. Other graphic cues (punctuation, capitalization)

When we define reading, perhaps simplistically, as "getting information from the printed page," we must remember that the elements above are complexly interrelated.

Elementary teachers are expected to teach children to read and to help them improve, refine, and apply their reading abilities. To do so, a teacher, school staff, or entire school district must decide on a sensible approach to teaching reading and in so deciding, choose appropriate instructional materials.

SELECTING MATERIALS

Before examining some specific approaches and their related materials, we wish to offer some guidelines for selecting and evaluating reading materials and programs. Some programs come wrapped in very pretty packages, and some publishing houses employ very articulate and persuasive salespersons. The wise teacher and administrator will carefully examine materials and programs before buying them. The following guidelines are intended to help individual teachers or text-selection committees composed of teachers, administrators, and students make wise selections.

Guidelines for Evaluating Reading Materials and Programs

1. Consider the underlying philosophy of the program. Does it reflect a word-frequency, decoding, or child-interest point of view about

initial vocabulary? (We discuss this aspect thoroughly next in this chapter.)

2. Consider the treatment of ethnic, racial, and sex groups. Do the reading selections and illustrations treat all groups equally and with dignity? Do the materials contain blatant and/or insidious prejudices or standardizations? Check carefully for discrimination shown by commission and *also by omission*.

3. Consider the interest value of the children's book—the quality of the literature, the variety of the content. Are the selections motivating, and do they extend children's experiences and ideas? How much time does the reading program devote to the enrichment of children's interests and attitudes? What is the quality of the suggested activities?

4. Consider the quality of any illustrations. Are they imaginative and enriching apart from the stories? With respect to item 1 above, do they develop or stifle open attitudes toward ethnic and sex groups?

5. Consider the development of word-identification skills. Is the program balanced and comprehensive? Is the sequencing of skills a good one? Are the suggestions for teaching useful and varied? Are the major word-identification skills, described in Chapter 7, included?

6. Consider the *emphasis* of the comprehension questions and activities. What levels are being developed, and how fully? Are the materials *intended* to help improve children's comprehension ability? Do most comprehension activities require only literal recall, or do they include the different comprehension skills described in Chapter 8?

7. Consider the usefulness of the teacher's manual. How valuable are the suggestions for skills work, questioning strategies, and reading-related activities? How varied are they? Is the manual well organized and easy to use?

8. Consider the recommendations made for individualization and grouping. Are suggested groups flexible or permanent? Do they form for varied purposes as discussed in Chapter 3? How helpful are the individualized procedures suggested?

Although these guidelines are not presented in any order of importance, we do feel that the second guideline must not be taken lightly by teachers or selection committees. For too many years, authors and publishers of children's materials seemed to have had a monolithic view of America. Only in the past decade or so have children's books seemed to reflect a discovery that ours is a pluralistic society, with black inhabitants as well as white. Only very recently have materials shown an awareness of Native Americans, Chicanos, and other minorities. Sex bias and stereotyping continue to be shortcomings of many published works, however. In Chapter 12, "Teaching the Linguistically and Culturally Diverse," a number of such factors are considered in greater depth.

BASIC APPROACHES TO READING

There are various ways to categorize the basic approaches to reading instruction and their accompanying materials. One way is to examine the sources of initial vocabulary. Answering the question "Where do 'first words' come from?" can provide rather quick awareness of the philosophy of reading underlying a given program. In essence, initial vocabulary—first words—can stem from one of three sources:

1. The words that children want to learn to read

2. Words that occur with such high frequency that children will encounter them again and again

3. Words that contain such consistent letter-sound relationships that they are easily "decodable."

Each of these sources of words reflects a philosophy of reading. The first source suggests that reading should be, from the start, intensely interesting and meaningful. The second source suggests that reading acquisition involves repetitive encounters with highly useful words. The third source views initial reading as essentially a decoding process, which is facilitated by repeated exposure to highly regular letter-sound correspondence patterns. Typical beginning words that might derive from each source are:

Self-selected		*High frequency*		*Letter-sound patterns*	
love	toothache	and	saw	Dan	hit
Angela	fight	the	she	can	pit
street	subway	are	not	fan	sit
Dad	weirdo	red	I	pan	kit

The following model shows the relationships of the three sources of initial vocabulary and includes examples of the basic approaches to reading instruction related to them.

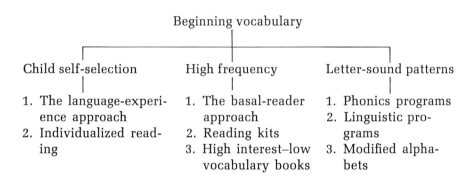

Beginning vocabulary

Child self-selection	High frequency	Letter-sound patterns
1. The language-experience approach	1. The basal-reader approach	1. Phonics programs
2. Individualized reading	2. Reading kits	2. Linguistic programs
	3. High interest–low vocabulary books	3. Modified alphabets

In Chapter 3 we discussed individualized reading and offered suggestions pertaining to material selection, record keeping, conferences, and varied grouping patterns. The term "individualized reading" has had many meanings and many manifestations. Certainly, all elementary teachers individualize at some times with all pupils. Many educators view individualized reading more as a *belief* about reading than as a tangible, definable instructional program.

Closely related to individualized reading, in fact perhaps the "purest" form of individualization, is the language-experience approach to reading instruction. Because of our belief in the psycholinguistic soundness of the language-experience approach as a beginning approach to reading, all of Chapter 6 is devoted to it. Consequently, the remainder of this chapter is comprised of descriptions and evaluations of some of the major approaches to reading which utilize published materials— approaches which stem from either a "high frequency" or "decodability" view of initial vocabulary selection.

THE BASAL-READING APPROACH

There is a nine-to-one chance that you were taught to read by means of a basal reader. It has been estimated that currently, more than four out of five children are instructed through this approach (Chall, 1967). Formerly referred to the "look-say" method, this approach is undergirded by a belief in a "controlled vocabulary" of high-frequency words. Most newer basal series, however, have a more balanced vocabulary criterion, with a higher evidence of decodable words introduced early.

In most published basal-reading programs, high-frequency (and other) words are introduced gradually and with sufficient repetition to ensure mastery. Word-identification skills and comprehension devices are introduced sequentially and gradually. The pupils proceed from the familiar to the unfamiliar within a tightly controlled scope and sequence.

Basal-reading programs are comprehensive and are designed to comprise the total program (though many authors and publishers urge the use of supplements as well) to help children progress from the status of nonreaders, through the stages of reading acquisition, into refined, fully developed mature readers. With such a goal, most basal programs contain a variety of printed material designed to span the elementary school experience from kindergarten to grade six or eight. Basal programs typically include a number (eight to fifteen or more) of basic textbooks, an equal number of accompanying workbooks, comprehensive teacher's manuals, supplementary books, magazines and wall charts, a variety of audio-visual aids, and a full assortment of pre- and posttests intended for diagnosis of reading needs and assessment of mastery of skills and materials. Capsule descriptions of some of the typical components of a basal program follow.

Prereading (Readiness) Materials

These usually consist of workbooks, story charts, perceptual-motor development devices, records or cassettes, games, and story books intended to improve the children's auditory and visual perception and discrimination, language development, interest, and other factors considered prerequisite to beginning reading. A typical readiness activity designed to reinforce visual-auditory-kinesthetic ability is shown in Fig. 1. In the exercise in Fig. 1, children are asked to say the name of the picture and to listen to its beginning sound. Then, in the space provided, they are to write the letter that represents that sound.

In many basal programs, children engage in readiness activities for a month or more before progressing to story books. Obviously, since some children enter school already reading, whereas others require extended periods of prereading development, the sensitive teacher does not "march" the entire class systematically through the entire program.

Visual-auditory-kinesthetic reinforcement of initial consonants: **c, m, h, j**   **31**

Fig. 1. A typical reading-readiness activity. (From *Teachers' Edition, My Sound and Word Book,* of the Reading 360 series, by Theodore Clymer and others, © copyright, 1969, by Ginn and Company (Xerox Corporation). Used with permission.)

Preprimers, Primers, and Readers

These are the basic reading books of the basal program. Beginning with very thin paperbacks containing perhaps 25 frequently repeated words, they progress to rather comprehensive literary anthologies for the older students. Typically, many illustrations are included, particularly in the early books, and many story characters are met time and again throughout the series. The newest basal series have abandoned tight grade-level labels (e.g., Book 2—Grade 2; Book 4—Grade 4, etc.) and include a greater number of books. Thus, first-grade children might be reading

Book 5, and older children presumably avoid the embarrassment encountered when a slow-reading fifth-grade child is assigned to Book 2. The two pages shown in Figs. 2 and 3 illustrate the type of basal-series content at a preprimer level and at a fourth-grade level, respectively.

Ben, you get the cat.

I'll help you get on the truck.

Tiger will come to you.

13

Fig. 2. Basal-series content at a preprimer level. (W. K. Durr, *et al., Tigers,* Boston: Houghton Mifflin, 1971, p. 13. Reprinted by permission.)

WHEELS
by Lisa Miller

Take a ride on your bike. Go for a drive in a car. Push a shopping cart. A bike, a car, a cart, all move on wheels. Wheels make things move easily.

Wheels help us to move things because they cut down *friction*. Friction is the force that makes objects hard to move when they rub against each other.

Little, highly polished balls called ball bearings, or roller bearings, help to reduce friction in many wheels. Instead of the wheel rubbing against its axle, it slides around smoothly on the roller bearings. Both the wheel and the axle touch only a tiny part of each ball. And the balls touch only a tiny part of each other. There is very little friction. That is why you can skate faster on ball-bearing roller skates than on learners' skates.

29

Fig. 3. Basal-series content at a fourth-grade level. (W. K. Durr, *et al., Kaleidoscope,* Boston: Houghton Mifflin, 1971, p. 29. Adapted from Lisa Miller, *Wheels,* New York: Coward-McCann, 1965. Reprinted by permission.)

Workbooks

Usually, a workbook accompanies each reading book. Workbooks contain practice pages to develop skills geared to the stories in the basic books. These practice pages contain various activities designed to teach or reinforce particular dimensions of comprehension, word-identification skills (e.g., phonics, structural analysis, and context), and study-reference skills (e.g., chart reading and the use of the dictionary). Ideally, children would be asked to do only those pages containing skills in which they are weak. Unfortunately, however, we have often observed teachers who require that *all* children in a group sequentially do *all* workbook pages (and just as bad, sequentially read all the stories in the story book). Certainly, such teachers have the best of intentions and do not want their pupils to miss anything essential. However, children *are* individually different, and frequent assessment would seem to lend guidance toward more appropriately assigned activity. Figure 4 shows a typical phonics activity found in a basal-reader workbook.

Teachers' Manuals

These are often excellent, invaluable guide books to the use of the reading books and workbooks. They contain numerous teaching suggestions and supplementary activities. Some contain specific questions for each of the stories and suggestions for diagnostic use of the materials. If used selectively, teachers' manuals can be extremely useful resources for instructional planning. The page reprinted from a teacher's manual (Fig. 5) demonstrates the type of detailed suggestions available in many manuals.

Tests and Supplementary Materials

Most programs include a variety of pretests, skill tests, story-end, unit-end, and total-book tests. Group tests for both diagnosis and assessment are usually available. Such supplementary materials as tapes, kits, extra story books, filmstrips, and posters are, to varying degrees, available with basal programs and are intended to add variety and interest in learning to read.

One of the key instructional strategies of basal-reading programs is ability grouping. Most programs suggest that a number of groups be formed (in practice, it is often three) comprised of children with similar reading ability as identified by testing and teacher judgment. The three-group plan has been with us for about 40 years, having commendably replaced whole-class instruction, which showed no cogni-

aei

Put a ring around the vowel letter whose
name you hear in the word for each picture.

Phonology: distinguishing among /ey/, /iy/, and /ay/
Have the pictures identified and, if necessary, help children with the directions.
They are to say the name of each picture to themselves and circle the vowel
letter whose name they hear.

19

"**Three Friends,**" pages 41-46

Fig. 4. A typical phonics activity from a basal-reader workbook. (E. L. Evertts,
et al., *A Time for Friends: Teachers Edition Workbook*, New York: Holt,
Rinehart and Winston, 1973, p. 19. Reprinted by permission.)

Extending interests

As an inducement for boys and girls who seldom visit the library table, you might recommend Augusta Stevenson's biography of the popular frontiersman, *Daniel Boone, Boy Hunter.*

Then, just for fun, select a few poems from Karla Kuskin's *In the Middle of the Trees.* Pupils will enjoy the personification in "The Tree and Me," the delightful last line of "The Hat," and the bit of nonsense called "Around and Around."

Pupils read biography of Daniel Boone . . .

and respond to poetry.

Encouraging personal reading

Because there will always be youngsters whose interests lead them to books bearing little relation to the theme of the unit, be sure to give these children a chance to share their enthusiasm for books they have read.

As a child talks about one of his favorites, he might use the illustrations to tell just enough about the story to tease listeners' curiosity, explain the problem facing the main character (without, of course, giving away its solution), or compare a story character or problem with one youngsters have read about in *More Roads to Follow.*

Children share independent reading interests.

Evaluating progress

The responses on pages 52-53 and 54 of the *Think-and-Do Book* will help you evaluate pupils' progress in using ideas gained through reading and in interpreting dictionary definitions and pronunciations. As children use pages 52-53, they must think about whether a particular individual evidenced a certain personal quality and decide which of the other people pictured had this same quality. The dictionary definitions of the qualities referred to are included on page 53.

Page 54 provides a means of testing each child's competence in using a short pronunciation key to determine the pronunciations of words found in a glossary or dictionary.

Pupils take informal tests in Think-and-Do Book.

Fig. 5. A typical page from a teacher's manual. (From *More Roads to Follow, Teacher's Edition,* by Helen M. Robinson, A. Sterl Artley, Marion Monroe, and Charlotte S. Huck. © 1964 by Scott, Foresman and Co. Reprinted by permission of the publisher.)

zance of individual differences. During the reading period of a basal program, the three groups of students typically alternate: (1) reading orally with the teacher and answering questions; (2) doing workbook pages at their desks; or (3) reading independently. However, we tend to disfavor ability grouping as a *total* grouping scheme and would recommend flexible grouping for various purposes, as described in Chapter 3.

The main instructional strategies within a basal program include: (1) developing background (discussing common experiences and activities related to the story to be read and highlighting new vocabulary to be encountered); (2) silent and oral reading of the story, discussing the story (to develop and assess comprehension), skill development (primarily by using the workbooks and supplementary materials); and (3) extended reading (referring to other stories or books related in some way to the story just read).

Some Criticisms of Basal Programs

In the past 15 years, a number of improvements have been made in basal readers, somewhat nullifying many of the criticisms traditionally leveled at them. Since some criticisms seem to remain valid and since others continue to be heard, it is worthwhile to examine the most prevalent ones.

1. The "three-group" organizational plan has been rather widely attacked by various reading authorities. Certainly, the three-group plan is not unique to basal readers. It is used with some other reading materials and in other subject areas. But most teachers who use a basal program *do* use a three-group approach, as they are urged to do by most basal teachers' manuals. The principal criticism of the plan is its rigidity. Few students tend to move out of a particular group, and they are therefore "tracked" for their reading instruction. Studies have shown that children who are placed in the low group in grade one are often still in the low group in the later grades. They start at the bottom and never really "catch up" with classmates who learned more quickly in the beginning (Bosman, 1972). Because students in the low group generally read "easier" material and spend a great deal of time on "skill and drill" activities, their interest in reading dissipates. Children quickly learn that they are in the "dumb" group and, following the Pygmalion theory—i.e., people tend to achieve the expectations set for them—respond in kind. Again, you are referred to Chapter 3, which offers alternatives to lock-step ability grouping in reading.

2. The materials contain overt and indirect discrimination against minority groups and women. Until the past decade, most basal-story

characters were clean, well-clothed, white suburbanites who owned only unbroken toys. Mother never worked and seemed to be perpetually in the kitchen. Father invariably worked in an office. Gradually, black characters (at first, light tan) began to appear in the basals, and in some current series one occasionally encounters a Chicano, a Native American, or an Asian. Figure 6 shows a multi-ethnic picture found in one such series.

Women have yet to be presented realistically in a majority of basal series, however. *Dick and Jane as Victims* (1972) and other publications have clearly demonstrated the sex stereotyping that exists. Women are found almost exclusively in the home (when they do work, it is as a teacher, nurse, or librarian) and are more dependent and passive. Boy-centered stories far outnumber girl-centered stories. It is encouraging to note that in the very newest basal series published, authors and editors have demonstrated a much sharper sensitivity about racism, ethnicism, and sexism.

3. Story content is dull, repetitive and nonliterary. People who level such criticism should attempt to write a children's literary masterpiece with a controlled vocabulary of 30 words. Because of the philosophical belief in gradual, sequential, repetitive introduction of high-frequency words, basal series have often contained quite uninteresting stories. Recently, greater variation in illustrations and photographs and in manipulation of print have helped increase the interest level of the materials. Figure 7, a page from the Sounds of Language series, exemplifies this.

Other criticisms have focused on the mismatch between "Primerese" (syntactic structures) and the language of children, and insufficient attention to decoding. Most recently published basal series show improvement in both of these areas.

Whatever the strengths and weaknesses of the basal-reader approach, elementary teachers should probably analyze critically two or three such series. Eighty to 90 percent of all elementary teachers are employed in schools which use one of the basal-reader series.

SUPPLEMENTARY MATERIALS

Most publishers of children's reading materials also market various reading kits, which are designed for a number of purposes. Some stress specific skill development; others stress comprehension development; others, literary appreciation; and some are multipurpose. Typically, kits afford a certain type of individualization in that no two children are likely to work with the same booklet, selection, or card at the same

On the Bus

"I know you.

You watch out for the cars."

"We are going to the zoo.

Are you going to the zoo?"

"I don't get to go.

I am here to get you on the bus."

Fig. 6. Nonwhite Americans are beginning to appear in basal readers. (D. M. Baugh and M. P. Pulsifer, *Let's See the Animals,* p. 9. Reprinted by permission. Copyright © 1970 by Noble and Noble, Publishers, Inc., and Materials for Today's Learning, Inc. Copyright © 1965 by Chandler Publishing Company. All rights reserved.)

The design of the type creates a mood that will be reflected in the reader's interpretation of the poem. As a matter of proof, just listen to the vocal freedom that children bring to the reading of this poem as compared to other, more traditionally typographically designed poems in the book. And don't be surprised if this *play* with print occurs in children's own stories in the next several weeks.

The bean was so hard, Susie dropped it in lard.

The lard was so greasy, Susie nearly jumped fleecy.

And when she came down,
She ran through the town.
The town was so big,
Susie jumped on a pig.
The pig jumped so high,
He touched the sky—
He touched the sky
And he couldn't jump higher,
But, oh,
what a ride had Susie Mortar.

Fig. 7. Imaginative use of illustrations and type can heighten students' interest in the material being presented. (B. Martin, Jr., *Sounds of Laughter,* Sounds of Language Series, New York: Holt, Rinehart and Winston, 1972, 1966, p. 55. Reprinted by permission.)

1   The young ruler was handsome, athletic, and courteous. He wanted a son, to be his companion and eventually to rule after him. He was disappointed when the new child in his family was a girl, for he knew that she could never be

A — companionable.   **B** — king.   **C** — courteous.   **D** — athletic.

2   Generally the dieting problem is an esthetic one — we want to build up flat areas or flatten built-up areas. Those who face this problem should buy a chart showing the amounts of calories, vitamins, etc., contained in basic foods. By controlling the number of calories in their diets, they can

A — learn better to enjoy food.   **C** — gain or lose weight.
B — increase their consumption   **D** — improve their health
of the basic foods.   permanently.

3   The glider is a type of airplane that is not equipped with power. It is launched by means of an elastic cord, a spring catapult, or a tow cable. Once in the air, the pilot endeavors to stay aloft by using

A — catapults.   **C** — radio controls.
B — turbojet engines.   **D** — air currents.

4   A newspaper reaches many people in a local area, whereas a magazine is usually read by people of similar interests

A — throughout the country.   **C** — in one age group.
B — in that same area.   **D** — and educational standards.

5   The United States is the only industrial nation of the world that has a large surplus of food. Few other countries, either agricultural or industrial, have methods of food production efficient enough to feed their increasing populations, much less to produce any surpluses. Until more countries do master efficient food-producing methods, many of the people in the world will have to

A — produce their food.   **C** — appeal to the United
B — go into industry.   Nations.
                                D — go hungry.

Fig. 8. A typical reading-kit activity. (From *Reading for Understanding, Junior edition,* by Thelma Gwinn Thurstone. © 1963, Science Research Associates, Inc. Reprinted by permission of the publisher.)

time. Materials in the kits (usually, a short reading selection together with comprehension questions or skill activities and a self-correcting answer key) are categorized according to level of readability or interest area or both. Readability level is usually determined by a combination of tabulating high-frequency words and examining syntactic complexity. Figure 8, from *Reading for Understanding,* Junior Edition, published by SRA, shows one type of kit activity. There are 400 such cards (with five items on each side) in this kit, graded on ten broad levels of difficulty.

Other supplementary materials include:

1. "High-interest/low-vocabulary" books—those of presumed interest to older children who have poorly developed reading ability
2. Reading machines designed to increase eye-span or reading speed
3. Boxes of games constructed to teach or reinforce specific word-attack or comprehension skills
4. Audio tapes, cassettes, records, and film strips intended to increase reading interest as well as ability
5. Newspapers, magazines, and wall charts designed to be readable and of interest to particular groups of children.

Few, if any, supplementary materials claim to be comprehensive reading programs, as the basal series do. Instead, they are prepared for specific purposes to aid and broaden the major reading program in the classroom.

LETTER-SOUND PATTERN APPROACHES

We have shown that certain approaches to reading instruction stem from a belief that initial vocabulary should consist of self-identified, high-interest words. Individualized reading was discussed in Chapter 3, and the language-experience approach is the subject of Chapter 6. On the other hand, the popular basal-series approach is built on the belief in the need for frequent repetition of a "controlled vocabulary" of high-frequency words. On the following pages we will describe some of the approaches that are based on a belief in letter-sound regularity and consistency in initial words.

It is not easy to differentiate between phonics programs (see Fig. 9) and "linguistic" * programs (see Fig. 10) except by the label on the package. Since both recognize that children have large speaking vocab-

---

* The term "linguistic" must be viewed in the simplistic sense in which it is used to label certain reading programs which stress decoding. The science of linguistics is concerned with phonetics, phonemics, morphemics, syntax, semantics, paralanguage, and other aspects of communication. "Linguistic" readers are concerned mainly with letter-sound relationships.

a

Use your train for a marker.
See how fast you can read these words.
Remember! It is better to be a good freight train
than a careless streamliner.

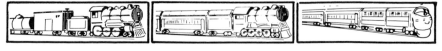

c a t	c a t	cat
c a n	c a n	can
r a n	r a n	ran
m a n	m a n	man
s a t	s a t	sat
h a d	h a d	had
b a g	b a g	bag
th a t	th a t	that
th a n	th a n	than
f a s t	f a s t	fast

Cut a marker.

Fig. 9. A page from a typical phonics program. (R. B. Montgomery and S. Coughlan, *Sound, Spell, Read: The Phonovisual Vowel Book,* Washington, D.C.: Phonovisual Products, 1955, p. 18. Reprinted by permission.)

ularies, both also view reading as a decoding process—one in which readers need to translate from the written code to the oral code. Consequently, both types of programs attempt to stress words in which letters consistently correspond to certain sounds, at least at the outset.

The Tops

Dan's mother has a box of tops.

The tops are for Dan, Jim, and Tim.

Dan sits and rubs his top with a rag.

Jim taps his top, and it hops a bit.

" Look, Tim," Jim said.

" The top can hop."

Tim hits his top with a mop.

It pops into a tin can.

The twins have to look for the tops.

Fig. 10. A page from a typical linguistics program. (From *Merrill Linguistic Readers, Level C,* by Wayne Otto, *et al.* Copyright 1975 by Charles E. Merrill Publishing Co.)

Both approaches gradually introduce irregularly spelled words and exceptions to previously learned patterns. There are some differences, however.

1. Some phonics programs tend to emphasize synthesis. Children are taught certain letter-sound associations in isolation and are then taught to "blend" them together to form words. In one sense this is a spelling approach to reading, since it stresses encoding rather than decoding (see Chapter 7). Synthesis does not require an encoding emphasis, since some activities involve sound-blending only. Most linguistic programs

stress spelling *patterns* or "word families" rather than isolated letter-sound relationships. In linguistic programs children tackle *cat, fat,* and *pat* as whole entities, whereas in synthetic phonics programs the emphasis is on c /c/ + a /ae/ + t /t/ = *cat.*

2. Phonics programs tend to stress memorization and application of rules or generalizations. With some programs teachers teach certain words and then ask the children to analyze the words to *discover* the rules or generalizations. With other programs teachers teach the generalizations directly. In either case, children are guided to learn, experiment with, and apply 20 or 30 or 60 or more generalizations.* Linguistic programs do not stress the learning of rules, but try to foster awareness of minimal contrasts in words, e.g., *man, map, mad; pan, man, can; pan, pin, pen.* They tend to stress high-speed recognition of high-consistency spelling patterns through repeated exposure.

Phonics Programs

There are several published programs that are similar to basal programs in that they are total programs. These phonics programs contain primers and readers, workbooks, manuals, texts, and supplementary components. They differ from the basal programs described earlier in their intensive emphasis on phonics. Vocabulary words are selected because of letter-sound consistency rather than frequency of occurrences.

In addition to total phonics programs, many supplementary charts, kits, games, and workbooks are on the market and are widely used. Teachers following a language-experience, individualized, or basal approach to reading sometimes find the need to emphasize decoding with certain pupils who have specific skill weaknesses. Although most reading educators support the necessity of aiding decoding ability (through supplementary materials), few advocate the use of total programs which may slight the other important word-identification skills delineated in Chapter 7.

Linguistic Programs

The first published linguistic program, *Let's Read,* was written by a linguist. To avoid distracting children's attention from the basic task believed imperative—decoding from printed word to sound—no pic-

---

* In an interesting study of 45 commonly taught phonics generalizations, Clymer found only 18 of them useful in that they applied to 75 percent or more of the words to which they supposedly related. Of these 18, only nine are widely applicable.

tures were included in the series. Nonsense words (synthetic words such as *dat* and *fam*) were used, as well as real words, and lists of words were included in addition to stories. The use of nonsense words can be seen in Fig. 11, a page from the *Let's Read* series. The series includes nine books intended for children in grades one to three. The stress is on grapheme-phoneme relationships in words, not in isolation.

az	av	az	ac	az
	az	af	az	as
daz	daz	das	daz	daf
	dav	daz	dal	daz
gaz	daz	gaz	gat	gaz
	gaz	gan	gaz	gad
haz	gaz	hap	haz	haz
	haz	haz	hag	han
laz	haz	laz	haz	laz
	laz	gaz	laz	lan

Fig. 11. The use of nonsense words in a linguistic program. (By special permission from *Let's Read 1* by Leonard Bloomfield and Clarence L. Barnhart, © 1963 by Clarence L. Barnhart.)

Since the publication of the *Let's Read* series in 1963, a number of other linguistic programs have appeared. Their similarities are greater than their differences. Some include pictures; some teach basic high-frequency function words; some place a greater stress on comprehension than did *Let's Read;* some introduce word-attack skills other than pronouncing. All of them, however, stress mastery of a limited number of consistent spelling patterns, with gradual introduction of less consistent or less frequent patterns. Most of these series include basic reading books, workbooks, and teachers' manuals. One program, aimed at Spanish-speaking children who are learning English as a second language, contains "culture-free" stories and themes to which children from diverse backgrounds can relate. Most of the published linguistic programs have been designed for beginning reading and include materials for only the first two or three grades. A recently revised linguistic program (Merrill) has added materials for grades four through six.

Another program, *Programmed Reading,* combines a "linguistic" (decoding) philosophy of reading with the instructional strategy of linear programming. It contains 21 illustrated books in which the children read and frequently respond in writing. Children check the appropriateness of their responses before moving to the next item. A sample page from this series is shown in Fig. 12.

Being a programed approach, *Programmed Reading* is highly (prescriptively) individualized. Since children work at their own pace, pupils in a given class may be reading in several programed texts, thus making it unlikely that any two children will be on the same page at the same time. After completing each programed workbook, the children read a small, hardcover storybook containing the patterns and words taught in the text. This series is intended only for children in the primary grades.

Summary

The emphasis in both phonics and linguistic approaches to reading is on decoding. Children come to school with thousands of words in their speaking/understanding vocabularies. Proponents of decoding programs tend to view reading *primarily as decoding,* i.e., reading is translating an unfamiliar printed word to its known, oral counterpart. Proponents believe that once they have mastered decoding, children are capable of reading on their own and of reading virtually anything they can handle conceptually; hence, many such programs are written only for children in their first few years in school. Both types of approaches and materials (phonics and linguistic) seek to facilitate the decoding process by beginning with high-consistency spelling patterns or useful generalizations. Others, who view decoding as a major hurdle to reading acquisition, have developed different strategies to reduce the problem.

MODIFIED ALPHABETS

The English language employs 26 letters, singly or in combinations, to represent about 45 phonemes (distinctive speech sounds), resulting in hundreds of letter-sound correspondences. For centuries, spelling re-

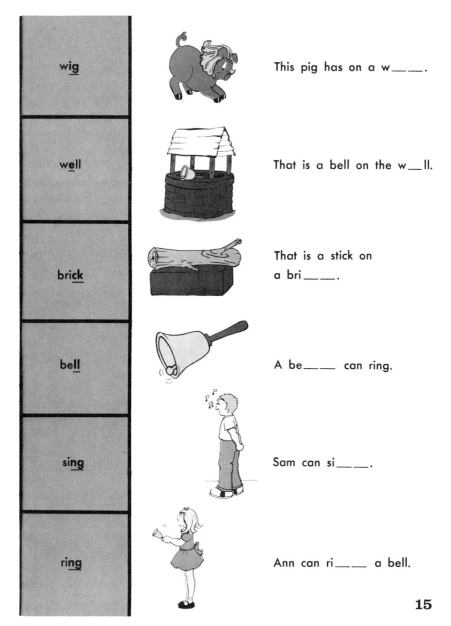

w**i**g	This pig has on a w＿＿.
w**e**ll	That is a bell on the w＿ll.
bri**ck**	That is a stick on a bri＿＿.
be**ll**	A be＿＿ can ring.
si**ng**	Sam can si＿＿.
ri**ng**	Ann can ri＿＿ a bell.

15

Fig. 12. A programed linguistic approach. (C. D. Buchanan, *Programmed Reading Book 4*, rev. ed. New York: Webster Division, McGraw-Hill (a Sullivan Associates Program), 1968, p. 15. Reprinted by permission of Behavioral Research Laboratories, Inc.)

formers have urged the adoption of a phonemic alphabet (one in which a given letter represents only one sound, and through which each phoneme is represented by only one letter). In his will, George Bernard Shaw left a sum of money to be used as prize money in a contest to see who could develop the most sensible phonemic alphabet. The irregularity of English spelling is bemoaned in innumerable poems:

> "I take it you already know
> of rough and bough and tough and though . . ."

Though many spelling reformers hold out hope that a new alphabet will be universally adopted for English, others have concerned themselves with helping children who are learning to read overcome the inconsistencies of letter-sound relationships. Two published programs, the i.t.a. (Initial Teaching Alphabet) and UNIFON, contain alphabets designed to *initially* help children learn to read. Both programs advocate transition from the modified alphabet to our standard alphabet (traditional orthography) during the child's first year of school. The i.t.a. contains 44 symbols (one for each phoneme in the author's dialect); UNIFON contains 40. Figure 13 presents the i.t.a. alphabet together with representative words. It should be noted that of the 44 "letters," 24 are taken directly from the traditional alphabet (q and x are omitted). Fourteen are combinations of traditional letters, and six are unique to i.t.a.

The i.t.a. and UNIFON approaches to reading are similar. After children have been taught the new alphabet, the sounds the different

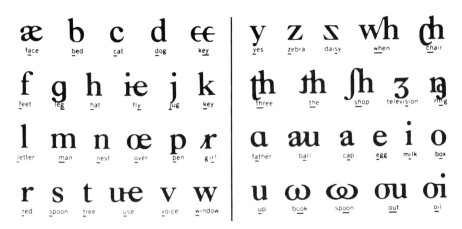

Fig. 13. The i.t.a. alphabet and representative words. (H. J. Tanyzer, "What You Should Know About the Initial Teaching Alphabet," *Hofstra Review* (Winter 1966): 1. Reprinted by permission.)

characters represent are taught so that the students can synthesize the sounds to form words. Proponents of modified alphabets contend that once the new alphabet (letter-sound correspondences) has been learned, children can read (decode) any words they encounter and can write any word in their speaking/listening vocabularies.

As stated previously, neither i.t.a. nor UNIFON is intended as a permanent alphabet. From the beginning, children are helped to make the transition to the traditional (irregular) alphabet, since many of the "new" letters were borrowed from the traditional. As children progress through the small books in the series, they increasingly encounter traditional—rather than modified—spellings. Teachers report that 60 to 80 percent of their pupils have made the complete transition by the end of first grade; the others complete it in second grade. For this reason, many schools using a modified alphabet assign a class to a teacher for two years—grades one and two—to ensure smooth transition. A reprint of a page from an i.t.a. reading series is shown in Fig. 14.

Modified alphabets have been criticized for several reasons. Critics contend that the meanings of many English words (homophones) are identified by their spellings (*road-rode; horse-hoarse; great-grate;* etc.) and that these differences are obliterated by a modified, phonemic alphabet. Others criticize the unavailability of sufficient printed materials (other than reading books) in the modified alphabet. Still others point out that ours is a highly mobile society, with one family in five moving yearly, and question the effect on a child who moves into or out of a modified-alphabet program in midyear. By contrast, proponents laud the ease with which children learn to read and comment favorably on the creative writing children are capable of, since they—at least theoretically—can write any word they know.

OTHER MODIFICATIONS

Two other approaches have attempted, through modifications, to reduce the problem of inconsistent letter-sound relationships in English. In one such approach, called *Words in Color,* the author identified 47 phonemes. Each phoneme is printed in the same color, regardless of its spelling. For example, in the words *be, bee, mean, either,* and *happy,* the [e] sound is always represented by the same color. Because of the similarity of the colors, however, some children may have difficulty discriminating the 47 different ones. Another system, DMS (diacritical marking system) utilizes diacritical marks—similar to those found in dictionaries—to facilitate letter-sound acquisition (mādɇ, mɑ̄ɨd). Gradually, the diacritical marks are used less and less frequently.

ſhe elefant and
ſhe muŋky

far awæ in ſhe juŋgl livd tɷ animal
frendſ—an elefant and a muŋky.

aull dæ loŋ ſhe muŋky wonted tɷ
cliem up treeſ and swiŋ kwickly from
wun branch tɷ anuſher.

ſhe elefant liekt tɷ wauk around ſhe
juŋgl and mæk a paſh in ſhe treeſ wiſh
hiſ truŋk.

Fig. 14. An i.t.a. story. (From the book, Book 5, *The Trick* by A. J. Mazurkie-
wicz and H. J. Tanyzer. Copyright © 1966 by Initial Teaching Alphabet Pub.,
Inc. Reprinted by permission of Pitman Publishing Corp.)

These are but a few of the many approaches to teaching reading. Auckerman (1971) describes dozens of other programs in his book on beginning-reading methods. Since 80 percent or more of the nation's classrooms utilize one or more of the major basal-reader programs, all of the many other approaches receive relatively limited use. This does not mean they are inherently bad or inferior. Many things besides philosophical considerations, quality, or effectiveness enter into the selection of materials and methods (habit, packaging, salesforce).

A FINAL WORD

This unit has been concerned with reading materials and methods. It must be reiterated that no method or material is a panacea. Nothing works best with all children; similarly, all things work with some children. A major research study of instructional approaches in reading analyzed 27 different comparative investigations (Bond and Dykstra, 1967). Some of these studies compared a basal program with a linguistic program; others compared i.t.a. with language-experience, etc. Virtually every type of comparison of the six or eight major approaches was made. Among the major conclusions were the following:

1. Children learn to read and others fail to learn to read in all the programs studied. Pupils learn by a variety of vastly different materials and methods.

2. No one approach was so distinctly better in all situations that it should be used exclusively.

3. A combined program, basal with supplementary phonics, was often superior to a single approach.

4. Children's reading scores sometimes varied more *within a method* than *between methods,* suggesting that the *teacher* and the total learning environment—not the materials or method—is the key variable.

Some excellent teachers use one approach, and others, equally excellent, use another approach. Sadly, some teachers achieve poor results (undoubtedly due to a combination of factors) regardless of method or material.

In seeking teaching positions, elementary teachers should carefully consider the approaches and materials that will be available to help them teach reading. They should ask themselves, "Philosophically and practically, can I teach at my highest level of ability using the approach or approaches used in this school?"

Suggested Activities for the Methods Class

Activity 1

1. Select one strand of materials from one published program. For example, if you choose Grade 2 from a basal series, collect all Grade 2 materials: the basic book(s), the workbook, the teacher's manual, the tests, and add supplementary materials.
2. Using the eight suggested guidelines presented on pp. 91–92 of this chapter, analyze the selected materials.
3. Prepare an oral report of your findings (supplemented with visuals, if you wish) to share with others in the class.

Activity 2

1. Analyze three or four of the many Dr. Seuss books. What seems to be their underlying philosophy? Why do you think they are so popular with many children?
2. Compare the books with three or four books from one of the published linguistic series. What are the similarities and differences?

Activity 3

Search through published reading programs and children's books for examples of racial, ethnic, or sex bias or stereotyping. The examples you find may be blatant or insidious and may be in the form of commission or omission.

Activity 4

Conduct a survey of teachers regarding material selection. Be sure to ask at least the following questions:

1. How are reading materials and methods selected in your school?
2. What criteria are considered in the selection process?
3. What differentiates a "good" program from a "bad" one?

Did you find uniform answers to question 3?

Activity 5

Using a teacher's manual from a published reading series, plan a lesson and then share your plans in small groups.

Teaching Suggestions

Suggestion 1

Gather reading books and workbooks from several published series—as many as you can find at a particular level. Ask a group of elementary children to examine the materials and decide which series they would choose if they could. Do not give them guidelines about what to look for; rather, let the discussion be very "free-wheeling." Listen carefully to their discussion (you may want to tape it). What kinds of things seem to be important to children in selecting materials?

Suggestion 2

Observe first-grade classrooms in which different basic approaches are being used. Note any differences you observe in how pupils respond to the reading act (i.e., they sound words out, they use good intonation patterns, they are keenly aware of the meaning of each sentence, they are skillful at using a variety of word-identification skills).

REFERENCES

Aukerman, R. C. *Approaches to Beginning Reading,* New York: John Wiley and Sons, 1971.

Bermont, Hubert. "A Bookman Speaks to Students," *Journal of Reading* **17,** 7 (1974): 524–526.

Bloomfield, L. "Linguistics and Reading," *Elementary English Review* **19** (April 1942): 125–30 and (May 1942): 183–186.

Bond, Guy L., and Robert Dykstra. "The Cooperative Research Program in First Grade Reading Instruction," *Reading Research Quarterly* **2,** 4 (1967): 5–141.

Bosman, D. "Mobility in Basal Reading Groups," Unpublished paper, University of Wisconsin, 1972.

Chall, J. S. *Learning to Read: The Great Debate,* New York: McGraw-Hill, 1967.

Clymer, T. "The Utility of Phonic Generalizations in the Primary Grades," *Reading Teacher* **16** (January 1963): 252–258.

Dick and Jane as Victims: Sex Stereotyping in Children's Readers, Princeton, N.J.: Women on Words and Images, 1972.

Huey, E. B. *The Psychology and Pedagogy of Reading,* New York: Macmillan, 1908.

Tanyzer, Harold J. "What You Should Know About the Initial Teaching Alphabet," *The Hofstra Review* (Winter, 1966).

We went to the
School Forest.
We saw lots of
trees.
We saw many animals.
We rode on a school
bus.
We had a good time.

If there is a strong correlation between listening/ speaking and reading ... if the teacher is to capitalize upon children's backgrounds, experiences, and interests in the initial structuring of the learning environment, and if learning theory states that one new variable should be introduced at a time, then the language experience approach approximates a sound method for developing learning ability for all children.

LOUISE MATTEONI

6 Using the Language- Experience Approach

The language-experience approach to reading is a method whereby the reading materials are created by actually recording children's spoken language. The approach mandates that reading be based on the language and the experiences of the learner. By wedding the child's experiences with language in the acquisition of reading fluency, the approach rests on the foundation of the child's interest. The child cannot help but be interested in reading, for what is read are the thoughts and experiences, words, and sentences of the child.

In Chapter 5 we mentioned that the sources of initial vocabulary in reading reflect the philosophy of the reading program. The first few hundred words a child learns to read generally reflect one of three opinions about beginning reading:

1. Beginning words should be the most frequent words in use, the words the child will encounter time and again.

2. Beginning words should be those with regular, patterned, letter-sound correspondences, e.g., *pit* and *sit,* thereby facilitating decoding from the start.

3. Beginning words should be those the child wants to learn to read, so that reading will be interesting and meaningful from the start.

The third point of view is the philosophy underlying the language-experience approach. The method does not downplay the need for children to learn high-frequency words and to learn to decode, but it does recognize the need for high interest in beginning reading. Further, the development of skill in reading is totally interrelated with the development of skill in listening, speaking, and writing. According to Allen (1968, pp. 1–2), the approach presumes that:

• the thinking of each child is valued, regardless of how limited, which leads to

• encouraging each child to express his thinking in many forms, but especially in oral language, which can be

• represented in written form by a teacher or by the child, which can be

• reconstructed (read) by the author and others, which leads to

• reading the written language of others from a variety of sources, which should

• influence the thinking and oral language of the reader so that his spelling, writing, and reading improve.*

When children enter school, they have a highly developed language ability. They have thousands of words in their speaking-listening vo-

---

* R. V. Allen. "How a Language-Experience Program Works," in *A Decade of Innovations: Approaches to Beginning Reading,* ed. E. C. Vilscek, IRA, Proceedings of the 12th Annual Convention, 1968, pp. 1–2.

cabularies. They use and understand most of the syntactic structures of their dialect of English, and they are capable of arranging words and structures to generate countless meaningful utterances which can be understood by others. Their various storehouses of linguistic ability will differ according to background and dialect, but few children enter school with a serious linguistic deprivation.

The language-experience approach is a way to teach *beginning* reading. No one suggests that children remain in such a program indefinitely. Though the approach has most often been used to teach young children to read, it has also been used effectively with nonreading older children and illiterate adults, as demonstrated by Paulo Freire. (Freire taught Brazilian peasants to read by beginning with words charged with political meaning and issues of vital importance to the learners.) But regardless of whether the approach is used with children or with adults, it is a beginning—a temporary—approach.

No two language-experience programs are the same. What happens in one classroom is different from what happens in another classroom, because of the peculiar mix of time, people, and circumstances and because the approach is tied to no particular set of published materials. There is, for example, no scope and sequence of skill instruction. There are few, or perhaps no, books used by all children in the class. A wide variety of individual and group activities occur. Nonetheless, there are instructional activities common to most classrooms using the language-experience approach.

LANGUAGE EXPERIENCE IN A NUTSHELL

There are at least six types of reading and related activities that are integral to the language-experience approach. Some are most effective as individual activities, whereas others may be used with groups. Each is briefly described here and then explained more fully in the remainder of the chapter.

1. Each day, individuals (or groups) tell the teacher the word(s) they want to learn. The teacher writes the words on separate pieces of paper and gives them to the child. The child studies the words, perhaps tracing and writing them, and then files them in a word box or writes them in a personal word book.

2. Simultaneously, individuals (or groups) dictate stories, events, or descriptions to the teacher, who records them—in the children's vocabulary and sentence structure—on the chalkboard or a sheet of paper. Later, the children read the stories back and read one another's stories. The stories can be recorded more permanently on

ditto paper for personal books or on large poster paper for a class "big book." In group situations, language-experience chart stories often arise from a common class experience, such as listening to a visitor, going on a trip, or caring for a classroom pet.

3. Sight vocabulary, phonics generalizations, structural elements, contextual awareness, and comprehension can all be taught by using the individually or group-dictated stories. In this approach there is no sequence for such skills; rather, they are taught and reinforced as needs and opportunities arise. For example, if a group story contains three or four words beginning with "t," a lesson on beginning "t" might be appropriate.

4. As children accumulate more words in their word box or word book, they begin to write their own stories (which they can also illustrate). The teacher and/or aide or volunteer serves as a resource person who provides help with needed function words (and, or, but, the, etc.), punctuation, and spelling.

5. Children practice reading the stories the teacher has written for them and the stories they have written themselves, before they begin to read the stories written by their classmates. Stories are read both silently and orally, in private (and in groups), and are often displayed in the room. Children help one another to read their stories.

6. Gradually, pupils begin to read small books, school newspapers, magazines, and other printed matter. Eventually, the great bulk of their reading is done in published rather than personal materials. For some children the transition to published material may begin after a few months; for others, it occurs later.

These six types of activities are, in a nutshell, the key ingredients of the language-experience approach. In the following pages, each of these components is examined in greater detail. A three-week first-grade lesson plan for the language-experience approach to reading is given in Chapter 13.

CLASSROOM PROCEDURES

Vocabulary

Sylvia Ashton-Warner (1963, p. 32) describes her language-experience approach, which she calls "organic reading," with Maori children in New Zealand. In discussing initial vocabulary, she states: "First words must have an intense meaning. First words must be already part of the dynamic life. First words must be made of the stuff of the child himself, whatever and wherever the child." For initial-reading words to have "intense meaning" and to be the "stuff of the child," they must be words the child chooses to learn to read rather than those emanating from some external source.

In most language-experience classrooms, the teacher meets briefly, but privately, with each child at least once a day in order to find out what word(s) the child would like to learn. The teacher writes the words on sheets of paper or note cards, and the child keeps the paper or card for practice and later use. Periodically, the child is tested on the words in the word box or vocabulary book; any that the child does not know are destroyed. This may seem a bit brutal, but it is based on the belief that if the chosen words *were* intensely meaningful, they would have been learned and remembered. Sometimes, a child will ask for a word because he or she overheard someone else ask for it, or for some reason other than interest in it. These are the words most difficult for the child to remember.

Pupils read, trace, and write the words independently. Occasionally, children work together in small groups, taking turns reading their words to one another and trying to read the others' words. Sometimes, children want to draw pictures of their words for a personal word-picture book or for display in the room. Later, the words become a vocabulary source for writing.

Experience Stories

Experience stories can be written by either individuals or groups. Although we prefer individually dictated stories, group stories must often suffice because the teacher has insufficient time to spend with each child. Nonetheless, group stories are often very successful and highly interesting to the children if they develop from a shared group experience.

Individuals or groups may dictate stories, questions, beliefs, poems —anything they wish—to the teacher, aide, or volunteer who serves as secretary or recorder. Individual stories should be recorded as legibly as possible on paper; group stories can be written on the chalkboard, tag board, or poster paper. Stories should be recorded as closely as possible to the child's syntactic structure and vocabulary, but words should never be misspelled. Spelling alterations can only cause later confusion when the same words are confronted in their accepted form. However, the closer the match between the language of the child and language of the printed matter, the easier it is for the child to read. Children who speak a nonstandard dialect and say "I be going" instead of "I am going," for example, should have their sentences recorded as they say them. Furthermore, it can be both frustrating and ego-damaging to continually be "corrected" when the dialect is personal and the same as that of family and friends. At a later point, after the child has learned to read, standard English can be taught as an alternative dialect (see Chapter 12).

Some teachers use language-experience stories to teach certain words *they* feel are important. They may want to do this because they know a word will be encountered in later reading or is pertinent to a season, holiday, or school event. In rephrasing the sentence of a child, they will occasionally substitute a word or two. If kept to a minimum, this may be harmless enough, but children will sometimes call the teacher on it: "I didn't say that!" If overdone, however, this practice defeats the whole purpose of the approach, because the children will realize that the stories are not their own, and they may lose interest in the whole approach.

The teacher often needs to provide punctuation. Punctuation in written material takes the place of accent and stress in oral language in helping to convey meaning. Few of us talk in discrete, serial sentences. Our thoughts are at times run-on and at times fragmented, but we are generally understood. In writing, we rely on punctuation marks to help us to be understood. Many times, sentences dictated by children will not be complete sentences, and the teacher will need to determine sentence boundaries and punctuate accordingly.

Many individuals and groups will need motivation for story dictation. They will need help in selecting a topic and in getting started. Some teachers keep a bulletin board or corner of the chalkboard for a display of suggested (not required) topics of the day or week. The following are some possible "story starters" which have been found interesting by many children.

What is red?	Halloween
What is blue?	Yom Kippur
What is happiness?	Christmas
What is spring fever?	Valentine's Day
What is coming soon?	A snowy day
Tell about a dream.	A summer day
Tell about a friend.	Birthdays
Tell about a trip.	Ghosts
Tell about a sad day.	Monsters
Tell about your wish.	Games
How would it feel to be a bubble?	Super cars
How would it feel to be a stallion?	Airplanes
How would it feel to be an astronaut?	Brothers/sisters
How would it feel to be a snake?	Teachers
How would it feel to be a puppy?	Yesterday
How would it feel to be a robot?	Tomorrow

This list is very brief and is intended only to suggest ideas. Teachers are encouraged to discover their pupils' interests as possible topics for individual and group story dictation. Shared experiences, such as field trips, school events, guest speakers, and the like, lend themselves well to group-experience stories. Recurring activities, such as lunch, recess time, the special teacher, and riding the school bus, are additional shared experiences. Similarly, any type of group or class planning of a trip or a project can be the focus of a group-experience story. The major challenge to the teacher in individual and group story-writing is to discover topics *of interest to the children* rather than those of interest to the teacher or those that might be useful because something is "needed."

The usual steps that are followed in writing an individual- or group-experience story are as follows:

1. Engage the child (children) in a discussion of the interest, topic, or event, and continue the discussion as long as interest is high. A few notes on the discussion may be kept for later reminders.

2. At some point in the discussion, the teacher says, "Why don't we write a story about [topic]. How should we begin?" The teacher then asks the child, or calls on the children, to suggest things that should be in the story. As sentences are offered, the teacher records them, using the words and sentence structures of the child, but supplying correct spelling and punctuation. Some teachers begin with a title; others ask for a title after the story has been finished. After the story has been written, read, discussed, and used to teach vocabulary or word-identification skills, it may be rewritten in a more permanent form to be reread later.

The following two stories were written in a first-grade classroom. The first was dictated by an individual; the second, by a group of eight children who had been on a field trip together.

Individual Story

The Corn

My Dad and Ma fighted last night.
He don't like food in cans.
Ma said "eat it."
Dad went to a farmer place.
He got corn on the cob.
All of us ate that.

Kirk

Group Story

The Library

The library was too quiet.
Teacher always went "Sh" "Sh"
The librarian was crabby.
Lots of good books are there.
And records and papers.
We each got a card and a book.
It was a good day.

Miss Barry's Class

Sometimes, the teacher will need to ask questions or make comments which help the pupils recall the event or the discussion. If the students' interest lags, the stories can be kept very short.

After the story has been written, the teacher reads it aloud to the child or group, pointing to each word so as to reinforce left-to-right, top-to-bottom sequence. Usually, group stories are next read in unison by the whole group. Then, volunteers are asked to read different sentences or the whole story. Children can be asked to point out specific words or specific sentences which answer questions posed by the teacher. As a follow-up activity, budding artists can draw a picture or do some other project based on the story.

If the story is done in a group, many teachers like to prepare mimeographed copies for each child to keep in a booklet. The booklets serve many purposes: they serve the pride of possession most children have; they allow for independent reading practice; they can be illustrated by each child as a seat-work activity; and they can be taken home by the pupils, to be shared with family and friends. In addition, if each story is rewritten on large tag board or poster paper, a class "big book" begins to grow. This can be used to teach word-identification and comprehension skills by referring back and forth among the stories. Some teachers make an extra copy of each story, which can be marked up and cut up as it is used to teach skills.

In a language-experience classroom, each child becomes an author and an illustrator, as well as a reader. On their first day of school, many children can take home and read to their families a short story they have written.

Word-Identification Skills

Some teachers criticize the language-experience approach because it doesn't equip children with the word-identification skills they need in order to become independent readers. It is true that skill instruction does not follow any predetermined scope and sequence. But this may be an advantage, not a disadvantage. There is no evidence to support *any* skill sequence in reading acquisition. Compare the sequence of skills in any two or three published reading series. According to Johnson and Pearson (1975, pp. 760–761):

The whole notion of a sequence or hierarchy of skills is, at best, a pedagogical convenience. While the idea may appeal to our sense of logic (just as we think of driving a car or riding a bicycle as a complex of sequenced subskills), there is precious little evidence to support the existence of separate skills, let alone separate skills which can be placed into a sequence or hierarchy. . . . Some begin with the alphabet, proceed through the consonants' sounds alphabetically and eventually teach some vowels, while others begin with rhyming elements and graphic shapes and dwell on the colors of the rainbow before looking at a few words and some letters. When sequences are committed to paper, the message teachers get is that there is some logical rationale for such sequences.

In the language-experience approach, skills are taught when an opportunity presents itself and as the children need them, rather than in some arbitrary sequences, but they *are* taught. There have been some teachers who wanted to go only half way with the approach, believing that children should function as "free spirits" and learn only those words and stories that meet their fancies. Such teachers have been remiss. Except for the few very bright children who are capable of making discoveries about language without assistance, most children need a good deal of help in developing word-attack and comprehension ability. If children read only words and a few sentences and are not asked questions or guided to discovery, their reading ability probably will not develop and frustration may set in.

Consider the following example by Dahl (1971, p. 11), a description of a word-identification activity in her language-experience program:

1. Example of a Group Skill

   After we recorded stories about our gerbils, students were asked to locate the word *gerbil*. When some of the children pointed to the word gerbils, a lesson in forming simple plurals was a natural thing and was easy for the class to understand. We then made plurals of many known words:

rat	bed	carrot	tail	cage
rats	beds	carrots	tails	cages

2. Example of an Individual Skill

   A little girl dictated the sentence—"Harriet can drink from a bottle." As *drink* was printed, the little girl said, "Drink, dream, drive—they all start the same, don't they?" Thus, our first lesson on blends was taught to an individual early in October.

3. Example of an Individual Skill

Student (dictating): "The rat didn't like her, so he went away."
Teacher (printing): "That rat did not. . . ."
Student: "Not 'did not,' I said 'didn't.' "

This provided a perfect opportunity to present contractions:

can not   did not   is not   have not

The prerequisite skills of visual and auditory discrimination (discussed in Chapter 4) can be taught and reinforced. For example, children can be asked to look in the story to find a word that begins, has the same middle letter, or ends with the letter of a word the teacher writes on the board. The teacher can say a word, e.g., bed, and ask children to raise their hands when they hear a word in the story that sounds like it, e.g., red. In addition, language-experience stories can be invaluable aids in teaching any of the phonics correspondences, structural elements, or contextual strategies that are described in Chapter 7.

Comprehension

In Chapter 8 we discuss many ways to improve children's ability to comprehend what they read. The suggestions pertain as much to language-experience stories as they do to printed stories. Listed below are the ten categories of comprehension skill we believe are most important. Though each skill is described in Chapter 8, we invite you to read down the list while asking, "How could this be done by using language-experience stories?"

1. To read sentences with the appropriate intonation patterns

2. To form mental pictures of situations or conditions that are described in a sentence or a longer passage

3. To answer questions about the facts or details presented in a sentence or a longer passage

4. To recall, with a minimum of prompting, the facts or details in a sentence or a longer passage

5. To paraphrase the central thought or main ideas in a passage

6. To identify cause-effect, comparison-contrast, sequential happenings, and other relationships between and among ideas

7. To summarize the content of a passage

8. To test the information or assertions given by the author against personal observations, logic of the information, and assertions given by other authors

9. To use a literary character, a description, or an opinion as a point of departure for creative thinking that goes beyond the presentation of an author (e.g., the creation of lines of dialogue between two characters, an extension of a story, a diary entry of a historical figure)

10. To identify specific characteristics of an author's craft (e.g., exaggeration, use of figurative language, deductive or inductive reasoning, detailed descriptions, vivid characterization, emotional appeals).

The first seven comprehension skills clearly relate to individual- and group-experience stories. Skills 8–10 become relevant when children read the works of others (a classmate, different group, or professional writer). The point is that for many—perhaps most—children, comprehension does not just happen. Children need to read orally with proper stress and intonation. They need to respond to questions that focus their attention and shape their thinking. The teacher in a language-experience classroom is charged with engaging the pupils in lively discussions of their own stories and those of others through the skillful use of questioning. Only two of the ten skills (3 and 4) deal with literal comprehension. Too often, teachers ask questions that require only recognition or recall of specific facts and details. The language-experience approach to reading lends itself very well to developing *all* of the important aspects of comprehension in reading.

Writing

Since the language-experience approach integrates the four language arts of listening, speaking, reading, and writing, writing is an integral part of the program. Writing begins with the pupils' copying words in their personal vocabularies and copying the individual- and group-experience stories they have dictated. As their vocabularies enlarge, the children begin writing sentences and stories of their own. At first, they will need adult help in supplying linking words and with spelling, punctuation, and capitalization. As they write more and more stories, they will want to read them to their classmates and others and, in turn, will want to read stories that others have written.

Children participate in the creation of group stories very early in the language-experience program. As their facility develops, they will be able to work with groups of pupils—without a recorder—in writing short plays and puppet shows, newscasts, weather reports, directions to visitors, poems, and songs. Throughout the program, reading and writing are closely related and are viewed as inseparable parts of communication, rather than as separate entities to be learned and used in isolation.

Printed Materials

The intent of the language-experience approach, like that of any other method, is to equip the child to survive in school and society by being able to read and to open the gates to the world of print from which pleasure, knowledge, and relaxation can be obtained. Furthermore, getting information from difficult textual materials is a task all readers have to cope with, e.g., the taxpayer struggling with tax-form instructions. Therefore, a wide variety of printed materials should be available in the classroom. Printed materials are easy to come by. The attic of the teacher, the storeroom of the school, the good will of family, friends, and parents can all be tapped. The school and public libraries often have rotating collections. Paperback books from children's clubs, discarded basic-reading series, magazines, books, maps, sheet music, library books, comic books—all can find a useful place in a language-experience classroom. One teacher we know has each child write to foreign embassies for free materials. His room becomes flooded with booklets, posters, and the like, and each child has the thrill of receiving some mail.

Children should not be discouraged from attempting to read any of the materials in the room, even if the teacher knows they are too difficult. Many times a strong interest will compensate for a lack of ability, and teachers are often surprised by what their pupils can read.

When they are ready and able, the pupils should move from reading their own writing to that of others. Some pupils will begin to do this early in the year, whereas others will need encouragement from the teacher. Book "sales," book displays, and book sharing can all help interest insecure readers in venturing from their own stories to those of classmates and those that are published.

Ideally, an individualized reading program, as we described in Chapter 3, should follow a beginning program based on the language-experience approach. Thus sometime between early first and early second grade, pupils will shift from reading stories written within the classroom to those written "outside." This does not mean that the use of experience stories ceases abruptly. Many children in the third and fourth grades continue to enjoy and profit from reading stories written by themselves individually and in groups.

But we have seen some very frustrated second graders who were placed in a basal-reading series in a traditional three-ability group program after an initial reading experience based on their own interests, language, backgrounds, and needs. Similarly, we have seen frustrated second-grade teachers who find it difficult to "place" children at some point in the scope and sequence when they have come out of a language-experience program knowing some "fourth-grade skills" but lacking some "first-grade skills." There is a need for teachers to communicate across the grades so that children don't fall between the cracks of disparate philosophies of reading instruction.

A FINAL POINT

We are often asked, "How do you evaluate, assess, or judge children's reading progress in such a program?" We think that too much attention in reading has been given to measurement at the expense of instruction and interest-building. There are many informal procedures for diagnosing reading strengths and weaknesses (some are described in Chapter 9), but the best measure, we feel, is whether or not the child is reading. Does the child like to read? Does she or he read widely? How fluent is the child's oral reading? If a child reads well orally and comprehends what is read, that may be enough to know. If the child does not, short, informal diagnostic tests can be given from time to time to individuals and small groups. However, it has been our experience that even on formal standardized tests, children from language-experience classrooms do as well—or as poorly—as children who have been taught with other approaches. We suspect that on less easily measured variables—interest in reading and a lifelong habit of reading—language-experience children fare somewhat better than do their counterparts in other programs.

For many teachers, the language-experience approach constitutes their total beginning-reading program. Other teachers, however, use various aspects of the language-experience activities (i.e., group-experience charts, word boxes) in conjunction with a basal, phonic-linguistics, or modified-alphabet approach. The language-experience approach is described in this chapter as a total beginning program. Teachers who prefer not to use language experience as the basic or total approach to beginning reading may find many of the activities we have described in this chapter useful supplements to whatever approach they do prefer.

Suggested Activities for the Methods Class

Activity 1

Divide into groups of five or six for microteaching. In each group select one person to be the teacher. Teachers should arrange a common experience for their groups and then lead a discussion which results in a group-experience story. When the story has been written, each group member should become the teacher to demonstrate how the story could be used to teach some aspect of word identification or comprehension.

Activity 2

Get the teacher's manual and workbook at the first- and second-grade levels from *two* commercial reading series. Compare the sequences of skills introduced in the two series. In a class discussion relate your findings to skill instruction in the language-experience approach.

Activity 3

Divide into teams to debate the following proposition: *"Resolved:* that a beginning teacher should not use a language-experience approach to reading. A first-year teacher should use a published basal or phonic/linguistic program."

Activity 4

Using either of the language-experience stories on pp. 127–128, identify some common elements that might be used for a skill lesson.

Activity 5

If it can be arranged, invite a panel of first-grade teachers to your methods class to discuss and compare the merits (and problems) inherent in the reading approach they use. If possible, invite teachers who use the language-experience approach, a basal reading series approach, a phonics/linguistics approach, and a modified-alphabet approach.

Teaching Suggestions

Suggestion 1

Observe a beginning-reading class in which the language-experience approach is used. Try to visit the same class three or four times during the year, to note the children's progress or lack of progress.

Suggestion 2

Take a group of children on a field trip or plan some other shared experience. Then generate a discussion which results in a group language-experience story. What difficulties do you experience in accurately recording the sentences as dictated? Give each child a mimeographed copy of the story.

Suggestion 3

Using the story your group has written, plan and teach a lesson based on some aspect of word identification and some aspect of comprehension.

Suggestion 4

Record an individual story dictated by one member of your class. Later, assemble the story in booklet form, one or two sentences per page, and ask the child to illustrate the story.

Suggestion 5

Rewrite the child's story, retaining the basic content but using as many different words and sentence structures as you can. Ask the child to read each version of the story orally, and note the differences in oral-reading fluency.

REFERENCES

Allen, Roach V. "How a Language-Experience Program Works," from *A Decade of Innovations: Approaches to Beginning Reading,* V. 12, Part 3, Newark, Del.: International Reading Association, 1968, pp. 1–2.

Ashton-Warner, Sylvia. *Teacher,* New York: Simon and Shuster, 1963.

Dahl, Sandra S. "The Language-Experience Approach: A Study and Implementation of the Method," Madison: The University of Wisconsin, unpublished monograph, 1971.

Freire, Paulo. *The Pedagogy of the Oppressed,* New York: Seabury Press, 1971.

Johnson, Dale D., and P. David Pearson. "The Weaknesses of Skills Management Systems," *The Reading Teacher* **28,** 8 (May 1975): 757–764.

Matteoni, Louise. "Developing Reading Ability Through the Language Experience Approach," in Thomas C. Barrett and Dale D. Johnson, *Views on Elementary Reading Instruction,* Newark, Del.: IRA, 1973, p. 55.

I wish to begin by stating that I still hold the somewhat old-fashioned conviction that written words are important in reading. I know it is more fashionable to be concerned with syntactic structure, semantic nuances, and phonological relationships as important planks in bridging the gap from printed surface structure to the writer's or reader's deep structures. And I agree that they are important. Yet without words they are meaningless.

DALE D. JOHNSON

7 Developing a Reading Vocabulary: The Skills of Word Identification

Have you ever wondered how many words you know? Have you ever thought about what it means to "know" a word? As a mature reader, the number of words you recognize in print may closely match the number of spoken words you understand. But when you were a young child, that was certainly not the case. Although each individual's vocabulary is unique, research tells us that you could intelligently speak and/or understand many thousands of words when you entered school as a five-year-old. Yet you could read (recognize in print) very few words, if any. Today, how many words can you read? If someone were to hold small flash cards in front of you, each with one word printed on it, how many would you recognize? That is, for how many words could you make a meaningful association if no clues were available for each word other than the five or eight or twelve graphic shapes we call letters, arranged in a linear sequence? Because of your background, you could probably read between 100,000 and 200,000 words, which means that you could recognize up to a fifth of a million words presented to you in isolation (Smith, 1971).

In Chapter 1 we stated that reading is much more than saying words, vocally or silently, as your eyes scan their printed forms. Indeed, reading is communicating; it is relating to a message that has been encoded by a sender for a purpose. Reading is a language process, a psycholinguistic process, that involves a sender and a receiver, intended and received meanings, and printed representations of the meanings (letters and their arrangements, grammatical patterns, punctuation marks, etc.). Although this chapter will focus on the printed forms of *words*—linear arrangements of letters—we urge you to remember that processing printed words is but one component of reading. Indeed, vocabulary development in reading is facilitated by three main "word attack" skills.

There are four language arts that can be classified in various ways. Two are considered "productive"; two, "receptive." Two involve the writing system of the language; two do not. Two are acquired at home; the other two, usually at school; i.e., two are "learned" and two are "taught." The four language arts, in the typical sequence of acquisition are listening, speaking, reading, and writing. Together, they comprise the essence of meaningful communication. All four are uniquely human. All four involve auditory codes; two involve graphic representations of those codes.

Writing systems for languages are comparatively new, having been with us for only three thousand years (Mathews, 1966). In fact, many of the world's languages today have no written forms. In Nigeria alone, more than 200 languages are spoken, but fewer than a dozen are written. Thus for many people, the development of a reading vocabulary is a phenomenon not yet imagined. Oral language is learned "naturally" through trial and error and reinforcement by fluent models.*

For written languages, such as English, the teacher has two major concerns regarding vocabulary development:

1. Children know (can understand and use) many more words than they recognize in print. How can children be taught to make the transfer from the unknown printed form of a word to the oral form to which they already attach meaning?

2. How can printed language be used to expand children's total vocabulary? What can be done if the child does not recognize the word in print or in its oral form?

This chapter will offer suggestions to help the beginning teacher with these objectives.

The terms "word attack," "word analysis," "word recognition," "decoding," "phonics," and "phonetics" are often used interchangeably in materials dealing with the teaching of reading. In essence, the terms refer to an assortment of skills and techniques a child may use to gain meaning from an unfamiliar printed word. Whatever we call these skills, however, the purpose is the same: to increase the child's reading vocabulary. Writers' meanings are lost and syntactic patterns are of little help in retrieving those meanings, when too many unknown words are confronted by the reader.

The enlargement of reading vocabulary is essential for developing reading fluency. Children enter school reading, perhaps, their name and a few other words. Those who become fluent readers learn another 100,000 or so words along the way. Obviously, each is not learned as a "sight word," but through the employment of various techniques. We advocate three word-recognition techniques as being most useful to children. In this chapter each technique will be discussed separately and then in conjunction with the others. Children rarely use only one technique, but by applying two or all three simultaneously, find the greatest efficiency in word recognition. Each technique is defined briefly now; later in this chapter, each is discussed in greater depth.

Phonics: The ability to relate symbols (letters) to sounds. Phonics instruction is concerned with helping children *pronounce* words,

---

* For an excellent discussion of different theories of a child's language acquisition, see Courtney Cazden's *Child Language and Education,* New York: Harcourt, Brace and World, 1972.

with the reasonable expectation that once pronounced, the child will recognize the word from his or her oral/aural vocabulary.

Structural analysis: The ability to identify meaningful components of words. Instruction in structural analysis focuses on helping children examine meaningful parts of words, e.g., prefixes, root words, suffixes, inflected endings, that are known in order to understand the total, seemingly unfamiliar, word.

Context: The ability to examine the material surrounding an unknown word in order to determine its meaning. Instruction in contextual analysis is aimed at helping children derive semantic or syntactic cues from preceding or subsequent sentences, or pictorial material, as a way of ascribing meaning to an unfamiliar word.

Examples of utilization of phonics, structure analysis, and contextual analysis are presented later in this chapter. Some reading-methods textbooks describe picture clues and "configuration" as word-identification techniques; we, however, consider picture clues as a type of contextual analysis. Further, we feel that configuration exercises (noticing the shapes of words, usually by drawing little boxes around them) are both inefficient and unhelpful.

The beginning teacher might well wonder how any word-recognition techniques can be taught before the child has some words in his or her reading vocabulary. With few exceptions, most children are initially instructed in reading with basic sight words. Ways of introducing basic sight words are discussed in the next section. The derivation of the initial sight words that are taught vary according to the teacher's underlying philosophy of reading. There are three major points of view:

1. The first words to be taught should be those that the children will encounter the most frequently in printed materials, e.g., "school," "home," "the," "under."

2. The first words to be taught should follow invariant letter-sound patterns, so that the children will not be confused by decoding, e.g., lip, ship, tip.

3. The first words to be taught should be those words that child *wants* to learn to read, so that reading will be meaningful from the start.

SIGHT WORDS

Our position is that reading instruction should commence with sight words—presented and written by the teacher; read, discussed, and used by the pupils—before the word-recognition techniques are introduced. Large numbers of sight words the children learn in their first years in school should be those in which they are interested. The use of language-experience stories (discussed in Chapter 6) is an excellent way to begin to teach a reading vocabulary. But self-selected words may not be sufficient to prepare children for the world of print. Therefore, it is important, we believe, to introduce those high-frequency words which the children will assuredly need as they begin to read books and materials written by others, but which they may not identify as words they want to learn in language-experience stories. Later, as phonic techniques are taught, sight words that follow particular patterns can profitably be presented. Thus, all three sources of sight words should be used by teachers in grades one, two, and three.

Johnson (1971) published a basic vocabulary for beginning reading, comprised of 306 words. The words were selected because they met two important criteria: (1) they were among the 500 most frequently occurring words in printed English; *and* (2) they were in the speaking-listening vocabularies of kindergarten children. Later, Johnson and Menzel (1975) tested a number of first- and second-grade children to determine which of the words were known by at least 70 percent of the children at each grade level. That study resulted in a list of 180 words considered to be first-grade words, and an additional list of 126 words considered appropriate for second grade. The two lists have become a useful source for sight-word instruction by primary grade teachers. We recommend that these words be taught as sight words along with self-selected "language experience" words. Naturally some teachers will prefer to teach some of the words as part of a context or phonics lesson. The important thing is that they become part of the child's instant-recognition vocabulary. Table 1 contains the first grade list arranged in alphabetical order; Table 2 presents the second-grade list.*

Although there are a number of ways to teach sight words, the techniques inherent in the language-experience approach to teaching reading (see Chapter 6) are commonly used. Many teachers use games to teach or reinforce the learning of sight words. For example, such popular card games as Bingo, Old Maid, Horse-race, Fish, Rummy, or Poker can be easily adapted to the particular words a teacher wishes to present. Ekwall (1970) describes a large number of vocabulary games, as does Spache (1973).

---

* Dale D. Johnson, "A Basic Vocabulary for Beginning Readers," *Elementary School Journal* **72** (October 1971): 31–33. Reprinted by permission of the University of Chicago Press.

142   **Table 1.** First-grade words*

a	day	I	off	table
above	days	if	old	than
across	did	I'm	one	that
after	didn't	in	open	the
again	do	into	or	then
air	don't	is	out	there
all	door	it	over	these
am	down	its		they
American		it's	past	think
and	end		play	this
are		just	point	those
art	feet		put	three
as	find	keep		time
ask	first	kind	really	to
at	five		red	today
	for	let	right	too
back	four	like	room	took
be		little	run	top
before	gave	look		two
behind	get	iove	said	
big	girl		saw	under
black	give	make	school	up
book	go	making	see	
boy	God	man	seen	very
but	going	may	she	
	gone	me	short	want
came	good	men	six	wanted
can	got	miss	so	was
car		money	some	way
children	had	more	something	we
come	hand	most	soon	well
could	hard	mother	still	went
	has	Mr.		what
	have	must		when
	he	my		where
	help			which
	her	name		who
	here	never		why
	high	new		will
	him	night		with
	his	no		work
	home	not		
	house	now		year
	how			years
				yet
				you
				your

* An alphabetized listing of the 180 words read correctly by at least 70% of the first-grade students tested.

Table 2. Second-grade words*

able	different	last	real	water
about	does	leave	road	were
almost	done	left		west
alone		light		while
already	each	long	same	whole
always	early		say	whose
America	enough	made	says	wife
an	even	many	set	women
another	ever	mean	should	world
any	every	might	show	would
around	eyes	morning	small	
away		Mrs.	sometimes	
	face	much	sound	
because	far	music	started	
been	feel		street	
believe	found	need	sure	
best	from	next		
better	front	nothing	take	
between	full	number	tell	
board			their	
both	great	of	them	
brought	group	office	thing	
by		on	things	
	hands	only	thought	
called	having	other	through	
change	head	our	together	
church	heard	outside	told	
city		own	town	
close	idea		turn	
company		part		
cut	knew	party	until	
	know	people	us	
		place	use	
		plan	used	
		present		

* In addition to the 180 words in Table 1, these alphabetized 126 words were read correctly by at least 65% of the second-grade students tested.

Whatever one's approach to teaching basic sight words, there are usually five steps involved, but not necessarily in the following order:

Seeing: The word is printed on the chalkboard, a flash card, or is used as a label or a picture caption.

Discussing: After the word has been read by the teacher and repeated by the children, a short discussion is held so that the word can be related, if possible, to the lives and experiences of the group. If, for example, the word is *pet,* children could be asked about their own pets or one that they would like to have.

Using: Pupils are asked to use the word in a sentence or to think of a synonym for the word. This is usually done orally, but at times may be used as a written assignment.

Defining: Providing a definition for a word is often harder than using the word in a sentence. But after the class has used the word in several sentences, it is not too difficult to arrive at a tentative answer to the question, "What does this word mean?"

Copying: Many elementary teachers have their pupils keep a personal dictionary of new words. Fernald (1943), in advocating a "kinesthetic" approach to reading, believes that writing a word reinforces its learning, and common sense bears this out.

These five steps are not used with every word, nor are all the steps used with each new word. The teacher is most in tune with her pupils and can best determine the amount of instruction needed for a given word. Chapter 9 discusses ways of measuring the various components of reading, including techniques for assessing vocabulary development. In addition to the five steps, it is always wise to discuss the *purpose* for learning the word; usually, it is because the word will be encountered in subsequent reading material.

It was mentioned earlier that mature readers have a sight vocabulary of some 100,000–200,000 words. If each had been taught to the learner as a sight word, the task would have been very laborious and would have taken several lifetimes. A major task for elementary teachers, therefore, is equipping their pupils with the means to learn new words independently. There are hundreds of techniques readers use, but most can be classified in one of three modes: phonics, structural analysis, and contextual analysis. The skills are rarely used in isolation, and often all three are used in combination to "unlock" a new word.

PHONICS

The English language has hundreds of thousands of words, and many new words are added to the language each year. Arranged in grammatical sequences we call sentences, the variations are infinite. Yet the total flow of language utilizes only a handful of distinctive sounds, called phonemes. Depending on the English dialect one speaks, a person uses between 44 and 48 distinctive speech sounds.

These 40-odd sounds, or phonemes, are represented in writing by an even smaller number of graphic shapes, the 26 letters of the Roman alphabet. But the relationships between letters and sounds in English are extremely complex. Many of the phonemes are represented by a variety of letters, singularly or in clusters; likewise, many of the letters singularly or in clusters represent many phonemes. These complexities make learning to decode (pronounce) and encode (spell) difficult for many children. The following phonemes typify this complexity:

1. *game, tray, train, they, great, gauge*
2. *fun, photo, tough, muffin*
3. *ground, soup, though, would, anxious*
4. *chin, machine, chorus*

The words in "1" and "2" are examples of sound-to-spelling ambiguity; the words in "3" and "4" demonstrate spelling-to-sound ambiguity.

Simplistically, phonics is concerned with but two sets of relationships: consonant letters, alone or in combination, as they represent consonant phonemes; and vowel letters, alone or in combination, as they represent vowel phonemes. The works by Hall (1961), Venezky (1971), and Berdiansky, *et al.* (1969) are recommended to those of you interested in the massive variety of letter-sound correspondences, arrangements, and sequences that occurs in English.

Teaching phonic elements and phonic generalizations to children is not as complex as it might first appear. Certain correspondences are much more predictable than others—they have fewer exceptions—and certain correspondences occur much more frequently than others do.

In the following sentences, all the consonants have been omitted and replaced by blank lines. Pause for a moment and try to read the sentences.

1. A _o_ _i_ _ _ _o_e _a_ _e_ _ _o _o_ _.
2. _ea_ _i_ _ _ea_i_ _ i_ _ _a_ _e_ _i_ _.

Most readers find this a very difficult, if not impossible, task. Now try to read the same sentences, this time with the vowels omitted.

1. _ r_ll_ng st_n_ g_th_rs n_ m_ss.

2. T_ _ch_ng r_ _d_ng _s ch_ll_ng_ng.

It is obvious that consonant letters are the significant identifiers in English. Furthermore, consonant letter-sound correspondences are considerably more consistent than vowels are. Teachers should be much more concerned that their pupils learn consonant relationships than vowels, though the latter should not be ignored, of course.

There is but *one* purpose for phonics instruction—to help children *pronounce* words they do not recognize in print, with the reasonable assumption that once they have pronounced the word, they will recognize it from their speaking-listening vocabulary. If the word is not within the readers' speaking-listening vocabulary, phonic analysis is of no use. Applying the phonics knowledge you learned, directly or indirectly, as a child, you will be able to pronounce the underlined word in this sentence:

"My dad gave me a new *plit.*"

Since *plit* is a contrived word, it is not in your speaking-listening vocabulary; though you can pronounce *plit,* it has no meaning for you. Teachers are wise to be skeptical of reading programs that advocate *only* one word-attack skill—phonics. Yet since children do have very large speaking-listening vocabularies, teachers would be remiss if they did not help their pupils learn ways to bridge the gap from unfamiliar printed words to their meaningful oral counterparts.

Although we do not advocate the direct teaching to pupils of the multitude of letter-sound correspondences, we do believe that it is essential for teachers to know all the major relationships. It is pointless to expect children to memorize 60 or 140 or 320 "rules" governing phonic correspondences. Yet if teachers are to guide their pupils to the most useful patterns, they need to become very familiar with the "code." In addition to the thorough works of Hall (1961), Veneky (1971), and Berdiansky (1969), two excellent books—Heilman (1968) and Durkin (1972)—are available in paperback and are valuable references for teachers in that they include the major patterns, suggested techniques, and patterned word lists. The books by Spache (1973) and Ekwall (1970), referred to earlier, also contain many proven techniques and games. The teacher's manuals of most commercial phonics programs and published basic-reading series contain numerous specific ideas; many teachers find them very valuable references.

Hundreds of specific phonics techniques have proved successful, and they can be categorized in four main ways:

Word families: Word families are sometimes referred to as phonograms, graphonemes, or spelling patterns. When teaching word families, the teacher introduces (in writing and orally) a few words which represent the family and asks the pupils to supply others. For example, to teach the family *-and,* the teacher might write *hand, land,* and *band;* the students might volunteer such other words as *stand, sand,* and *gland.*

Analytic phonics: After children have learned a number of sight words containing a particular letter-sound correspondence, they are asked to *discover* the relationship. For example, after they have learned *dog, Dick, bad, weed,* and *dime,* they are asked what all those words have in common. Through questioning, the students are helped to discover that all the words contain the letter *d,* which represents the /d/ sound. This technique is also called the *inductive method,* and we recommend it as the *first* introduction to phonics. Things learned through discovery are usually learned best.

Synthetic phonics: The children are specifically taught certain letter-sound correspondences and are then asked to synthesize them—to blend them—into words. For example, once the children have learned the sounds of *s, n, p,* and *i,* they are asked to blend them to form *pin, sip, sin, nip, pins, spin.* In essence, this is a spelling approach to phonics and is of questionable value in the early grades. Children come to school wanting to learn to read, not wanting to memorize tiny sound segments. Besides, this is not the way mature readers read.

Patterns: Certain phonics generalizations are highly reliable and occur frequently enough to be of use as a technique for teaching. A few examples of reliable generalizations are: (1) in syllables ending in a vowel, the vowel is usually long, e.g., *be;* (2) in consonant-vowel-consonant syllables, the vowel is usually short, e.g., *cat;* (3) any time a vowel is followed by two identical consonants, it is short, e.g., *rabbit;* (4) the letter *c* is pronounced /s/ before *e, i,* and *y,* e.g., *cent,* but is pronounced *k* elsewhere, e.g., *cap;* final silent *e* marks the preceding vowel as long, e.g., *pin-pine; mat-mate; cub-cube; not-note.* Children are directly taught the major patterns of the language; after each pattern has been introduced, children are exposed to new words to which the pattern can be applied.

What Should be Taught

The major letter-sound correspondences,* patterns, and phonics generalizations, i.e., those that we believe are of the highest value to young readers, are:

1. Major single-letter consonant correspondences:

   b–book, d–dance, f–funny, h–heart, j–Jim, k–king, l–lemon, m–money, n–new, p–party, qu–queen, r–roll, v–violin, w–water, y–yes, z–zebra.

2. Phonics generalizations related to the remaining single-letter consonant correspondences:

   a) "Soft" c or g before e, i, and y (cent, city, cycle, gem, agile, gymnasium); "hard" c or g elsewhere (candy, cotton, cupid, success, game, gone, guild, suggest.

   b) Initial s usually has the sound heard in sow, see, and Saturday (exceptions: sure and sugar).

   c) The sound of t is usually that heard in tent, Tom, and melt; in -tion endings, however, it has the sound of nation or action.

   d) The letter x represents three main sounds—/ks/, /gz/, /z/—(tax, fix, box; exit, exam; xylophone). All of these sounds are identifiable by their position within the word.

3. Major consonant cluster correspondences:

   a) *Digraphs*—consonant digraphs are two-letter clusters which represent a sound different from the sound of each individual letter, e.g.:

   sh—shoe, bush, worship
   ng—song, wing, long
   ch—chew, chop, chat or chorus, choir or chef, machine
   th—thin, bath or this, bathe
   ph—phonograph, photo

   b) *Compounds*—compound consonants are two identical, adjacent consonants. With the exception of cc and gg, compound consonants always represent the sound of one consonant (rabble, ladder, jiffy, belly, dimmer, funny, happen, narrow, savvy, dizzy, buccaneer or accept, egg or suggest).

---

* Letters don't *have* sounds; they *represent* sounds. However, in teaching children, it is often less confusing to refer to the sounds of letters.

c) *Blends*—consonant blends are strings of two or more consonant letters whose sound is a composite of each individual letter's sound. Most consonant blends follow one of three patterns: (1) a consonant plus *l* (black, glue); (2) a consonant plus r (brown, grass); (3) *s* plus a consonant (spot, stick).

d) *Silent letters*—certain consonant clusters contain a silent letter, e.g.:

kn—knee, knife
mb—comb, bomb
ten—fasten, often
wr—wrath, wrong

4. Major single-letter vowel correspondences. Johnson (1973) argues that on the basis of frequency of occurrence and consistency of pronunciation, the vowel letters should be introduced in the following sequence:

i—if, pin, mitten; mild, isle, bind; bird, sir, dirt

a—act, match, sand; about, alone, among; ape, bake, sale; want, call, star

o—hot, bond, copper; of, above, glutton; note, bone, explode; off, coffee, log; for, bore, cord

u—ugly, much, glutton; cute, puny, muse; tube, tune, dude; bull, put, pull; fur, burp, curdle

e—bed, melt, tend; jacket, pocket, ticket; blaze, came, date; item, given, often; he, she, be; her, fern, herb.

The vowels listed above are suggested as a sequence for each vowel, not between vowels. In other words, we do *not* suggest that all the sounds related to *i* be taught before the first *a* correspondence is taught.

5. Phonics generalizations related to single-letter vowels:

a) A vowel between two consonants in a word or syllable is usually "short," e.g., pin, cap, hot, bug, bed.

b) A vowel before two or more consonants is usually "short," e.g., wish, graph, much; blotter, lettuce, happen; itch, hospital, wrestle; cinder, dampen, bumper.

c) A vowel followed by a final consonant plus e is usually "long," e.g., pine, date, dope, cute, cede.

    d) A vowel at the end of a one-syllable word is usually "long," e.g., go, me, she.

    e) When it occurs in the final position of a word, the letter y functions as a vowel. In one-syllable words, it has the sound heard in my, try, cry. In words of two or more syllables, it has the sound heard in baby, happily, serendipity.

6. Major vowel cluster correspondences. For many years an erroneous generalization has been taught, namely, "When two vowels go walking, the first one does the talking." According to the generalization, when two vowels are together, only the "long" sound of the first one is pronounced. However, since that rule is true for only four or five vowel clusters (out of 61), it should never be taught. Instead, the following vowel clusters, together with words representing their *major* sounds, occur often enough in common words to be worth teaching:

io—nation, lion
ea—teach, bread, great
ou—ounce, though, soup, would
ee—see, been
ai—pain
au—because, laugh
oo—moon, book
ow—own, cow
oi—coin
ay—play

7. Phonic syllabication. Sometimes it is useful for children to divide words into shorter elements so as to facilitate pronunciation. Syllabication *can* be helpful in pronouncing words, but often that purpose has not been made clear enough. It is meaningless to ask children to draw lines between parts of words *unless* they are then expected to pronounce the parts as they attempt to identify the whole word. Three syllabication generalizations can be helpful aids to pronunciation:

    a) In vowel-consonant-vowel (VCV) patterns, divide before the consonant, e.g.:

       a/way, ta/ken, sli/my

b) In VCCV words (excepting digraphs and compounds), divide between the consonants:

cin/der, ham/per, can/dy

The exceptions:

ma/chine, ha/ppen.

c) In words that end in consonant *le,* divide before the consonant, e.g.:

ta/ble, un/cle, can/dle

Most elementary teachers instruct their pupils in all of these phonic correspondences at one time or another. They do so using games, skill sheets, alliteration exercises (Peter Piper picked a peck . . .), and a variety of other activities designed to teach and reinforce the major letter-sound correspondences. Phonics is sometimes thought of as dreary, but it can be a good deal of fun if taught in short doses and by a number of techniques. The teacher must concentrate on correlating the phonics skills with the other reading activities. If phonics instruction, in separate "skill and drill" sessions, is regularly isolated from reading for pleasure and information, it can quickly lose its appeal, and children will fail to see how phonics can help them to become better readers.

Our approach to phonics instruction is simple. As soon as children have learned three or four sight words containing a particular letter-sound correspondence, pattern, or phonics generalization, the words should be written on the board. Children should read each word orally, listening carefully to its sound. The teacher should then ask the class what the words have in common. Once pupils discover the: (1) correspondence (the *b* in *bed, Bill,* and *grab*); (2) pattern (the short vowel before the final *-tch,* as in *itch, hatch, witch*); or (3) generalization (the soft *c* before *e, i,* or *y* pattern, as in *cell, city, bicycle*), they should be encouraged to volunteer other words to which it applies. These other words, in turn, are added to the list on the chalkboard, read orally, discussed, and sometimes written in the students' individual dictionaries. Later, the learning is reinforced through appropriate activity sheets, games, and exercises. When the pattern is found in words encountered in subsequent reading, it should be pointed out to the children. This basic inductive teaching strategy can be varied and used flexibly throughout the elementary grades.

A phonics test for teachers appears at the end of this chapter. If you can pass it, you probably have the background knowledge required of a good phonics teacher; if you cannot, you may need to brush up.

STRUCTURAL ANALYSIS

As was pointed out earlier, the smallest distinctive sound segments of English are called phonemes. There are about 45 phonemes in the English language. The smallest units of meaning are called morphemes, of which there are hundreds of thousands. Some words *are* morphemes, but other words contain several morphemes. The word *car,* for example, is a morpheme referring to a vehicle. The word *cars,* however, has two morphemes—*car* plus an "s," which signifies plural. *Foot* and *ball* are separate morphemes, but when combined they form a new morpheme, *football. Unhappiness* has three morphemes; *unrealistically,* four. The term "white elephant," though two words, is only one morpheme.

Few primary grade teachers use the term "morpheme" with their pupils. However, most teachers teach the principles of structural (morphemic) analysis. Stated simply, structural analysis amounts to scrutinizing unfamiliar words for familiar meaningful parts, i.e., root words, affixes, and inflected endings. Children in a first-grade class may be able to read the word *help,* but may stumble when they encounter *helping, unhelpful,* or *helpless.*

The *major technique* used to improve structural analysis is word building, or extension. Known words are reviewed, extended by the addition of affixes, and used in sentences constructed by the pupils:

play–played–playing	*long*–longer–longest
jump–jumped–jumping	*black*–blacker–blackest
lock–unlock–locker	*rub*–rubbed–rubbing
wind–unwind–winding	*sad*–sadder–saddest

It is not helpful to teach long lists of suffixes and prefixes and to require that their definitions be memorized. Some affixes have several different meanings (often subtle) when new words are formed. For example, the *un* in *untie* and *undo* means something different from the *un* in *unable* and *unwilling.* Likewise, some morphemes (meanings) are spelled in a variety of ways; for example, the morpheme *not* is represented by the prefixes *unable, impolite, disloyal, inactive,* and *illegible.* Variant meanings of affixes are best discovered through the use of context, though a few occur with sufficient frequency to merit separate instruction through word building, e.g., *untie, unlike, unhappy, unclean, uncertain.*

Certain structural components occur so frequently in English words that they should be taught directly and reinforced as needed. We advocate an inductive approach (similar to that described in the phonics section) to help children discover the following basic structural patterns:

1. Plurals—cats, dishes, days, babies
2. Past tense—walked, helped, planted
3. Continuous tense—walking, helping, planting
4. Comparisons—smooth, smoother, smoothest, younger, youngest
5. Contractions—isn't, didn't; I've, we've; they're, you're
6. Compound words—football, streetlight, sidewalk.

The important thing is to help children develop a mind-set, an attitude, for examining unfamiliar words in order to discover their meaningful parts as a means of recognizing words. However, instructing children to "look for the little words within the big word" can be very misleading; in fact, it can be detrimental to word recognition. Many small "words" assume entirely different sounds (as well as meanings) when they are only syllables in longer words. For example, look for the "little words" in the following: *father, some, brown, mother, great,* and *wine.*

Thousands of words are derived from root words in conjunction with other root words, inflections, or affixes. To attempt to teach each of them as a sight word would be a monumental waste of time. The more practice children have at: (1) building new words from known words, and (2) subdividing unfamiliar words into meaningful parts, the more likely they will be to use the elements of structural analysis in their daily reading.

CONTEXTUAL ANALYSIS

Using surrounding context to identify an unfamiliar word can be defined as "making an educated guess." "Figuring out a word by the way it's used in the sentence" is a typical definition of contextual analysis. Context clues, if the reader knows how to look for them, help define an unfamiliar word by providing syntactic, semantic, typographic, and stylistic clues. These clues reduce the number of possible alternatives for the unfamiliar word. When context clues are used in conjunction with phonic and structural analysis, many unfamiliar printed words can be rather quickly defined. Consider the synthetic words in the sentences on the following page.

1. His new *cromp* had tall handlebars.
2. Mary *blinched* further than Tom did!
3. Dick, who is center on the basketball team, is *glanner* than Mike.
4. The raisin *lortin* was soft, fluffy, and still warm from the oven.

A young reader would be rather certain that the unknown word in the first sentence is a noun, because of its sentence position. Furthermore, "tall handlebars" restricts the noun to a class of vehicle. The reader might tentatively decide that the word "cromp" means "bicycle" and see if the definition is confirmed in subsequent sentences. By using context and structural analysis in the second sentence, we know that "blinched" is a past-tense action verb that describes some form of covering distance. "Blinched" probably means "jumped" or "hopped." Similarly, it is quite clear that "glanner," in the third sentence, means "taller." Finally, "lortin," in the fourth sentence, is quite likely a type of pastry.

In recent years a number of researchers have identified different kinds of contextual clues useful to readers (Ames, 1965; Dulin, 1969). However, more than three decades ago Artley (1943) succinctly identified ten categories of contextual aids:

1. Typographical (quotation marks, parentheses): He got a new bicycle (a yellow Schwinn) for Christmas.
2. Structural (syntactic) (appositives, non-restrictive clauses, signal words: Prognostication, predicting events, is a popular pastime.
3. Substitute words (synonyms, antonyms): The antennae, or feelers, help a cockroach sense direction.
4. Figures of speech (similes, metaphors): The typhoon brought buckets of rain.
5. Subjective clues (tone, mood, intent): On the cloudy, gray November day, I felt dejected.
6. Pictorial representation (pictures, diagrams, charts): The girls' scores surpassed the boys'.

7. Word elements (roots, affixes, inflections): He did it unthinkingly.
8. Direct explanation or definition: An itinerant preacher is one who travels about saving souls.

9. Inference: Tom was a foot taller and 30 pounds heavier than Carl. He overwhelmed him in the match.

10. Background of experience of the reader: He ripped off a candy bar at Rennebohm's Drug Store.

Direct instruction in each subcomponent of each of the categories is not recommended. The child does not need to know the terms that describe these aids in order to use them. Instruction in contextual analysis should be geared to generate thinking—intelligent guessing—about the probable meaning of an unfamiliar word rather than formally teaching language characteristics.

There are a great number of teaching techniques available for strengthening the use of contextual analysis. Some materials contain adequate context clues, but others do not. The teacher should examine material carefully to see that it can be used to meet the purpose of the lesson. Furthermore, the materials should reflect the language patterns of the child as much as possible.

Emans and Fischer (1967) conducted a study of six kinds of instructional activities that utilized deletions. Children were asked to read sentences and to provide the missing word in each sentence. Their results showed a significant hierarchy of exercises, from the most difficult to the easiest, for children in grades three to ten. The hierarchy, used in reverse order (easiest to most difficult), might be used as an instructional sequence in developing contextual ability. Their hierarchy is:

1. (Most difficult) No clues given other than context.

   "The _____ of a turkey are not tasty."

2. Beginning letter given.

   "The f_____ of a turkey are not tasty."

3. Length of word given.

   "The _ _ _ _ _ _ _ _ of a turkey are not tasty."

4. Beginning and ending letters given.

   "The f_____s of a turkey are not tasty."

5. Four word choices given.

   "The _____ of a turkey are not tasty."

   gizzard   feet   wings   feathers

6. Consonants given.

"The f_ _th_rs of a turkey are not tasty." *

Teachers often utilize variations of exercises such as these in helping children to make use of context. Other approaches to the development of contextual-analysis skills are based on the use of complete sentences with unknown real words or contrived nonsense words. In Emans' exercises, above, children are asked to supply a missing word. In the following exercise they are asked to define a word in a completed sentence.

1. Matching. Match the correct definition with each sentence.
   a) He made a *run* in the game. _____   1) a hole or tear
   b) Her stocking has a *run* in it. _____   2) a score in baseball

2. Circle the word.

   Jerry *twanked* Terry in the shins.
   kissed   killed   kicked

3. Rewrite the sentence, substituting a new word.

   The big, brown *Quabbo* had long claws.

4. Idiomatic expressions rewritten.

   The teacher said, "Get on the ball."
   "Get on the ball" means _____.

These exercises, and many more like them, are designed to help the child "tune in" to the sentence and broader context as a source of word identification. By looking at a combination of factors—the grammatical "fit" of the word, available meaning clues within or around the sentence, and available phonic or structural clues—children can add many new words to their vocabulary and can identify many known words.

SUMMARY

Teachers who want to improve their pupils' word-recognition skills so that their sight vocabularies will grow larger need to be concerned about the three broad categories of word-recognition skills: phonics,

---

* Robert Emans and Gladys M. Fisher, "Teaching the Use of Context Clues," *Elementary English* **44** (March 1967): 243–246. Copyright © 1967 by the National Council of Teachers of English. Reprinted by permission of the publisher and the author.

structural analysis, and the use of context. Children must be encouraged to be flexible; they must not develop an overreliance on one type of skill. They must be shown how two or three skills can be used simultaneously. Fluency in reading and size of reading vocabulary go hand in hand. The more one reads, the larger one's reading vocabulary becomes; the larger one's reading vocabulary, the more *likely* that one will choose reading as a leisure pastime activity. Teachers need to demonstrate regularly that word recognition and vocabulary development are inherent components of increased reading ability.

Suggested Activities for the Methods Class

Activity 1

Assume that you are trying to select words that will help you teach or reinforce the various word-attack skills. Study each of the following words and decide if it would be most helpful in stressing phonics, structural analysis, or context. Work in groups of two or three students so that you can discuss your choices as you proceed.

cue	pain	walking	babies	unhappy
center	tear	sow	cliff	bookcase
plant	baseball	nation	wind	pine

Phonics	*Structural analysis*	*Context*
1.		
2.		
3.		
4.		
5.		

When each group has finished, tally the results for each of the 15 words on the chalkboard. For example:

	Group 1	2	3	4	5	6	7
cue	con	con	phon	con	phon	con	con
center							
plant							

On which words was there total agreement? Where was there diversity of opinion? Why? What does this suggest?

Activity 2

Using Eman's hierarchy (see pp. 155–156) of context formats, write two different sentences for one word of your choice, e.g.; (1) "A Cooley is a valley open
at one end only." "The house was nestled in the Cooley." (2) "A _____
is a valley open at one end only." "A c_____ is a valley open at one end
only." "A _____ is a valley open at one end only." The class should divide itself into groups, and each group should prepare the sentences for one
word. After you have written the two sentences (each in *six formats*) for your
word, write all 12 sentences on separate sheets of paper. Distribute a different
sheet to 12 of your classmates. Afterward, tabulate the results, by format, for
the entire class. Did your results (adult readers) parallel Emans' results (children)? Were formats 4, 5, and 6 easier to do than formats 1, 2, and 3? Why
or why not?

Format	Group 1	Number correct 2	3	4	5	6	Total correct
1. (No clues)	2	1	3	0	0	2	8
2.							
3.							
4.							
5.							
6. (All consonants)	5	6	8	8	5	7	39

Question: Are "fill-in-the-blanks" formats, which require writing (encoding), legitimate exercises for building skill in reading (decoding)?

Activity 3

Select one letter-sound correspondence pattern or phonics generalization
from those described in this chapter. Prepare a short microteaching lesson,
using the inductive approach, and present it to four or five of your classmates
for evaluation.

Activity 4

Develop a short microteaching lesson that encourages simultaneous use of
phonics, structural analysis, and context.

Activity 5

Complete the following "Word Identification Test for Teachers."

Word Identification Test for Teachers, General Directions

This test is divided into five parts: consonant correspondences, vowel correspondences, phonic syllabication, structural analysis, and contextual analysis. In all, there are 49 questions. Score two points for each correct answer to determine percentage correct. On the first 39 questions, write a brief statement indicating the generalization or reason for your response. These written statements will not be scored, but should be discussed.

Part I: Consonant correspondences. Read each synthetic word on the left. Note the underlined letter(s). Circle the word on the right whose underlined letter(s) represents the same sound. Below each item, write the generalization which applies.

1. ceft   sugar   kiss   sell

2. cupe   king   sew   sure

3. galp   measure   gym   pig

4. genn   gone   agile   raquet

5. tuce   wash   sand   Ken

6. bition   hat   battle   dish

7. frax   seem   kitchen   sacks

8. quan   choir   ark   wag

9. rebbing	ledge	bend	dent

10. fax	zebra	sticks	eggs

11. gliph	hophead	cuff	cup

12. knilp	now	kite	acne

13. cump	ship	sin	kin

14. gome	log	garage	lock

Part II: Vowel correspondences. Read each synthetic word on the left. Note the underlined letter(s). Circle the word on the right whose underlined letter(s) represents the same sound. Below each item, write the generalization which applies.

1. peff	bed	came	she

2. laup	fuse	baby	gone

3. gite	bird	mild	pin

4. toib	book	bone	boy

5. dunt	tube	put	much

6. moad	open	coin	out

7. frage	sand	want	bake

8. wot	bond	of	off

9. wapple	game	call	black

10. de	her	team	tend

11. chy	lip	tree	pine

12. frotion	away	mild	lion

Part III: Phonic syllabication. Read each synthetic word and draw a line dividing it into syllables. Write the generalization below the word.

1. mapen

2. dochone

3. finter

4. flotten

5. boncle

Part IV: Structural analysis. Draw a line dividing each synthetic word according to "meaningful" parts (which may or may not be pronounceable parts). Below each word, explain why you divided where you did.

1. unwok

_____

2. rothing

_____

3. lidenalk

_____

4. narthless

_____

5. moltn't

_____

6. glennest

_____

7. palps

_____

Part V: Contextual analysis. Read each sentence and note the italicized word. Circle the word it replaces from the choices below.

1. Mary bought an old *flabber* (a wood-burning range) at the auction.

        icebox   stove   fireplace

2. The swarm of *moopies* destroyed the farm.

        locusts   trout   singers

3. Being much heavier than Ruth, Anna *brizzled* her in the match.

        overwhelmed   tied   defeated

4. His cheeriness was *rantwilious* on this heart-rending occasion.

        needed   out of place   typical

5. On the gray, cloudy February evening, I felt very *seroptick.*

        cold   hopeful   lonely

Read the short paragraph that follows, and write a word that fits in each blank space.

Actually, the conventional reading (6) _____ that have dominated the (7) _____ of reading for decades (8) _____ not get at the (9) _____ logical processes operating in (10) _____ passage or work such as (11) _____ by Hearn.*

Answer Key

Part I	Part II	Part III	Part IV	Part V
1. sell	1. bed	1. ma/pen	1. un/wok	1. stove
2. king	2. gone	2. do/chone	2. roth/ing	2. locusts
3. pig	3. mild	3. fin/ter	3. lide/nalk	3. overwhelmed
4. agile	4. boy	4. flo/tten	4. narth/less	4. out of place
5. sand	5. much	5. bon/cle	5. molt/n't	5. lonely
6. dish	6. open		6. glenn/est	6. skills
7. sacks	7. bake		7. palp/s	7. teaching
8. choir	8. bond			8. do
9. bend	9. black			9. basic
10. sticks	10. team			10. a
11. cuff	11. pine			11. that
12. now	12. away			
13. kin				
14. log				

Teaching Suggestions

Suggestion 1

Prepare, teach, and evaluate *three* word-attack lessons with the child you are tutoring or the group you are teaching. College-level reading textbooks or elementary school instructional materials written for children may be used for reference.

Suggestion 2

Prepare a game to teach or reinforce either sight vocabulary or certain phonics generalizations. Write a short paper explaining the *purpose* of the game, the instructions, and an evaluation of its strengths or weaknesses, based on your use of it with your pupils.

---

* George Henry, *Teaching Reading as Concept Development,* Newark, Delaware: IRA, 1974, p. 18.

Suggestion 3

Prepare an instructional session intended to introduce one or more structural-analysis features. Write a statement of objectives, procedures, and materials. After teaching the lesson, evaluate it in terms of its effectiveness and interest to pupils.

Suggestion 4

Write a short story with 10 or 15 synthetic nonsense words which you think can be identified through the use of context. Write and number the real words in lists below the story. Have your pupils read your story and supply the real word (or number) above the synthetic word replacing it. Next, prepare an item analysis (how many children missed each word?) and evaluate the lesson on that basis.

REFERENCES

Ames, W. S. "The Development of a Classification Scheme of Contextual Aids," *Reading Research Quarterly* **2** (1966): 57–82.

Artley, A. S. "Teaching Word Meaning Through Context," *Elementary English Review* **20** (1943): 68–74.

Ashton-Warner, Sylvia. *Teacher,* New York: Bantam Books, 1967.

Berdiansky, Betty, *et al. Spelling-Sound Relations and Primary Form-Class Descriptions for Speech-Comprehension Vocabularies of 6–9 Year Olds,* Inglewood, Calif.: Southwest Regional Laboratory, 1969.

Cazden, Courtney. *Child Language and Education,* New York: Harcourt, Brace and World, 1972.

Dulin, Kenneth LaMarr. "New Research in Context Clues," *The Journal of Reading* **13,** 1 (October 1969): 33–38.

Durkin, Dolores. *Phonics, Linguistics and Reading,* New York: Columbia University, Teachers College Press, 1972.

Ekwall, Eldon. *Locating and Correcting Reading Difficulties,* Columbus, Ohio: Charles E. Merrill, 1970.

Emans, R., and G. M. Fisher. "Teaching the Use of Context Clues," *Elementary English* **44** (March 1967): 243–246.

Fernald, Grace. *Remedial Techniques in Basic School Subjects,* New York: McGraw-Hill, 1943.

Hall, Robert. *Sound and Spelling in English,* New York: Chilton, 1961.

Heilman, Arthur W. *Phonics in Proper Perspective,* Columbus, Ohio: Charles E. Merrill, 1968.

Johnson, Dale D. "A Basic Vocabulary for Beginning Readers," *Elementary School Journal* **72** (October 1971): 29–34.

————. "Suggested Sequences for Presenting Four Categories of Letter-Sound Correspondences," *Elementary English* **50** (September 1973): 888–896.

————. "Word Lists That Make Sense and Those That Don't," speech presented at Symposium XXVII of the International Reading Association annual conference, New Orleans, May 3, 1974.

Johnson, Dale D., and Emily Menzel. "Grade Level Recognition of Johnson's Basic Vocabulary for Beginning Reading," *The Elementary School Journal* (in press).

Mathews, Mitford. *Teaching to Read: Historically Considered*, Chicago: University of Chicago Press, 1966.

Smith, Frank. *Understanding Reading: A Psycholinguistic Analysis of Reading and Learning to Read*, New York: Holt, Rinehart and Winston, 1971.

Spache, Evelyn B. *Reading Activities for Child Involvement*, Boston: Allyn & Bacon, 1973.

Venezky, Richard. *The Structure of English Orthography*, The Hague: Mouton, 1971.

In correct reading (1) each word produces a correct meaning, (2) each such element of meaning is given a correct weight in comparison with the others, and (3) the resulting ideas are examined and validated to make sure that they satisfy the mental set or adjustment or purpose for whose sake the reading was done.

E. L. THORNDIKE

8 Teaching Comprehension

Within the simplest of conceptual frameworks, reading comprehension may be defined or explained as a dialogue between an author and a reader. The written language is the vehicle that permits the dialogue to occur when the two are far apart in space or time. Although words may be mouthed or sentences scanned visually, no reading comprehension has occurred until the two persons communicate via the medium of print. And, of course, the proof of the pudding in most reading activities lies in the ability to communicate with an author while reading silently rather than orally.

Most people are able to recall one or more totally unproductive reading experiences. The person who reads a page of print too soon after an argument with another person may find that the "reading" activity has produced several good counterarguments, but no notion of the information on the page. The reader's eyes have been with the words, but the mind has not. Or, a person with no background in anatomy and physiology may read a detailed explanation of the measurement and interpretation of diastolic and systolic blood pressure without gaining any insight into the subject. Indeed, it is possible that an erroneous interpretation of the information presented may result. To use another example, a person may read material that is poorly written and for that reason gain nothing. The writer whose words are not precisely chosen, whose sentence structure is awkward, or whose paragraphs are not unified and coherent may fail completely to transfer his or her knowledge and feelings to the readers. Finally, most good readers can recall an instance when they read a passage orally for an audience without first reading it silently and found that their audience learned more about the subject than they did. They were so intent on a good oral-reading performance that they failed to attend to or reflect on the ideas in the material they were reading.

Reading comprehension, then, depends on many factors: (1) the reader's ability to attend to the printed ideas; (2) the reader's background knowledge to which new information must be added; (3) the quality or lucidity of the writing itself; and (4) the reader's purpose or goal in reading the material. Thorndike (1917, p. 332) says: "... we should not consider the reading of a textbook or reference as a mechanical, passive, undiscriminating task, on a totally different level from the task of evaluating or using what is read ... the demands of mere reading are also for the active selection which is typical of thought. It is not a small or unworthy task to learn 'what the book says.' " *

---

* Edward R. Thorndike. "Reading as Reasoning: A Study of Mistakes in Paragraph Reading," *Journal of Educational Psychology* **8** (1917): 332. Copyright 1917 by the American Psychological Association. Reprinted by permission.

Definitions and models of the process of reading comprehension can be found in nearly every textbook concerned with the teaching of reading. However, no one really knows precisely how the transfer of ideas and feelings from an author to a reader takes place. In fact, the complexity of the process is such that investigations of the many factors involved in the production and interpretation of printed material have produced more assumptions and hypotheses than definitive answers. For this reason, all teachers must be highly suspect of instruments, materials, approaches, and models that purport to define, teach, or assess reading comprehension in a straightforward, no-nonsense manner. Stimulus-response models, information-processing models, behavioral objectives, standardized or criterion-referenced tests, reading-assessment systems, kits and workbooks that conceptualize, test, or teach comprehension as one would conceptualize, test, or teach word recognition—all, in our view, tend to be too simplistic for the phenomenon of comprehension. Suffice it to say that a number and variety of interacting factors appear to affect reading comprehension.

THE READER

A student takes from a reading selection in relation to what she or he brings to it. We learn most about those subjects we already know something about, for which we are motivated to learn more, and for which we have the necessary learning skills. "Readiness" is a concept that applies not only to beginning-reading instruction, but also to any reading experience, regardless of the maturity of the reader. Therefore, students' basic skill development, their concept of reading, their attitude toward reading, and their overall intellectual development are all factors in how well they comprehend any given reading selection.

Basic Skill Development

Although it is true that words often have little meaning until they are embedded in the context of other words, a child must have some knowledge of the meaning of individual words in order to get meaning from sentences, paragraphs, or whole selections. Davis (1944) sorted out and labeled nine skills judged by the reading authorities he consulted to be basic to reading comprehension. They are the following:

1. Knowledge of word meanings
2. Ability to select the appropriate meaning for a word or phrase in the light of its contextual setting
3. Ability to follow the organization of a passage and to identify antecedents and references in it

4. Ability to identify the main thought of a passage

5. Ability to answer questions that are specifically answered in a passage

6. Ability to answer questions that are answered in a passage, but not in the words in which the question is asked

7. Ability to draw inferences from a passage about its contents

8. Ability to recognize the literary devices used in a passage and to determine its tone and mood

9. Ability to determine a writer's purpose, intent, and point of view, i.e., to draw inferences about a writer.

In order to obtain the intercorrelations of scores in the nine basic skills, 240 multiple-choice items were administered to a large number of college freshmen. The analysis of the data showed clearly the importance of the knowledge of word meanings in reading comprehension. Davis reported, "Component I is clearly word knowledge (skill 1). Its positive loading in each of the nine basic reading skills reflects the fact that to read at all it is necessary to recognize words and to recall their meanings" (p. 191).

Therefore, the process of reading comprehension begins at the level of knowing word meanings. Until children have learned to recognize and apply meaning to a vocabulary of words, they cannot begin to comprehend ideas. However, the number of words in that vocabulary need not be more than four or five (e.g., "I have a dog." "Maria is happy.") before the teaching of comprehension can be started. Our recommendations for the teaching of a reading vocabulary are delineated in Chapter 7. A list of basic comprehension skills that we believe need specific teaching in the elementary school appears later in this chapter, along with our recommendations for materials and activities to teach each of the skills listed.

Concept of Reading

Underlying the development of basic comprehension skills is the child's concept of reading. Since this topic is discussed in some detail in Chapter 1, we will mention it only briefly here. The reader who is not looking for ideas is likely not to find any. There is no shortage of students, at all academic levels, who perceive the giving of a good oral-reading performance as the mark of a good reader. Generally, this perception can be traced to an instructional program that overemphasized oral reading. There is also no shortage of students who have never learned to become emotionally involved in their reading.

The concept of reading as a task of translating words and sentences to the sounds they represent or as a simple matter of covering all of the words on a page with one's eyes to enable the answering of objective questions at the end of the selection interferes with reading comprehension. Children must "hear" the words of the author and "see" in their mind's eye the pictures described. Furthermore, for maximum comprehension, they must read with the intention of using their reading experience for a specific purpose, such as discussing the material with another person, writing about it, drawing a picture relative to it, or doing some other reading-related activity. How a child perceives the purpose of reading, then, is a factor in comprehension.

Attitude Toward Reading

The attitude of the student toward reading in general or toward a particular selection is another factor in comprehension. Students who have had pleasant, nonthreatening experiences with reading are more likely to be open to an exchange of ideas between an author and themselves. Students who perceive themselves to be poor at understanding what they read or who see printed material as threatening to their self-concepts or social status are likely to have considerable anxiety interfering with their comprehension. Most people have experienced the deterioration of their language-arts skills under emotional stress. Certain materials cause more stress in students than in others. The reading of arithmetic problems, for example, is often very difficult for students who don't like arithmetic or who perceive themselves as poor arithmeticians. These same students may do quite well at getting information from material they feel comfortable with or from material that deals with a subject they are especially interested in. Hunt (1970, p. 147) says: "Every observant teacher has seen the highly motivated reader engrossed in a book which for him is obviously of considerable difficulty. But because interest and involvement are high, he persists in the pursuit cf ideas and he gets some."

Some students for various reasons simply don't like to read anything. They approach every reading assignment with reluctance. Consequently, they finish each assignment with an understanding of the material in direct proportion to the enthusiasm with which they attacked it. This is a major factor in poor reading comprehension for many students and has some definite implications for teaching reading (discussed in Chapter 10).

Intellectual Characteristics

The range of intellectual development within a group of students at every academic level is large. This range results from differences in both innate intellectual potential and environmental circumstances. Accordingly, the range of comprehension ability within any group of students is at least as wide as, and usually wider than, the range of intellectual development within the group. Although factors other than intelligence, defined in a broad sense, play a role in reading comprehension, there is a high positive correlation between intelligence and reading ability, as best we can measure those two developmental attributes at the present time. Harris (1970, p. 24) says, "Correlations between intelligence test scores and reading achievement in the first grade tend to be substantial in size, although not as large as in higher grades."

No comprehension occurs until the ideas that are newly encountered are fitted into the reader's existing framework, organization, or storehouse of knowledge. Consequently, teachers need to be certain that a child's intellectual development is ready for the material he or she is expected to comprehend. According to Ausubel (1964, p. 223): "Subject matter content can at best have logical or potential meaning. Potential meaning becomes converted into actual meaning when a particular individual, employing a meaningful learning set, incorporates a potentially meaningful proposition or unit of information within his cognitive structure."

Perhaps the best way to ascertain the "match" between a child's cognitive development and the reading material is to elicit from the child the material that has been read. In effect, this amounts to a language-experience approach (discussed at some length in Chapter 6). To reiterate here, the teacher provides an experience likely to evoke oral comments from the child (a trip to the airport, an animal brought into the classroom, a picture, or a film), solicits and records the child's comments, and asks the child to read them. Using this approach for children's beginning instruction in reading comprehension is, in our opinion, the best way to begin the reading-comprehension process. As the child's instruction continues, care must always be taken to select materials for which the child has a background of relevant experience or to give the child the experiential background necessary for comprehending the assigned materials.

THE WRITER

Reading comprehension is not entirely dependent on the reader. The writer, too, is responsible for the communication that does or does not take place with the reader. Writing is not simply "talk written down." Very few, if any, writers express themselves in writing as they would in speaking. The limited punctuation system that exists for the writer of English to signal meaning is often a poor substitute for the gestures, facial expressions, vocal emphases, and other cues to meaning that would be used in speaking the same ideas. The writer must depend on the reader's ability to "tune in," as it were, to the language both are familiar with. In a sense the writer must write so that the reader "hears" the intonation patterns that signal much of the meaning in the English language. By way of illustration, we invite you to reread this paragraph and to "listen" to yourselves as you do so.

Students who are learning to read should be instructed with material that is selected carefully from the standpoint of the author's craft as well as the relevance of the subject matter. Words should be used with precision, sentences should be constructed so as to avoid ambiguity, and paragraphs should be focused, unified, and coherent. Smith (1973, p. 43) says:

There is no substitute for good material. Interesting characters, vivid descriptions, unified and coherent paragraphs permit students to empathize, visualize and think through an idea with an author. The producers of some developmental materials have devised elaborate word attack cues, comprehension questions, work sheets and other instructional aids for material that is poorly written or not relevant to the experiences and interests of the students. Attractive packaging sometimes hides dull, meaningless material that students can do little more with than repeat or answer simple questions about.*

Teachers should not assume that short, choppy sentences are easier to comprehend than are longer ones which are more like their students' oral-language patterns. Surely, long sentences with subordination, negations, or other complicated constructions are not suitable for children in the initial stages of learning to read. But neither are short, artificial

---

* Richard J. Smith. "Developing Reading Maturity in the Elementary School," *The National Elementary Principal* **LIII** (November 1973): 43. Copyright 1973, National Association of Elementary School Principals. All rights reserved.

constructions, which may be judged "easy" according to a formula for measuring reading difficulty but are in fact difficult to read. For most children who are learning to read, sentences that contain some modifying elements and perhaps some simple coordination or subordination will aid their reading fluency and hence will help them to get the maximum amount of meaning from the material they are reading.

THE TEACHER

The quality of the material used to teach children comprehension skills is certainly a major factor in their development of those skills. However, the importance of the teacher in the learning process cannot be overemphasized. We wish to stress this point, although it may seem obvious. We are concerned with what we see as an increasing tendency to produce and buy instructional "packages" that at least implicitly, and in some cases explicitly, purport to do the whole job of teaching comprehension. Commercially developed basal series, kits, workbooks, and other collections of selections at specified grade levels of difficulty have flooded the marketplace. They all come with prepared postreading questions or other comprehension exercises; many include answer sheets or cards that allow each student to correct his or her own responses and to proceed through the materials at his or her own pace. Although these materials may be helpful in the process of teaching comprehension skills, complete reliance on "canned" questions and exercises deprives students of more appropriate and more beneficial questions and exercises prepared by the teacher according to the interests and needs of the students at any particular time in this reading development. Teachers should be careful not to relinquish one of their most important responsibilities, the construction of good comprehension activities and tests. Authors of developmental reading materials cannot possibly anticipate all of the needs of distant students or plan reading-related activities that capitalize on the current interests of those students.

Initial Instruction

As we stated earlier, we recommend that formal instruction in reading-comprehension skills be started with sentences or "stories" dictated by the students themselves. This language-experience approach enables students to learn a sight vocabulary of words from their own experiential background, words that are expressed in sentence patterns easily recognized by the students when they see the words written down. We do not recommend that the reading process be begun as a process of sounding out words which are recognized as meaningful language after the sounding-out process has been completed. From the beginning of their instruction, children should be more keenly aware of the ideas in print than of the individual letters or words on the page.

Sentences that are dictated by the children, printed for them by the teacher, and read by the children should always be discussed. We recommend that the "discussion" be precisely that. Although some specific questioning about the factual content of the material is not harmful, an overemphasis on the asking and answering of specific questions can cause students to become dependent on teachers' questions for their responses to reading selections. In the beginning stages, teachers should include questions that permit open-ended as well as "correct" responses. For example, the following language-experience story was dictated by a first grader. The questions that follow the story seem to use good examples of discussion questions.

> We saw a picture. It was about some kids on a playground.
> The kids was having fun because they was laughing.

1. Read the words in your story that tell where the kids in the picture are playing.
2. What made you think the kids were having fun? Did you explain this in your story?
3. What do you think those kids' names might be?
4. What do you like to do most on the playground?

Prereading Instruction

After children have learned some vocabulary and have learned to read orally with reasonable fluency, the emphasis of their comprehension skill development should be on silent reading. Oral reading is necessary for diagnostic purposes and to aid in the formation of certain basic skills, but the true power of comprehension is developed during silent-reading experiences. However, in order to maximize their chances of having a productive reading experience, children need guidance before they begin a selection.

There are three major reasons for the strategy of giving students prereading assistance in comprehension skills: (1) to motivate them to read or to get them interested in the selection; (2) to give them the background information they will need to comprehend the selection (e.g., help with difficult vocabulary, some acquaintance with concepts, sentence structure, or aspects of the author's craft they are likely to be unfamiliar with); and (3) to give them specific purposes or goals for reading the selections (e.g., to be able to recall the sequence in which a series of events occurred, to find a central thought or several main ideas, to locate facts to support a particular viewpoint). If students are properly prepared for a reading selection, then the postreading activities can be used to enrich the reading experience, not to hold a postmortem for it.

TEACHING SPECIFIC COMPREHENSION SKILLS

Except for a subsection on teacher-constructed reading-comprehension tests, the remaining discussion in this section is focused on the teaching of the comprehension skills we believe need to be specifically taught in the elementary school. In all, there are ten such skills.

1. To read sentences with the appropriate intonation patterns

2. To form mental pictures of situations or conditions that are described in a sentence or a longer passage

3. To answer questions about the facts or details presented in a sentence or a longer passage

4. To recall, with a minimum of prompting, the facts or details in a sentence or a longer passage

5. To paraphrase the central thought or main ideas in a passage

6. To identify cause-effect, comparison-contrast, sequential happenings, and other relationships between and among ideas

7. To summarize the content of a passage

8. To test the information or assertions given by an author against personal observations, logic, or the information and assertions given by other authors

9. To use a literary character, a description, or an opinion as a point of departure for creative thinking that goes beyond the presentation of an author (e.g., the creation of lines of dialogue between two characters, an extension of a story, a diary entry of a historical figure)

10. To identify specific characteristics of an author's craft (e.g., exaggeration, use of figurative language, deductive or inductive reasoning, detailed descriptions, vivid characterization, emotional appeals).

The nine skills enumerated in the list compiled by Davis, which was presented earlier in this chapter, and the ten in our list are similar in both content and number, and you will undoubtedly note the similarity in the behaviors that are enumerated in both lists. However, comprehension can and has been divided into many more than the nine and ten skills in the two lists. Scope and sequence charts from basal series and assessment systems typically include many more, for example. Although we do not find fault with longer lists that specify finer aspects of the broader behaviors in our list, we believe that careful teaching of the ten skills we enumerate will encompass those that are included in more specific breakdowns. In other words, many subskills are learned as part of the learning and practice of these ten skills. The overlapping of comprehension skills and the reinforcement they give to one another is obvious to any teacher who watches children learn to extract meaning from print. The fact is that comprehension skills are not learned in a one-two-three order. By the same token, not all skills need to be taught formally. Most teachers can attest to children's ability to summarize a reading selection before they were formally taught "summarizing." A reader simply cannot draw inferences from a passage without comprehending the factual information presented or interpret words or phrases appropriately without being aware of the meaning of the larger context in which they are embedded. For example, consider the admonition "Let sleeping dogs lie" in the following two paragraphs:

A dog often develops a strong loyalty to his "family." Some dogs will permit children to play roughly with them and even hurt them without complaining. However, dogs have been known to behave violently when suddenly awakened. Children should be taught to *let sleeping dogs lie.*

Someone once said, "I've had many troubles, most of which have never happened." Sometimes, people stir up troubles that would never surface if they were left to time. Perhaps the best advice for most worriers is, "Let sleeping dogs lie."

Our suggestions that follow regarding instructional materials and activities for teaching the behaviors we specify are by no means exhaustive. However, they should provide teachers with some specific ideas for teaching what we believe are the comprehension skills students need to learn to become good readers.

1. *Students must learn to read sentences with appropriate intonation patterns.*

   Oral reading is probably the only way to teach students to read with appropriate intonation patterns. Stories in basal series or language-experience stories are good materials with which to get students started with expressive reading. As their reading vocabularies and other reading skills develop, they can be given additional instruction with letters-to-the-editor, short plays, poetry, and narratives written in the first person. The assumption is, of course, that their feel for the flow of printed language as experienced in oral reading will transfer to silent reading, where vocalization will be replaced with subvocalization. An overemphasis on expressive oral reading can cause students to develop the bad habit of reading orally to themselves. Therefore, expressive oral reading should always be followed by silent reading for specific purposes. The teacher should frequently direct students, e.g., "Read the next sentence silently to find out why Bobby was so happy when he woke up."

   In the very beginning stages of reading instruction, most children seem to need to express orally the words they are learning in order to translate them into the sounds they represent. In the beginning stages, this is a somewhat deliberate, halting process. However, most children soon fall in with the rhythm of the sentences, especially if they are asked to read the sentences or lines of dialogue just the way they would read them to someone who couldn't see the book or just the way they think the character would have said them. Sometimes, the teacher may need to read the passage aloud; to attain the objective, the children then model the teacher's expression. It is important that the teaching of this skill be done with short passages. One or two sentences is about all that beginning readers are able to read with good expression. As they become more skillful, the length of the passages may be increased to a paragraph or two. However, expressive oral reading is a fatiguing activity, and teachers should never push students beyond their ability to do a good job. Bumbling, tumbling, and stumbling around with words never helped anyone become a fluent reader.

   After students have developed the ability to read silently, all oral reading should be preceded by "aided" silent reading. Students should be given an opportunity to read silently and to get help from their teacher with any words, sentences, or ideas they do not feel confident about. The teacher's job is to give them the help they need before they read for an audience. If the teacher is working with a group, each member should be given a different passage or a different excerpt from one passage to prepare for oral reading. The teacher then acts as a resource person for all of the students during the preparation time. When everyone is ready, the students should take turns, with each student reading the passage she or he prepared. When one student is reading, all other students should have their books closed so they can be good listeners. The teacher, whose book should remain open, should be prepared to give students help if they begin to falter, and such help should be immediate. Students should be given immediately a word they don't recognize or a phrase that is giving them difficulty. While a child is reading for an audience is not the time for teaching word-attack skills; rather, this is the time for helping the student give the best possible oral reading performance. Frequently, but not so often that the continuity of the selection is destroyed, some time should be devoted to having the students paraphrase, answer some questions about, or discuss the content of the passages that were read and listened to. The postreading focus on the ideas that were read will train students to be good listeners and will give those who read the material aloud a real purpose for reading with good expression.

2. *Students must learn to form mental pictures of situations or conditions that are described in a sentence or a larger passage.*

Forming mental images as one reads is important because so much of what is written requires visualization in order to be comprehended. For example, literary characters, geographic regions, steps in a laboratory procedure, and many other things and processes that are described in writing demand that the reader form a mental image of them. The reader who translates the words without mentally forming the images they describe is likely neither to be impressed by nor to remember the selection. Indeed, one possible cause of indifferent or reluctant readers is that they were never taught to develop their own mental pictures as they read. Children learn to comprehend television and movies by using the pictures created by someone else. To comprehend and enjoy written material, children must learn to create their own pictures.

One strategy for teaching children to form mental pictures as they read is to ask them to tell more about a character, situation, or process than is revealed by the author. For example, "It was summer and Bob and Erica were going shopping. What do you think they were wearing?

What do you think Erica's mother was wearing? Do you think the bus was full? How many people were on the bus? What did the bus driver look like?" Obviously, material that includes pictures is not appropriate for this kind of activity.

Another good instructional practice for training students to read with pictures in their minds is to use materials with accompanying illustrations. The pictures can be examined and discussed before the students read the selection and, when it seems advisable, referred to during the reading of the selection. Some authors feel strongly that pictures should not be used as part of the instructional-reading program. However, we feel that pictures can be, if used properly, beneficial in helping certain students develop powers of visual imagery as well as in motivating them and giving them a correct mental set for the reading selection.

Finally, students may be asked to draw pictures of characters, settings or situations described in their reading material. If they are told before they read that they are going to draw a picture of Suzy at her birthday party, they are more likely to visualize the party as they read about it.

3. *Students must learn to answer questions about the facts or details presented in a sentence or a larger passage.*

Classrooms abound with students who gain no more than a general impression from the material they read, and for some material and for certain reading purposes this is sufficient. However, much in-school and out-of-school reading contains a good deal of factual information and many details that are important for a good understanding of the subject matter being communicated.

Teachers should examine the material their students are going to be assigned to read so as to discover the specific facts and details that are important for a good understanding of the selection. Prereading questions can then be constructed and presented to the students to help them recognize and attend to important information as they read. For example, a teacher might write the following questions on the chalkboard and tell the students to find the answers to them as they read: (1) Why did Billy want to be on time for school? (2) What was Mrs. Thomas afraid might happen? (3) What did Robert give Billy?

Teachers must use good judgment about the information they focus students' attention on and the number of prereading questions they ask. The information should be of consequence to the understanding or enjoyment of the selection, and the number of questions should usually not exceed three.

Certainly, postreading questions about facts and details in a reading selection are also beneficial in training students to attend to and recall information. However, prereading questions are probably better for training students; postreading questions, for evaluating the effects of that training.

4. *Students must learn to recall with a minimum of prompting the facts and details in a sentence or a longer passage.*

There is a substantial difference between being able to answer specific questions about information in a selection and being able to recall details and facts without the aid of direct questions as prompts. The latter is more indicative of reading maturity. However, instructional materials and teachers frequently emphasize, or focus exclusively on, the former.

Postreading discussions in which students are asked to recount the selection in as much detail as they can remember are helpful in developing students' recall powers. During these sessions the teacher usually says no more than, "Tell me (or us) as much as you can about what you have just read." After the student has done so, the teacher says, "Is there anything else you can remember about the story?"

Students become progressively better at unprompted recall as they get practice in doing it. Teachers should always adjust the length of the selection to the student's ability and should not expect 100 percent recall. If students are working in a group, each one can be asked to supply one or two bits of information recalled from reading the selection. It is sometimes advisable for the teacher to add to the information supplied by the students if something of importance has been omitted. However, students should never be faulted for their failure to remember *all* the important facts and details in the selection. Generally, students' achievement at this task is better if they know beforehand that they will be rewarded for being able to recall the content of the selection.

5. *Students must learn to paraphrase the central thought or main ideas in a passage.*

No idea is truly our own until we put it into our personal language. Being able to repeat an author's exact words may be a manifestation of a good memory, but it does not require true understanding. Most people can remember having memorized a poem, prayer, or excerpt from a historical document without really knowing the meaning of the message. Similarly, identifying and reading aloud the topic or other important sentence in a paragraph does not guarantee understanding. The best manifestation of true understanding of the central thought or main ideas in a passage is the ability to put the passage aside and express the essence of the message, using one's personal vocabulary and personal manner of expression.

Obviously, the skill of paraphrasing major ideas cannot be taught without material that contains a central thought or major ideas, and some material does not. With appropriate material, however, students can be asked to put the material aside when they are finished reading it and to discuss, in their own words, what they believe the author was most concerned about communicating to them. During these discussions students can be guided to suggest applications of ideas to different people or different situations and to put in their own words any inferences they drew from ideas that were implied but not directly stated. For example, teachers might ask if the generalization that people build their houses out of material that is easiest for them to find or to make suggests the kind of home that would be prevalent in areas with abundant forests or in desert areas. Or, teachers might ask what the author who was being ironic really meant by, "You can buy anything with money."

Sometimes, it is helpful for students to state what they believe to be a fair representation of the author's point of view or major assertion and then search the selection to find information that supports that point of view or assertion. Another good exercise, with suitable material, is to ask the students to state what they believe might be contrary points of view or counterarguments to the ideas expressed by the author.

6. *Students must learn to identify cause-effect, comparison-contrast, sequential happenings, and other relationships between and among ideas.*

Probably the best way to teach students to detect relationships between and among ideas is by direct questioning. For example, students may be asked why Bruce thought no one liked him, why the family decided not to take a vacation together, how Mary was different from Jean, what happened first, second, and third. As is true of teaching most comprehension skills, such teaching is often maximally effective if it is done as a prereading activity. For example, students may be asked to read to discover what caused the fish in Crooked Lake to die, or to find out whether Jason or Tom was the better friend, or to learn the four steps in building a campfire in the proper order.

Teachers should preview material to find opportunities to focus students' attention on words that signal specific relationships. They might ask students what the words "because," "however," "but," "then," or "finally" signify. Students who learn to respond correctly to the precise relationships signalled by function words will read with much better comprehension than do students who miss these signals.

7. *Students must learn to summarize the content of a passage.*

Perhaps the best indication of a student's comprehension of a passage is the ability to summarize it. This is a difficult task and one which is frequently not taught or not taught well. Because of its difficulty, summarizing should probably not be specifically taught until students have mastered, or learned to a high level of mastery, the six skills that were discussed previously. After they have learned less difficult skills, students should be taught how to summarize selections both orally and in writing. Often, teachers need to prepare summaries of selections students are going to read. The summaries, which serve as models, can be studied by the students both before and after they read the entire selection. After studying model summaries, students should be given many opportunities to produce summaries of selections and to compare their summaries with those of the teacher and other students. Teachers should be careful not to teach summarizing as a "unit," but rather to give students instruction in this important skill frequently throughout their school years. Teachers should also be careful not to discourage students who have great difficulty pulling the necessary ideas from a selection together into a suitable summary, but rather to find as much good in each student's attempts as possible.

8. *Students must learn to test the information given or the assertions made by an author against personal observations, logic, or the information and assertions presented by other authors.*

The teaching of this skill can be begun early in a child's reading development. Cartoons, comics, silly poems, and exaggerated characters can all be used to help a child notice the difference between writing that is true to the world as it exists and writing that reflects an author's individual perceptions of that world. Questions such as, "Do you think that's really what would happen?" or "Do you think anyone would give someone an elephant for a birthday present?" call students' attention to the fact that they can read something and get the message without actually believing it or incorporating it into their own value system.

As children develop their reading ability, the decisions and behavior of characters in stories can be discussed and judged as likely or unlikely to occur and as being moral or immoral. Ultimately, children should read letters-to-the-editor columns, editorials, personal essays, poems, advertisements, and other material that presents personal values and biases. Such information can be checked against reliable references, and the assertions or implications can be discussed to see whether or not they meet the tests of accuracy, fairness, and logic. The students can read the same news story in different papers, noting the various choices of words and impressions given by the writers. All in all, children can and should be given many opportunities to evaluate the ideas they encounter in print and to discuss their evaluations with other people who have read the same material.

9. *Students must learn to use a literary character, description, or opinion as a point of departure for creative thinking that goes beyond the presentation of the author.*

Torrance (1965, p. 431) says, "A good story, biography or other reading material is likely to evoke many ideas and questions which can send the reader far beyond what is read." Smith (1969, p. 431) has suggested the following criteria for questions that help students think beyond the limits of a story or other selection: (1) they ask for information not in the story (e.g., "What do you think Basil will be like when he is in high school? Will he still tease other kids? Will he be an athlete?"); (2) they ask for the reader's personal ideas (e.g., "If you were a character in this story, what would you tell Sally to make her feel better?"); (3) they do not attempt to evoke responses that can be evaluated as correct or incorrect; (4) they focus on what the reader can produce, e.g., a different character, a different setting, lines of dialogue, or other creations.

Teachers must always realize that some students are much more creative than others, but that almost all students enjoy and profit from expressing the creativity they do have. The creation of some kind of product relative to a reading selection helps students to understand, remember, and enjoy the selection. Their creations should be fostered in an atmosphere of genuine interpersonal respect and accepted as highly personal expressions of unique individuals, regardless of the quality or degree of creativity in those expressions.

10. *Students must learn to identify specific characteristics of an author's craft (e.g., exaggeration, figurative language, deductive or inductive reasoning, detailed descriptions, vivid characterization, emotional appeals).*

One characteristic of a mature reader is the ability to recognize, interpret, and appreciate nuances in an author's style. The materials written for children reflect the stylistic preferences of the people who wrote them. Students should have their attention called to the unique ways in which certain writers express an idea. In addition, students often need help in interpreting figurative language, hyperbole, similes, metaphors, passages that set a mood, and other distinguishing characteristics of an author's craft. Teachers should examine the materials their students are reading to find examples of an author's style that may be particularly interesting or that may present interpretation difficulties. Usually, the benefit to the student—in terms of comprehension and appreciation of the passage—is greatest if these examples are identified and briefly discussed or explained before the student reads the passage. As students become more facile at recognizing and interpreting specific stylistic devices, instruction in this aspect of comprehension can be shifted from prereading to postreading.

TEACHER-MADE COMPREHENSION TESTS

Reading comprehension can be measured with formal standardized tests, which we discuss in Chapter 9. However, many educational benefits can also be derived from the making and the taking of teacher-constructed comprehension tests. Teachers become more aware of the need to teach specific skills; they use their knowledge of their students' needs and interests, thereby personalizing the tests; and they are likely to look more carefully at students' responses on tests they themselves prepared and to adjust their instructional programs accordingly. Students have the benefit of having the person who taught them also evaluate them; and if the tests are well constructed, students can learn a great deal about the many personal benefits of reading.

A good teacher-made comprehension test should meet the following criteria: (1) it should help teachers become familiar with their students' comprehension strengths and weaknesses in terms of the goals of their instructional program; (2) it should help students learn more about the reading process and about themselves as readers; (3) it should enrich the students' reading experience; and (4) it should help students learn more about the selection about which they are being tested. In other words, the test itself, if carefully constructed, is an excellent learning experience for both teachers and students.

When teachers construct tests to measure students' comprehension ability, they should have clearly in mind the specific skill or skills they wish to measure, they should provide for students to express their personal interpretations or reactions to the selection, and they should make the test interesting. By way of illustration, the following comprehension questions all rely on information in this chapter for their answers. Note that each question measures one of the skills in our list of ten. Together, they might comprise a comprehension test that meets the criteria we recommend that a comprehension test have; however, in most instances one test would not attempt to measure all of the skills focused on in the following test.

1. Look back through the discussion in this chapter and find one sentence that you think would be spoken with special emphasis if it were read aloud. Use slashes (/) to indicate the places where a good reader would probably pause, and underline any words that would probably be stressed.

2. Draw a picture or describe in words how you imagine a first-grade teacher might use a language-experience approach with students. (You may look back to refresh your memory before answering this question.)

3. What did Davis find to be the most important skill or the major component in his study of nine basic comprehension skills? (Do not look back.)

4. How does the "writer" figure into or play a role in a student's comprehension? (Do not look back.)

5. State in your own words what you believe is the central thought or two important ideas in the subsection entitled "Attitude Toward Reading." (You may look back to refresh your memory before answering this question.)

6. What might cause a student to render a fine oral reading of a passage but not comprehend the material he read? (You may look back.)

7. In a sentence or two, summarize the material presented in the subsection entitled "Intellectual characteristics." (You may look back.)

8. In our discussion of "initial instruction," we say, "We do not recommend that the reading process be begun as a process of sounding out words which are recognized as meaningful language after the sounding-out process is completed." What reasons can you offer either in support of or in opposition to this point of view? How do you think reading specialists who do recommend a synthetic phonics approach for beginning reading support their recommendation?

9. Create a five-sentence language-experience story that you think

serves as a representation of the kind of story that third graders might dictate after a visit to the airport.

10. Characterize this chapter as a piece of written discourse. Is it persuasive, emotional, objective, slanted, or does it possess other obvious or subtle characteristics? See if you can find specific words, phrases, sentences, or paragraphs to support your assessment.

SUMMARY

Basal series and other commercially produced instructional materials are designed to help teachers teach and test reading comprehension. They are for the most part valuable aids for the teacher of reading, especially the beginning teacher. However, teachers should also be familiar with the basic comprehension skills that students need to learn and should become skillful at selecting materials and planning instructional activities to supplement the developmental reading materials and activities that are available from publishing companies.

Suggested Activities for the Methods Class

Activity 1

Read the following selection from *The Prophet* by Gibran (1965, p. 56). Then respond to the questions that follow it. Be prepared to share your responses with other members of your group or your class.

ON TEACHING

Then said a teacher, Speak to us of Teaching.
    And he said:
    No man can reveal to you aught but that which already lies half asleep in the dawning of your knowledge.
    The teacher who walks in the shadow of the temple, among his followers, gives not of his wisdom but rather of his faith and his lovingness.
    If he is indeed wise he does not bid you enter the house of his wisdom, but rather leads you to the threshold of your own mind.
    The astronomer may speak to you of his understanding of space, but he cannot give you his understanding.
    The musician may sing to you of the rhythm which is in all space, but he cannot give you the ear which arrests the rhythm nor the voice that echoes it.

And he who is versed in the science of numbers can tell of the regions of weight and measure, but he cannot conduct you thither.

For the vision of one man lends not its wings to another man.

And even as each one of you stands alone in God's knowledge, so must each one of you be alone in his knowledge of God and in his understanding of the earth.*

1. Select the lines you think best state the need for individualizing instruction.

2. Identify an audience (one or more listeners) with whom you would like to share this selection.

3. Read the selection again as you would read it to the audience you identified. Imagine yourself reading it in your best oral-reading voice. Would you or would you not welcome the opportunity to do this?

4. How much do you value this selection (greatly; somewhat; not much; not at all)?

5. State the central thought in "On Teaching" in your own words.

6. Can you suggest any reason why a teacher might disagree with the central thought in "On Teaching" and perhaps even take strong exception to it?

After you have shared your responses to the six questions above with other members of your group or class, discuss the following with them:

1. What specific comprehension skill does each of the six questions focus on?

2. Does this test meet the criteria of a good comprehension test?

Activity 2

Construct a comprehension test for the short selection below, either individually or in small groups. Compare and evaluate the individual items you construct and each test as a whole. Identify the specific comprehension skill each item is measuring.

Match Game
by
Richard J. Smith

A drop of sweat plopped on the court as the tired player bent over to tie the new white tennis shoes that were finally resting. Those shoes had been dodging and darting, running and stopping for almost two hours. They were new

---

* Reprinted from *The Prophet,* by Kahlil Gibran, with permission of the publisher, Alfred A. Knopf, Inc. Copyright 1923 by Kahlil Gibran; renewal copyright by Administrators C.T.A. of Kahlil Gibran Estate, and Mary G. Gibran.

shoes, and they felt good. But they had to be tied just right. This could be the final game of the final set and they had to be ready to move fast.

For three years the weary player in white had been waiting to win the big match. Now the white canvas shoes were planted behind the baseline, waiting for the first serve of what could be "match game." The ball slammed in fast, but out of court. The shoes moved closer to the baseline for the second serve. It was in, and the shoes moved forward. The player's arm slammed the ball back across the net. On the other side another tired player reached for the slam but missed it completely. Fifteen-love, three more points and the match could be over. The shoes looked a little worried as they stood waiting for the next service.

The next serve came in fast and low. The white shoes carried the tired player to the inside line of the alley where a sharp backhand drove the ball to the toes of the shoes of the opponent across the net. Those shoes moved fast but not fast enough, and the ball ended up tangled in the net. Thirty-love. Just two points away from victory.

Winning two quick points put some pep into the feet in the new shoes. And they shifted sideways a little, waiting for the next service. An ace, but the shoes skipped backwards and lobbed the ball high into the air. The lob was returned, but not fast; and a smooth forehand shot made the score forty-love. One point to go.

Now the shoes danced nervously, waiting behind the baseline.

The serve was in, the return was deep into the backcourt. The ball crossed the net again. Now the new shoes leaped into the air and a racket slammed the ball back. The other pair of shoes was obviously not ready. They stumbled, a racket stretched out and the ball died on its strings.

The new shoes sailed across the net to permit the winner to shake hands with the loser. Julie didn't even hear the salesman ask her mother if the new shoes would be cash or charge. The cheering of the crowd was too loud in her ears.

Activity 3

Construct a comprehension test for Chapter 9 in this text. Each test should require no more than 30 minutes to complete. Working in pairs, exchange tests, complete them, and confer with each other about the answers and the strengths and weaknesses of each test.

Teaching Suggestions

Suggestion 1

1. Select a story from a basal series or a different piece of writing that is suitable for the ability and the interests of the students you are teaching. Examine the selection to discover which two or three comprehension

skills could be taught by using the selection (e.g., correct interpretation of figurative language, recognition of cause-effect relationships, discovery of central thought).

2. Write a statement of your objective for each skill in terms of what behavior you hope to elicit from your students. For example, "The students will be able to verbalize that when the author wrote 'Billy walked to school like a turtle,' Billy wasn't really walking like a turtle, but rather very slowly." Or, "The students will be able to tell me that Billy was walking very slowly because he didn't want to be in the play."

3. Plan instructional activities that will help you elicit the desired behavior from your students. For example, I will ask the following questions: (1) Try to get a picture in your mind of Billy walking to school. Do you think he was really walking like a turtle? Why did the author say he was? (2) Find the sentence that tells why Billy was walking so slowly. Would the word "and" in that sentence give us the same idea that the word "because" does?

4. Observe carefully the length of time students need to answer your questions or complete the exercises you assign. Observe also the eagerness or the reluctance with which they respond to your tasks. Finally, observe the way in which you react to their responses (e.g., quick praise, matter-of-fact acceptance, spontaneous follow-up questions or discussion).

5. Evaluate the entire teaching experience in terms of your objectives, your planned activities, your students' behavior, and your reactions to their behavior in the instructional setting.

Suggestion 2

Select a story from a basal series or from other material suitable for your students. Without referring to any suggested instructional practices or accompanying comprehension questions, construct a comprehension test for the selection. Take into consideration the interests and ability of your students. Have your students read the selection and complete your comprehension test. Discuss with them which question they most enjoyed answering and which was least enjoyable. Ask them if they think the comprehension test helped them understand the selection better. Ask them if they would have preferred to see certain or all of the questions before they read. Would having the questions before reading be more or less helpful with other kinds of material? Finally, compare your test with any activities and/or tests that the authors of the instructional materials have suggested, if any exist for the selection you used.

REFERENCES

Ausubel, David P. "Some Psychological Aspects of the Structure of Knowledge," in *Education and the Structure of Knowledge,* ed. Stanley Elam, Chicago: Rand McNally, 1964, pp. 221–249.

Davis, Frederick B. "Fundamental Factors of Comprehension in Reading," *Psychometrika* **9** (September 1944): 185–197.

Gibran, Kahlil. *The Prophet,* New York: Alfred A. Knopf, 1965, 1923.

Harris, Albert J. *How to Increase Reading Ability,* 5th ed., New York: David McKay, 1970.

Hunt, Lyman C. "The Effect of Self-selection, Interest, and Motivation upon Independent, Instructional and Frustration Levels," *The Reading Teacher* **24** (November 1970): 146–151, 158.

Smith, Richard J. "Developing Reading Maturity in the Elementary School," *The National Elementary Principal* **LIII** (Nov./Dec. 1973): 42–45.

————. "Questions for Teachers—Creative Reading," *The Reading Teacher* **22** (1969): 430–434.

Thorndike, Edward L. "Reading As Reasoning: A Study of Mistakes in Paragraph Reading," *The Journal of Educational Psychology* **VIII** (1917): 323–332.

Torrance, E. Paul. "Guidelines for Creative Teaching," *The High School Journal* **XLVIII** (1965): 459–464.

Assessment, however, is secondary to instruction. It comes into being only when a decision must be made, and then only when it can provide information not obtainable by less expensive means.

RICHARD L. VENEZKY

9 Diagnosing and Evaluating Reading Growth

We have long believed that well-intentioned reading specialists and elementary teachers spend too much time testing reading and not enough time teaching it. Perhaps that is a fault of their college remedial-reading courses, which tend to dwell more on how to test the many facets of reading ability than on ways to develop reading skills. Perhaps so much testing is done because teachers feel a need to be precise in an era of accountability. Perhaps it is because there are so many hundreds of reading tests available.

Diagnostic testing is a legitimate concern of teachers. If a child's strengths, weaknesses, and interests can be ascertained precisely, it should follow that more appropriate instructional activities can be planned. The term "diagnostic teaching" is relatively new. It implies that sensible testing and good teaching go hand in hand. It suggests a test-teach-retest instructional sequence. Unquestionably, teachers need information about their pupils, information that can facilitate their instructional planning; however, much of the testing that goes on in school may be unimportant as far as teaching is concerned. Testing can be a waste of time for a number of reasons, ranging from the purpose of testing and potential use of the results to the type of information yielded by the tests or to the poor quality of the tests themselves. We are not opposed to testing. To the contrary, we strongly support a good testing program *when* the tests provide information directly applicable to improved reading instruction.

In this chapter we talk briefly about the usual reasons for testing, the types of tests available, and the methods of testing reading. We examine some of the problems of test-item construction and selection, and we recommend and describe some testing procedures we feel are useful to classroom teachers.

PURPOSES FOR TESTING

The many reasons why school people give reading tests can be classified into three broad categories: comparative assessment, program evaluation, and diagnosis. These three purposes are arranged in order of increasing usefulness to teachers, albeit decreasing preponderance in practice. Comparative assessment is probably of least use to teachers, but it is the type of testing done most frequently. Accordingly, diagnostic assessments are most useful to classroom teachers, though they are often done with least frequency.

Comparative Assessment

Comparative assessment is usually done to help administrators make decisions about personnel or the allocation of resources. Annual assessment in reading and such other areas as math and language is undertaken by most school districts. More recently, state departments of public instruction have begun to conduct statewide reading assessments, and the federal government has also underwritten a national assessment in reading.

The testing instruments usually used are norm-referenced standardized tests (described later) or specially developed criterion-referenced tests. Standardized tests typically yield two or three types of information (rate, vocabulary, comprehension), with scores expressed as grade-level equivalents or percentile ranks. Such gross measures may be helpful for comparing performance between Milwaukee and Madison, or between Longfellow and Elmwood Schools, or between Teacher Jones and Teacher Brown. But the scores are not very useful and may be misleading for teachers who want to help the pupils in their class improve their reading. Problems of validity and reliability associated with group-standardized tests are discussed later in this chapter.

In some cities, mean or median scores for each grade level in each school in the district are published in the newspapers. Inevitably, a few schools, usually those in the high-income neighborhoods, look very good, whereas schools in the poorer areas across town look bad. The implication is that children in the former schools are blessed with better teachers than are those in the latter. In fact, just the opposite could be true.

Children in the more affluent neighborhoods may come to school rich in experience, in ownership of large numbers of children's books, and with the good fortune of having been read to by their parents for years. With such children, a teacher's job might be relatively simple. In contrast, some children in the poorer neighborhoods may enter school having had virtually no experience with books and reading. Their teachers, through very hard work, may achieve significant success in *gradually* developing the students' reading ability and interest. Yet the test scores of the low socioeconomic children would compare unfavorably with those of the former group.

Assessments at the school district and state levels are presumably done to assist decision makers in determining which schools need more money or which teachers need in-service help or termination. Both reasons seem legitimate, as long as the probable causes for poor performance or good performance are analyzed carefully. An assessment score must never be taken at face value (though it often is by the general public when it appears in a newspaper). Questions that must be asked about the assessment include the following: Was the content of the test compatible with the goals of instruction? Did the test items really measure what they purported to measure? What was the experiential background of the children taking the test? What were the test-taking conditions?

Before undertaking an assessment, the planners need to clearly resolve such concerns as: How will the results be used? How and to whom will the results be disseminated? What is the cost-benefit ratio? Will the amount of instructional time lost to test administration be compensated for by the information gained? Is the information to be gained really needed for decision making, or is sufficient information already available? Many school systems, perhaps out of some sense of tradition, administer batteries of achievement tests every year and then neatly file away the results. Yet when the intended use of a comparative assessment is clearly understood and the assessment is designed accordingly, the information gained can be very helpful to instructional decision makers in evaluating personnel and allocating resources.

Program Evaluation

Program evaluation is usually done at the classroom or school building level. Nearly every basal-reading series comes with a full testing component related to the materials and the objectives of the program. The purpose of program evaluation is to assess the effectiveness of a particular set of materials, an innovative program, a new set of procedures, or some other explicit part of the instructional program. Broad, standardized achievement tests are not often used. Instead, tests written to relate specifically to the program or to certain materials are given. These tests are often developed by the teacher or school district, but if the program to be evaluated is commercially published, a set of tests is typically available from the publisher.

Program evaluations can be very valuable in helping a teacher, principal, or school system decide whether to keep, modify, or discard a program or innovation. For example, school system A, after using reading series X for five years, decides to give series Z a try. The promotional literature has made series Z seem worthwhile trying. Some schools or classrooms in the system may be designated as "pilot" centers to try out the new program for a year or two before a decision to adopt it systemwide is made. Except for the pitfalls of the "Hawthorne effect," such a strategy is sensible. The Hawthorne effect suggests that results seemingly related to a new program or innovation may not be due to the program itself, but rather to the novelty of doing something that is different.

As another example of program evaluation, after teaching phonics with workbooks for two years, Teacher B designs a phonics program based on group and individual games and periodically devises short tests to determine whether or not the children are learning through the new approach. The teacher gives these tests to determine whether the new approach is effectively helping the pupils to learn phonics.

In school C, teachers begin to worry in November that their pupils don't really like to read. Therefore, an attitude-interest inventory is administered. For the next three months, pupils spend some time two days a week in free, independent reading. Then, the attitude-interest inventory is given again to see if they like reading any better than they did in November.

In our view, program evaluations such as those in the three examples above can be very worthwhile and should be undertaken from time to time to evaluate old programs as well as innovations.

Diagnosis

Diagnostic testing is the most immediately useful to elementary teachers and reading specialists. Such tests yield information explicit enough to be used in the day-to-day instructional program. Published diagnostic tests are available for both individuals and groups. Rather than yielding only gross scores, such as comprehension and vocabulary, they provide detailed information about specific skills strengths and weaknesses. For example, diagnostic tests of comprehension may evaluate a pupil's ability to: (1) recall facts and details; (2) infer character traits; (3) predict outcomes; (4) determine reality or fantasy; or (5) any of a number of other, rather discrete comprehension skills. The publication edited by Tuinman (1976) includes critical reviews of a large number of published diagnostic reading tests. Reading teachers concerned with the selection of diagnostic reading tests should refer to this collection of detailed reviews.

Most diagnostic testing in the classroom is done through informal procedures and teacher-made tests. Informal testing can ascertain the interests of the pupils and can also pinpoint specific strengths and weaknesses in the various components of word identification and comprehension. Some informal procedures lend themselves to group administration but others must be used only with individuals. At the end of this chapter we present a detailed informal diagnostic test designed for use with children whose reading ability ranges from beginning to about a sixth-grade level. You may want to modify this test to meet your own specific diagnostic testing needs.

TYPES OF READING TESTS

Reading tests can be categorized and labeled according to four criteria:

1. *How are they administered?* Must they be used with individuals or can they be given to groups?

2. *Who constructed them?* Are they published, standardized tests, or are they teacher-made?

3. *What do they measure?* Are they global achievement tests, which yield information about only the broadest aspects of reading? Or, are they diagnostic tests which show ability with the smaller sub-components of reading?

4. *What do the scores mean?* Are the scores *norm-referenced*—do they compare pupils with some previous sample of test takers by giving a grade-level, percentile, or stanine score—or are they *criterion-referenced,* providing scores not in reference to other test takers but denoting a level of proficiency? The score on a norm-referenced test tells how well the test taker did in relation to a national sample of test takers. The pupil's raw score is converted to some type of comparative score, such as a percentile rank or a grade-level equivalence score. The score on a criterion-referenced test relates to a specific predetermined objective (criterion) or set of objectives. The criterion score does not compare the test taker with anyone else. Instead, it indicates whether or not a child has achieved a certain level of proficiency. When test givers are most interested in comparing children, they use norm-referenced tests. Criterion-referenced tests are more frequently used for diagnostic purposes, when the teacher is interested in discerning how well a child has learned a particular thing.

These four questions apply to any reading test. For example, hypothetical test A is an individually administered standardized test of phonics knowledge which yields criterion scores. Hypothetical test B is a group-administered standardized general achievement test which gives grade-level equivalence scores. Hypothetical test C is a group-administered teacher-made test of cause-effect relationships which provides a criterion score.

The teacher's purpose will determine the type of test to be used at a given time. If a teacher wants to test everyone in the class, a group test will take much less time than an individual test. If a published test is available that will provide the kind of information wanted, it will cost money, but it will save some test-construction time. If information is needed about the pupils' ability to use structural analysis, a global test of comprehension will not suffice. If it is important to determine whether or not children have mastered a specific list of sight words, a criterion test is appropriate.

When selecting published standardized tests, teachers should read carefully the technical data in the manuals, particularly the information about validity, reliability, and the norming-population samples. Validity is the extent to which a test actually measures what it says it measures. For example, a test that says it measures word *meaning,* but which requires children only to circle a word pronounced by the teacher from among a choice of four words, is invalid; it is a test of word recognition, not word meaning. Reliability is the extent to which a test is consistent with itself in whatever it measures. For example, if the same paragraph comprehension test were administered to a group of children weekly for a month and yielded mean scores of 90, 20, 50, and 10, it is unreliable. The teacher can't be confident of the scores, because there is little consistency. In terms of a norming sample, if a test yields a grade-level score based on a sample of 200 children at each grade level in a Los Angeles suburb, the score is meaningless—except perhaps to Los Angeles suburbanite children or children who are like them in any variables that might affect the scores. A norming sample should be cross-sectional and representative of all types of schools and children if it is to be used with cross-sections of children. In summarizing *Reading: What Can be Measured?,* Farr (1969, p. 212) says:

Much of the research reviewed in the monograph has cast considerable doubt on the validity and reliability of all testing instruments in general and group standardized tests in particular . . . [but] . . . tests can make a valuable contribution to classroom practice if the test user is aware of their limitations: the test consumer should know *why* he wants to use tests and *for what* he is testing.

Before describing some inexpensive, informal testing procedures that we feel can be helpful to classroom teachers, we present some illustrative problems related to test-item construction. We hope that as teachers construct their own tests, they will be able to avoid some of these problems.

PROBLEMS OF TEST-ITEM CONSTRUCTION

Consider the following types of sample questions, which resemble questions frequently found on published reading tests.

Comprehension Questions

Instructions to Pupils: Read this paragraph and then answer the questions which follow. [Paragraph omitted.]

1. The elephant was very ——————.

   noisy   hungry   big

2. The monkeys played in the ——————.

   trees   sandbox   driveway

3. A kind old man cleaned the ——————.

   plate   cages   zebra

4. He let us feed the ——————.

   fish   children   animals

5. We had fun at the ——————.

   zoo   parade   circus

In this test, the child's task is to read the paragraph and then answer the questions. We have omitted the paragraph, but invite you to answer the questions. Chances are you scored "100," with answers of *big, trees, cages, animals,* and *zoo.* The test purportedly measures reading comprehension, but we think it tests previous experience or prior reading. When children can answer all or most questions without having read the passage, something is wrong with the test.

Decoding Exercises

Teacher says:

"As I say a word, circle the word that begins with the same sound."

ball	boy	girl	dog
leaf	go	now	lap
pull	sing	pack	flat

This test supposedly measures *decoding* ability, the ability to supply the sound of a letter or, simply, the ability to pronounce. At its best, however, this test measures *encoding,* the ability to spell. The child *hears* a sound and is asked to designate its spelling. At its worst, the test is a measure of sight vocabulary. The child's knowledge of words rather than of letter-sound correspondences may be what is being measured. Johnson (1973) recently addressed this type of testing error:

One of the major problems with many word attack tests, particularly tests of phonics ability, is that they involve encoding, or spelling, rather than decoding, or pronouncing. The sets of grapheme-phoneme correspondences for encoding and decoding are often quite different. For example, if you were asked to write /Kɔθ/ on your paper, you would have two choices for the initial consonant, *coth* or *koth* (*coth* would be proper because /K/ is spelled *c* in initial position before O except in borrowed words) and several choices for the medial vowel, *coth* (scoff), *cauth* (cause), or *coath* (broad). On the other hand, if you were shown the word *coth* and asked to pronounce it, other choices are available: /kaθ/ (mop), /Koθ/ (both), /Kɔθ/ (moth), or /Kəθ/ (mother). The point is clear: decoding and encoding correspondences are not always bidirectional. Therefore, tests in which the examiner reads a synthetic word and the children are asked to respond, either from among choices or in writing, are not accurately measuring word attack *decoding* skills. There is nothing wrong with testing encoding if one is interested in spelling ability, but testing should fit the purpose of the instruction. To measure childrens' ability to use phonics generalizations in pronouncing unfamiliar printed words, tests requiring decoding should be used. Failure to do so could cause teachers to plan instructional programs which do not match the skill needs of their pupils.*

To be useful to the teacher, tests must measure what they say they measure.

Inferential Comprehension Questions

Where would you probably see the following sign?

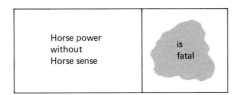

A. On a highway
B. On a gymnasium floor
C. At a racetrack for horses
D. In a grocery store

The intended answer (A) would probably be chosen far less often than (C), because of the use of the antiquated term "Horse sense." The language of the test must match the language of the test taker.

---

* Dale D. Johnson. "Guidelines for Evaluating Word Attack Skills in the Primary Grades," in *Assessment Problems in Reading*, ed. Walter H. MacGinitie, Newark, Delaware: IRA, 1973, pp. 24–25. Reprinted by permission.

These are but a few examples of the kinds of test items that can yield erroneous information about a child's reading ability. Another problem with test-item construction is that of deciding *which format* to use to measure a given skill. For example, in order to test word knowledge, we can ask a child to:

1. Read the word and circle a picture of it.
2. Look at a picture and circle the word for it.
3. Read the word and circle a definition.
4. Read the word and circle a synonym.
5. Read the word and circle an antonym.
6. Read the word in context and circle a definition, synonym, or antonym.
7. Read a sentence and supply the missing word.
8. Read a sentence and circle the missing word.

If the target word is *circle,* for example, it seems that a child could convincingly demonstrate a knowledge of the word *circle* with some of the above tasks, but reveal an ignorance of the word with some of the other tasks. Also, with multiple-choice formats, accuracy or inaccuracy may be greatly influenced by the other response choices.

The intent of the foregoing is to encourage teachers to examine carefully the kinds of test items contained in a test under consideration. Similarly, when constructing their own tests, teachers must continue to ask, "Do the items measure what they are supposed to?"

RECOMMENDED INFORMAL TESTING PROCEDURES

Thus far, we have considered some potential problems with tests and testing. In the remainder of this chapter we describe some informal tests and procedures which many teachers have found useful. The four types of measurement we discuss are: interest/attitude inventories, cloze tests, informal reading inventories, and informal diagnostic tests.

Interest/Attitude Inventories

Teachers need information about how their pupils feel about reading and the kinds of things that interest them. (Chapter 10 is devoted to the importance of fostering positive attitudes toward reading.) What we like to do, we do often and usually become quite good at. What we do not like to do, we avoid as much as possible. Related to attitude is interest. If a child can read about those things she or he is interested in, chances are that the child will read more avidly and will develop increasingly positive attitudes toward reading.

Some awareness of children's attitudes and interests can be gained rather simply. Attitudes can often be discerned through direct observation. How often does the child read during free time? Does the child go to the library frequently? How "tuned in" is he or she during the class reading period? When given the opportunity, does the child select reading over some other leisure-time activity?

Some teachers have developed rather elaborate attitudinal survey instruments. Typical attitudinal questions include:

Directions to pupil: Read each statement and circle the answer that describes how you feel:

1. I like to check books out of the library.

   Strongly agree   Agree   Sometimes   Disagree   Strongly disagree
2. I'd rather watch TV quiz shows than read a book.

   Strongly agree   Agree   Sometimes   Disagree   Strongly disagree
3. I like to read at night before bedtime.

   Strongly agree   Agree   Sometimes   Disagree   Strongly disagree

Teachers of very young children or nonreaders can use the same technique by reading the questions to the children and having them circle an appropriate "face."

Teacher: "I like to check books out of the library."
Pupil page

Dulin and Chester (1974) have developed and validated a four-part instrument for assessing the attitudes toward reading of intermediate through high-school-age children. An excerpt from their scale is reprinted in Fig. 1. Children are asked to mark one of five boxes nearest to the activity of their choice.

In many ways, it seems more sensible to assess pupils' attitudes toward reading *specific* things than to determine their *general* attitude about reading. Some children like to read only comic books; others like poetry or novels or the sports page or astrological charts. "Liking reading" may often depend on what the child's purpose is and what is being read. The most pertinent assessment of a child's attitude toward read-

Which would you rather do?

This . . .		*or*		*this . . .*
1. listen to the radio				read a book
2. read a book				clean up around the house
3. play a musical instrument				read a book
4. read a book				shine your shoes
5. write a letter				read a book
6. read a book				watch television
7. play with a pet				read a book
8. read a book				take a nap
9. do some work around the house				read a book
10. read a book				read a magazine
11. draw or paint a picture				read a book
12. read a book				fix something to eat
13. call a friend on the phone				read a book
14. read a book				play a solitary game
15. read a newspaper				read a book
16. read a book				look at pictures
17. do a crossword puzzle				read a book
18. read a book				work on a craft or hobby project
19. work on a school				read a book
20. read a book				listen to records

Fig. 1. The Dulin-Chester attitude scale.

ing is his or her responses to specific selections or materials. No one should be expected to respond equally positively to all types of reading. Smith and Barrett (1974, pp. 180–181) have developed a short inventory, easily administered, which measures attitude toward particular selections.

1. I enjoyed reading this selection.

    _____ Strongly Agree
    _____ Agree
    _____ Uncertain
    _____ Disagree
    _____ Strongly Disagree

2. This selection was boring.

    _____ Strongly Agree
    _____ Agree
    _____ Uncertain
    _____ Disagree
    _____ Strongly Disagree

3. This selection held my attention.

    _____ Strongly Agree
    _____ Agree
    _____ Uncertain
    _____ Disagree
    _____ Strongly Disagree

4. I disliked reading this selection.

    _____ Strongly Agree
    _____ Agree
    _____ Uncertain
    _____ Disagree
    _____ Strongly Disagree*

To ascertain students' reading interests, the best procedure is to ask them what they are interested in. This can be done elaborately, through a questionnaire, or informally, during a conversation. Some teachers ask open-ended questions; others provide lists which the pupils can check off. Typical interest inventory questions include:

1. Do you have hobbies? What are they?

2. What places do you like to visit?

3. What pets or animals do you like?

---

* Richard J. Smith and Thomas C. Barrett. *Teaching Reading in the Middle Grades*, Reading, Mass.: Addison-Wesley, 1974, pp. 180–181. Reprinted by permission.

4. Name your favorite TV shows.

5. Name the books you have enjoyed most.

6. What do you like to read about?

7. What was the best time you ever had?

Information about children's interests and attitudes is important for teachers to have. Children who avoid reading or dislike it need special attention and motivation (see Chapter 10). Once the child's interests are known, he or she can be helped to locate books and articles which relate to those interests. Reading has too often been viewed as "skilling and drilling." Our schools have prepared too many children who *can* read but who do not read. The teacher who wishes to improve children's feelings about reading and wants to help them find interesting things to read will profit from the use of informal interest and attitude inventories.

Cloze Testing

The cloze (closure) procedure has most often been used to measure comprehension of a particular passage. With this procedure, a passage from a book is mimeographed, with every *nth* word deleted. Three passages of about 100 words each are deleted from near the front, middle, and end of the book; then, the items are systematically deleted. Most users of this procedure delete every fifth word, but that is an arbitrary number. The child's task is to read the passage and write the missing word on the blank line. Cloze procedure "purists" argue that only *exact* replacement of the deleted words should be counted correct and that a correct score of about 40 percent indicates that a child is able to comprehend that material. This judgment is based on statistical analyses which separate good and poor readers as correlated with scores on other reading tests.

In addition to providing a guideline with respect to how "readable" a book will be for a given child, the cloze procedure can be used diagnostically. Errors, words that are not exact replacements of the deleted words, can be analyzed to see if they are semantically and/or syntactically appropriate. A child who misses all the words in terms of exact replacement but whose responses constitute reasonable synonyms probably has no reading problem, in our judgment, or at least has a different kind of problem from a child whose answers are semantically bizarre or ambiguous or who leaves a half page of blank lines.

We invite you to familiarize yourself with the cloze procedure by reading the following short cloze passage and inserting the missing words.

> Information-getting groups are _____ not formed before the _____ of grade three, although _____ may be exceptions and _____ should be exceptions for _____ who develop good reading _____ younger than most children _____."

If your responses were *usually, end, there, indeed, children, ability,* and *do,* you scored 100 percent, with exact replacement. If you substituted *normally, close, there, undoubtedly, pupil, skill, do* (or any other reasonable synonyms), we think that you are able to comprehend this material. If, on the other hand, your answers were *coming, three, green, once, pizza, clotheslines, block,* for example, you have either a reading problem or a sense of humor.

We recommend the informal use of the cloze procedure as a means of determining the approximate "fit" between the child and the book and as a way of diagnosing the child's semantic-syntactic contextual "sense."

Informal Reading Inventories

In its most informal application, the use of an informal reading inventory simply means having the child read orally while the teacher notes the kinds and number of oral-reading errors; after the child has finished reading, the teacher asks some comprehension questions. The following kinds of questions are intended to serve as guidelines in denoting the types of reading problems a child might have:

1. While reading aloud, does the child mispronounce words, thereby indicating phonic weaknesses?
2. Does the child substitute inappropriate words, thus indicating a lack of contextual awareness?
3. Does the child attend to punctuation marks or read right through them?
4. Does the child hesitate to the point of frustration?
5. When the child regresses or rereads, is the error corrected (a good sign) or repeated (a bad sign)?
6. Does the child omit entire words or phrases?
7. Despite oral-reading errors, does the child know the answers to the

questions that were asked; that is, did the child comprehend the passage?

A good deal of the literature on the informal reading inventory suggests that its label is a misnomer—that the procedure is, indeed, quite formal. General informal inventories have been published—which seems a contradiction—and most basal-reading series include an informal inventory to accompany their books.

Ostensibly, the procedure has two functions: (1) the placement of a child in a particular book which she or he is capable of reading, and (2) the diagnosis of specific reading problems. Betts (1946) published what has become the most widely used evaluation criteria for informal reading inventories. With reference to the placement of a child in a particular book in a basal-reading series, Betts describes three categories of "match":

1. The independent level, at which a child is able to read a book with no assistance

2. The instructional level, at which a child can read with the teacher's assistance

3. The frustration level, at which a book is so difficult that the child becomes frustrated trying to read it.

Betts' criteria for a passage of about 100 words are:

Oral reading	Comprehension	Level
99% accuracy	90% correct	Independent
95% accuracy	75% correct	Instructional
90% accuracy	50% correct	Frustration

Recently, Powell (1971) has questioned the validity of Betts' criteria and has suggested that they are too stringent and that pupils' scores will vary according to the type of material and their interest in it. We concur with Powell, believing that the child's interest and the type of material can cause significant variance in performance on supposedly similar passages.

In practice, selections from each level of a basal-reading series are mimeographed and comprehension questions are written. In an individual setting, the child reads to the teacher from one copy, and the teacher records the errors (sometimes called miscues). Then, the child responds to the questions and according to the criteria above, is assigned to a book in the series.

We think that it's sensible for a child to demonstrate capability in handling a book before being expected to read it. But we think that rigid adherence to a rather arbitrary set of criteria constitutes over-formalization of a most useful informal procedure. It seems much simpler to just ask the child to read to you from the book. To facilitate diagnosis of specific oral-reading problems, it would be useful for the teacher to have a mimeographed copy of the selection—or else just a blank sheet of paper—on which to record the number and types of errors. In sum, we support a very informal use of the informal reading inventory.

Informal Diagnostic Tests

An informal diagnostic test is a loose collection of nonstandardized, nonnormed, and usually teacher-made, short tests which attempt to pinpoint specific strengths and weaknesses in a child's reading. An example of an informal diagnostic test is given at the end of this chapter.

This type of test can include as many or as few subtests as the teacher thinks are important. The test is rarely given in its entirety; if it is, its administration is usually spread over two or more sittings. Most parts of the test are designed for use with individual children. The test is rarely given to everyone in the class, but is instead used only with children who seem to evidence some reading problems.

The subtests of an informal diagnostic test typically include:

1. Some measure of the child's reading attitude and/or interests
2. A list of sight words the teacher feels are important
3. A crude measure of reading "grade level"—usually comprising graded vocabulary or oral paragraphs
4. Several tests of phonics correspondences, i.e., consonants, vowels, digraphs, clusters
5. Tests of auditory and visual discrimination for young children
6. Measures of structural analysis
7. Measures of contextual analysis
8. Common reversal words
9. Leveled reading passages, followed by different types of comprehension questions.

Since informal diagnostic tests are not norm-referenced, criterion scores are yielded in terms of the specific elements of the test. For example, a child might demonstrate that she or he knows all of the major consonant correspondences except the variant sounds of c and g. This tells the teacher not to worry about consonants in general, but rather to concentrate on *c* and *g*. If a child demonstrates ability with compound words and prefixes, instruction in structural analysis can focus on suffixes and inflected endings.

Informal diagnostic tests provide the information needed to plan appropriate reading activities for individuals or small groups of children. They are not intended to tell the teacher how Johnny is doing in relation to other second graders in the nation. We encourage teachers to develop the kinds of informal subtests (perhaps like that at the end of this chapter) needed to meet the goals they have set according to the program they are using.

SKILLS-MONITORING SYSTEMS

In the past few years a new development in testing has entered the reading arena. For a variety of reasons related to increased interest in the individualization of instruction, the resurgence of nongraded instruction, and a need for instructional precision (which stems partially from taxpayers' demands for accountability), a number of publishing houses have developed rather elaborate skills-monitoring systems. These systems, whether commercial or developed locally, share several components: (1) a set of sequentially ordered objectives for the reading skills to be monitored; (2) sets of test items and subtests to measure each objective; (3) a statement about what level of test achievement is considered "mastery" of the objectives; and (4) a resource compendium keying the objectives to related published materials. The intent of these systems is worthwhile; they are designed to help teachers determine who knows what and who doesn't, so that instruction can be geared to individual needs.

The total testing package in some of the skills-monitoring systems is voluminous, ranging from two or three dozen to more than 100 discrete tests. Most systems require that a sizable number of pretests be administered at the beginning of the school year. In addition to the *amount* of testing time inherent in the use of these systems, several other of their features are troublesome. We are most concerned with the rather arbitrary division of language components and the lack of research data supporting the selection (or deletion) of the minute subskills tested. We have seen teachers spend considerable amounts of time teaching and reteaching the minute subskills at the expense of reading broadly and for pleasure. By having so many tests available to them (and the worth of many of them remains undemonstrated), too great a concern for the "atomistic" at the expense of the "global" has developed. In short, we would rather see a child read a book for a half hour than spend that time working on the *ou* vowel cluster.

We subscribe to the six criticisms that have been directed at program-independent skills-monitoring systems by Johnson and Pearson (1975, pp. 758, 763), two of which are summarized below:

A point we wish to consider is the psycholinguistic naiveté evident in skills management systems in reading. We know that language systems—the phonology, grammar and lexicon—are interdependent. In essence, language is indivisible; yet SMS's would seem to fractionate it and destroy its essential nature. Because of the interdependence of the language systems, there is really no possible sequencing of skills . . .

In summary, can SMS's provide a reasonable framework for establishing an accountability system for teaching reading? The answer at this point is *no*. There are too many unverified assumptions underlying SMS's. In principle, SMS's may be the ideal alternative for assessing student progress in reading. But, until some *basic research and evaluation* of the systems is conducted, they must be viewed only as one of many alternatives (and a very expensive and time-consuming one, at best).

We believe that if teachers carefully pick and choose from among the various subtests of any monitoring system, they will be able to compile a useful battery which can be used in the same way an informal diagnostic test is used. Our main concern with monitoring systems is that they may encourage teachers to overemphasize skill-and-drill work at the expense of reading for pleasure and interest. They may also contribute to the pool of citizens who can read, but don't.

SUMMARY

A considerable amount of reading testing is done in schools—too much, we think. The major purposes for testing include comparative assessment, program evaluation, and pupil diagnosis. Many kinds of published tests are available to teachers, and many kinds of teacher-made tests can be constructed. With standardized tests, there are sometimes problems of validity and reliability. Certainly, teacher-made tests can also be invalid and unreliable. We recommend the use of informal testing procedures which look at attitude and interest as well as the major subcomponents of reading skill. We think that good teaching develops from a foundation of appropriate diagnosis.

Suggested Activities for the Methods Class

Activity 1

Using any basal-reading series or other set of graded material available in the Instructional Materials Center (IMC) or from a nearby school, select six passages (grades one to six) of about 100 words in length to be used as an informal reading inventory. Prepare a set of comprehension questions for each passage.

Tape record a child orally reading the passages from your informal reading inventory. Divide into groups of six or eight and listen to the tape recordings. As you listen, mark the oral-reading errors on a mimeographed copy of the passages.

Activity 2

Divide the methods class into small groups and construct two small tests for use with beginning readers. One test should measure word meaning; the other, literal comprehension. Compare and discuss the tests you have developed.

Activity 3

Have each class member analyze one published reading test. Write a critique of the test, based on the following:

1. The purpose of the test
2. The means of scoring it
3. The quality of the test items
4. The nature of the norming sample and reported data (in the manual) on reliability and validity.

Activity 4

Individually, develop a short instrument for assessing either the reading attitudes or the reading interests of primary-grade children. In small groups, compare your instruments in terms of comprehensiveness, usefulness of the information yielded, and ease of administration.

Teaching Suggestions

Suggestion 1

Select two or three children who you suspect are retarded in reading development and administer the following sample informal diagnostic test to them individually. You may wish to give subparts of the test on different days so as to avoid pupil fatigue.

Suggestion 2

After you have given the informal diagnostic test, summarize on index cards the child's basic weaknesses and reading interests.

Suggestion 3

Plan and teach a series of lessons geared to the reading interests and needs evidenced by the children's performance on the informal diagnostic test.

Informal Diagnostic Reading Test

This instrument is designed to be used in various ways. Subparts of the test may be given to all children in the class if you suspect weakness or need information in a given area. The entire test may be used with disabled readers. Subparts of the test may be reproduced in different formats to add some variety to the test sessions. The pupil will need a copy of the test, and the teacher will need a copy on which to record errors.

Part 1. Interest Inventory: The questions may be read to the child, with the teacher recording the responses. The inventory may be mimeographed and administered to groups if everyone can read well enough to answer the questions.

1. Do you have a library card?   yes   no
2. How often do you visit the school library? _____
3. How often do you visit the public library? _____
4. What games do you like? _____
5. What are your hobbies? _____
6. Name two movies you liked. _____ ; _____
7. What are your two favorite TV shows? _____ ; _____
8. What places do you like to visit? _____
9. What animals do you like best? _____
10. What kinds of things do you like to read best? _____
11. Name two books you liked best. _____ ; _____
12. What magazines do you read? _____
13. What things do you like to study? _____
14. Where would you like to go on vacation? _____
15. Where did you have the most fun? _____

Part 2. Word Recognition—Reading Level: This test provides a rough guide to a child's reading level. The child begins reading the words in list A and continues with each list until he or she misses two or more words in a list. That level is probably too difficult for the child, who would therefore be more comfortable with books at the previous level. The levels are: A—preprimer; B—primer; C—first grade; D—second grade; E—third grade; F—fourth grade; G—fifth grade; H—sixth grade.

A	B	C	D
red	a	today	nothing
can	get	mother	should
look	and	first	street
see	said	keep	only
up	ride	over	together
go	run	came	believe
are	will	after	called
in	like	right	thing
little	here	seen	start
down	stop	under	place

E	F	G	H
accident	marvel	insult	jolt
invite	remain	miracle	parcel
package	admire	panic	distinguished
raise	shrug	skied	annoy
continue	doubted	weird	metropolitan
anchor	flicker	suggestion	typical
scratch	stable	apprentice	essential
disappear	weave	sprawl	associate
arrive	creature	title	pottery
plow	geography	delegate	efficiency

Part 3. Letter Names: Have the child read the letters of the alphabet, both in upper-case and lower-case. Circle those the child does not know.

S	C	D	W	X	Q	B	A	I
Z	J	U	R	L	M	T	F	E
H	G	F	K	O	N	Y	V	
a	q	e	l	u	r	o	j	t
d	w	g	c	b	k	n	z	x
f	m	y	s	h	i	p	v	

Part 4. Consonants—Digraphs and Blends: Ask the child to give the sound of each consonant or consonant cluster. (Although this tests sounds in isolation,

we do *not* advocate teaching sounds in isolation.) Children will insert a following vowel with some consonants. For example, they may pronounce /p/ as /pə/, /t/ as /tə/, etc. This is natural and should not be considered an error.

Consonants:

f	p	m	t	s	qu	c	j	n
d	r	x	y	v	b	k	z	g
h	w	l						

Digraphs:

ng   ph   sh   ch   th

Blends:

fl	pl	br	sk	sw	st	tr
cl	sm	gr	spl	cr	tw	str

Part 5. Vowels and Vowel Clusters: Real words and synthetic words containing short-vowel, long-vowel, and vowel-cluster correspondences are intermixed. If errors are made, note the incorrect pronunciation.

pote	leap	deat	maid	jal
nabe	nation	grue	cow	kibs
fud	nook	beed	awl	nep
bute	coy	lete	flout	zin
foil	mot	jowl	dite	vie
faip	stray	noab	maul	ting

Part 6. Reversals: These words are often reversed by children with a reversal problem. Record the reversals as the child reads the words orally.

was	ten	rat	saw
lap	won	no	pot

Part 7. Structural Analysis: The synthetic words are clustered by compound words, words with prefixes, and words with suffixes. As the child reads the words, record any errors.

Compound Words:

supperjumper	talkmobile	bucketdrop
paperenter	daycase	stopwalk
footsucker	jellyhanger	dropnose

Prefixes:

untooth	exgate	inleft
projump	recar	enhop
desaw	conbook	prenow

Suffixes:

boatous	meatly	treetion
foolful	spooner	cropness
pinkling	lightance	schoolest

Part 8. Contextual Analysis: There are three parts to this subtest. The first involves homographs. As the child reads each sentence orally, note whether context is being used to provide the correct pronunciation of the homographs. The next two parts use the cloze procedure. The first story is from a first-grade book; the second, from a fourth-grade book. The child is to read the story and supply the missing words. This may be done silently in groups or orally, with the teacher recording the words for the child. Accept any word that is semantically and syntactically appropriate.

Homographs:

1. Wind the clock before you go to bed.
2. They read the book before.
3. She had a tear in her coat.
4. It is time to sow the oats.

Context:

1. Context Clues

   Katy has a good time on the farm.
   Her grandmother _____ a garden.
   Each _____ Katy worked in the _____.
   That was fun.
   And there were animals on the _____.
   There _____ chickens.
   There were _____ cows.
   _____ was a big dog.
   And there was a little white _____.
   Katy liked the kitten best.
   Each day she _____ with it.
   That was _____, too.
   One morning Katy's mother _____,
   "Katy, we must _____ home tomorrow.
   Soon it will be time for _____."   13 responses

2. Context Clues

   Mrs. Weaver awakened that morning with a bad headache. She managed to _____ down to the kitchen in her dressing gown and _____ breakfast for Mr. _____, who always had to catch a _____ for the city, and for Milly and Tommy, who had to be at _____ by a quarter of nine. When they were all

_____, she made some _____ butter and jelly sand-
wiches, which she _____ in waxed paper and left on the table
for the children's _____ in case she wasn't able to come down-
stairs again. She knew Milly could get the milk out of the _____
and the cookies from the jar. Milly was very capable. When she had
_____ her work, she went slowly upstairs and lay down again
in _____. Her _____ hurt her very much.

For a good while the house was perfectly _____; then she
began to hear something. It _____ like soft little velvet pat-
pats on the stairs. At first she _____ it was the throbbing in her
head she heard; then the small, strange sounds _____ a bit
louder in the upper hall and stopped. Very slowly she _____ her
eyes. There in the _____ sat a brown rabbit. It appeared to
be like any other good-sized _____ she had ever seen except
that this one wore _____.

21 responses

Part 9. Comprehension: Ask the child to read the story silently; if the child
cannot, you read it aloud. Then ask the questions, and have the child respond
orally. This will indicate to you the type of comprehension that the child has
difficulty with. The stories are ordered according to grade level.

1. Story 1. Comprehension—Primer

   Fred and Toby liked to go fishing with Dad.
   This time they would be out in the woods for three days.
   They would stay in a little house in the woods.
   It was time for supper when they got to the little house in the woods.
   After they ate supper, Dad said, "We'll want to get up in time to get lots of fish.
   So we must go to sleep soon." *

Questions

Literal: How long will Fred and Toby be out in the woods?
Inferential: Will they catch many fish?
Evaluative: Could this be a true story?
Appreciation: Have you ever been on a fishing trip?

2. Story 2. Comprehension—first grade

   Sometimes little boys get tired of being little boys.
   They don't like being told what to do!
   "Eat your supper."
   "Put your toys away."
   "Get right to bed!"

---

* W. Durr, J. LePere, and M. Alsin. *Rainbows,* 2d ed., Boston: Houghton Mifflin, 1975,
pp. 120–121. Reprinted by permission.

One day a little boy named Jerry was tired of hearing things like that.

He wished he could be something that was never told anything.

But what should it be?

He ran outside and sat down by a tree.

He thought about what he would like to be.

Just then, a leaf came down.

Right on Jerry's head.*

Questions

Literal: What was Jerry tired of?
Inferential: What did the leaf make him think of?
Evaluative: Discuss why this story should be about girls as well as boys.
Appreciation: Tell about things you have wanted to be.

   3. Comprehension—second grade

The Boy and the Whistle
by Elizabeth Ireland

Once upon a time, and nobody knows when, so maybe it was just pretend, there was a little boy with a whistle. He played it ever so much of the time. He could play "Rory of the Hill" and lots of other songs.

One very cold day, the little boy was going outside to play.

"You be sure and stay right close to the house," his mother said. "You don't want to get lost, do you?"

"No, Mother," the little boy said.

So off he went outside, dressed in his warmest clothes—for it was bitter cold. He had his whistle in his pocket.†

Questions

Literal: Why did his mother want him to stay close to the house?
Inferential: What will he do with the whistle?
Evaluative: What is meant by "maybe it was just pretend?"
Appreciation: Tell me about the coldest day you can remember.

   4. Story 4. Comprehension—third grade

Doctoring An Elephant
by William Bridges

Sudana was sick.

The zoo doctor heard about it from the gateman when he drove into the zoo that morning. He heard about it again from the Monkey House Keeper, who shouted that he was wanted over at the Elephant House right away. And he got the news a third time as he drove up to the front of the Animal Hospital in the center of the zoo.

---

* Inez Rice. *A Long, Long Time,* New York: Lothrup, Lee & Shepard Co./Morrow, 1954. Reprinted by permission.
† Elizabeth Ireland. "The Boy and the Whistle," *Humpty-Dumpty Magazine,* March 1954. Reprinted by permission.

Since three people had been told to let him know about Sudana's illness as soon as he arrived, the doctor knew that the matter was rather important. He snatched up his black bag of emergency medicines. Then he hurried out to the animal ambulance and roared away.*

Questions

Literal: Who told the doctor about Sudana's illness?
Inferential: What do you think caused the illness?
Evaluative: Is there really such a thing as an animal ambulance?
Appreciation: Describe an elephant you have seen.

5. Story 5. Comprehension—fourth grade

In Rome there was once a poor slave whose name was Androclus. His master was a cruel man and so unkind to him that at last Androclus ran away.

He hid himself in a wild wood for many days; but there was no food to be found, and he grew so weak and sick that he thought he should die. So one day he crept into a cave and lay down, and soon he was fast asleep.

After a while a great noise woke him up. A lion had come into the cave and was roaring loudly. Androclus was very much afraid, for he felt sure that the beast would kill him. Soon, however, he saw that the lion was not angry but that he limped as though his foot hurt him.

Then Androclus grew so bold that he took hold of the lion's lame paw to see what was the matter. The lion stood quite still and rubbed his head against the man's shoulder. He seemed to say, "I know that you will help me."

Androclus lifted the paw from the ground and saw that it was a long, sharp thorn which hurt the lion so much. He took the end of the thorn in his fingers. Then he gave a strong, quick pull, and out it came. The lion was full of joy. He jumped about like a dog and licked the hands and feet of his new friend.†

Questions

Literal: Why was the lion in pain?
Inferential: How do you think the lion will show his happiness to Androclus?
Evaluation: Does this story seem to be believable?
Appreciation: Have you ever helped an animal or a person who was in need? Tell about it.

6. Story 6. Comprehension—fifth grade

The Valiant Chattee-Maker
by Christine Price

Long and long ago, in a terrible storm of thunder, wind, and rain, a mighty Tiger took shelter in a village. Wet and bedraggled, he lay down against the wall of an old woman's hut. The old woman was very poor, and the rain was coming *drip, drip, drip* through the thatch of her tumbledown house.

---

* From William Bridges, *Zoo Doctor*, New York: William Morrow, 1957. Reprinted by permission.
† From *Favorite Tales of Long Ago* by James Baldwin. Copyright 1955 by E. P. Dutton & Co., Inc., and reprinted with their permission.

The Tiger could hear her moving about inside, dragging her belongings out of the way of the leaks in the roof and muttering to herself, "Oh, what shall I do? I'm sure the roof will come down! If an Elephant or a Tiger walked in, he wouldn't frighten me half as much as this Perpetual Dripping!"

The Tiger's tail began to twitch. "This Perpetual Dripping," he thought, "must be something very dreadful. Can it be an animal bigger and stronger than an Elephant?"

Just at that moment, through the darkness and the rain, a man came running down the road between the houses. He was the village Chattee-maker, a poor man who earned his living making earthen jars and waterpots. He had lost his donkey, and his wife had sent him out in the storm to hunt for it. "How can you carry your chattees to market without a donkey?" she cried. "Off with you, and don't come back till you find him!" *

Questions

Literal: Where did the Tiger take shelter?
Inferential: Can you describe the Chattee-maker's wife?
Evaluative: How do you know this is not a true story?
Appreciation: What was the worst storm you can remember?

7. Story 7. Comprehension—sixth grade

The old crone drew herself up in her rags, and her eyes flashed, and she looked mighty proud.

"And who made that storm, I ask you?" she said. "I did. D'you hear?"

"I'm sure you did, Grannie, but don't get excited; it's bad for you. Now, what about getting some sleep? I should be up early tomorrow morning and—"

"Oh, thunderbolts and whirlpools!" she screamed in a passion. "Is there no way in this world of making what must be said plain?" And she smashed her fist on the bottom of the pot which lay upturned between them, so that it broke the clay and went right through. Mugimba thought it best to say nothing to this, and so he watched her sit back and suck her knuckles and close her eyes and mumble to herself until she grew calmer. Then she began again, speaking very slowly and carefully.

"Listen," she said. "Just listen, and if you wish me well, don't speak, and I will teach one fool of a man to better himself if it is the last thing I do!"

And so she did.†

Questions

Literal: What did she smash her fist on?
Inferential: Describe the old crone's looks.
Evaluative: Does the writer create believable characters?
Appreciation: Have you had any experience with black magic, voodoo, or ESP?

---

* From *The Valiant Chattee-Maker* by Christine Price. Copyright © Christine Price 1965. Reprinted by permission of Frederick Warne & Co., Inc.
† Adapted from Humphrey Harman, *African Sampson,* New York: The Viking Press and Hutchinson Publishing Group, 1965. Reprinted by permission.

Part 10. Sight-Word Recognition: Use the first- and second-grade word lists found in Johnson's "Basic Vocabulary" (Chapter 7, pp. 142–143). Ask the child to read each word, thus determining those you might want to teach as sight words.

REFERENCES

Betts, Emmett A. *Foundation of Reading Instruction,* New York: American Book Company, 1946.

Dulin, Kenneth L., and Robert Chester. "Which Would You Rather Do?" unpublished manuscript.

Farr, Roger. *Reading: What Can Be Measured?* Newark, Delaware: International Reading Association, 1969.

Johnson, Dale D. "Guidelines for Evaluating Word Attack Skills in the Primary Grades," in *Assessment Problems in Reading,* ed. Walter H. MacGinitie, Newark, Delaware: International Reading Association, 1973, pp. 21–26.

Johnson, Dale D., and P. David Pearson. "The Weaknesses of Skills Management Systems," *The Reading Teacher* **28,** 8 (May 1975): 757–764.

Powell, William R. "The Validity of the Instructional Reading Level," in *Elementary Reading Instruction: Selected Materials,* 2d ed., ed. Althea Beery, Thomas C. Barrett, and William R. Powell, Boston: Allyn and Bacon, 1974, pp. 89–95.

Smith, Richard J., and Thomas C. Barrett. *Teaching Reading in the Middle Grades,* Reading, Mass.: Addison-Wesley, 1974.

Tuinan, J. Jaap, ed. *Review of Diagnostic Reading Tests,* Newark, Delaware: International Reading Association, 1976.

Venezky, Richard L. *Testing in Reading: Assessment and Instructional Decision Making,* Champagne, Ill.: National Council of Teachers of English, Monograph, May 1974, pp. 24–25.

...the humane teacher cannot stop when his students "recognize" words and "comprehend" stories. He must acquaint children with the greatness inherent in their civilization.

JOHN STOOPS

10 Fostering Positive Attitudes Toward Reading

The printed word is surely one of the "greatnesses" inherent in our civilization. Statistics on the number of volumes stored in any major library, on the number of newspapers and magazines in circulation, or on the circulation, storage, and retrieval of ideas in print are outdated before they are reported. The continuous activity in producing and processing printed materials is a phenomenon that has grown and become increasingly complex despite the development of nonprint communications media in our technological society. The ease with which we utilize supermarkets and the postal service is a tribute to human genius with the printed word, as are the New York City Public Library system and the advertising and greeting card businesses. Anyone who contemplates the utilization of reading and writing in the world must be impressed with the role they have played and continue to play in human development.

The underlying theme of this chapter is that to be able to read is a highly valuable asset in our society and that as intelligent beings, children will learn to value reading if they are taught with that objective in mind. Although instructional reading materials comprise a relatively small part of the total complex of printed materials, their role is not without great significance. Without them and the trained teachers who use them, the vast complex of printed materials available would exist only for the small percentage of people who learn to read without the assistance of instructional materials and trained teachers. The point is that the key to the vast resources of printed materials for the majority of people rests with the educational system we have developed. Teaching children to read is undoubtedly one of the major goals of our society, which has determined that all children must have the opportunity to enrich their lives as well as they are able to, through the medium of print.

Teaching children to read is not as unidimensional as the phrase seems to imply. A child without reading skills is deprived of participating fully in his or her civilization. A child with the necessary skills, but with little or no desire to use them, is likewise deprived. Therefore, teachers have the dual responsibility of developing in their students both reading skills and positive attitudes toward reading; and the two are more interdependent than independent. That is, no one can learn to value reading without having many satisfying reading experiences; and no one can become a facile reader without valuing reading enough to spend many hours learning and strengthening the requisite skills. The task of the teacher is to teach and strengthen skills in a context which attracts children to reading and in a manner that extends the attraction beyond the immediate instructional setting. The ultimate goal is to have a society of people at all ages who can and do tap the printed resources at their disposal for life enrichment of one kind or another. In short, teaching children to value reading as a source of information and/or pleasure is an important objective of the elementary school reading program.

In previous chapters we explained that some children develop reading skills more rapidly and to a higher level of sophistication than others do. The same is true of the development of children's attitudes toward reading. For various reasons, which will become clear when we offer suggestions for fostering positive attitudes toward reading, some children like to read from their first attempts with beginning-reading materials, and others do everything in their power to avoid reading of any kind. As is true of all human behavior, most children would probably score somewhere near the middle on an attitudinal scale stretching from "loves to read" to "avoids reading like the plague."

We believe that only a small percentage of children cannot be taught to value reading if they are taught with that objective in mind. Some will undoubtedly learn to prize reading above all or most of the other greatnesses our civilization has to offer. But to insist that all do, or to show disappointment with those who fall short of that high standard may cause those who think reading is only "Okay" to feel guilty or unintelligent and to move closer to "avoid" on the attitudinal scale we referred to earlier. In short, teachers must be as realistic about individual development in attitudes toward reading as they are about individual development in reading skills. To expect too much or to expect too much too quickly may lead to as unfortunate consequences as to expect too little.

Attitudes develop slowly and are reflections of the entire value system of a child. To expect to shape values and influence attitudes with gimmickry and exhortations is unreasonable. Only many personally satisfying encounters with relevant materials and enthusiastic people will do the job.

Krathwohl, *et al.* (p. 81) say:

...exhortations, a rational argument for a particular behavior, and passive participation of a group of persons is likely to lead to little more than an awareness of the new material and perhaps even some intellectual conviction about the appropriateness of the new behavior. However, for any major reorganization of actual practices and responses to take place, the individual must be able to examine his own feelings and attitudes on the subject, bring them out into the open, see how they compare with the feelings and views of others, and move from an intellectual awareness of a particular behavior or practice to an actual commitment to the new practice ... What is suggested here, if specific changes are to take place in the learners, is that the learning experiences must be of a two-way nature in which both students and teacher are involved in an interactive manner, rather than having one present something to be "learned" by the other.

The secret of teaching to foster positive attitudes toward reading lies not in attractive bulletin boards, catchy slogans, or prizes for those who read the most books, although these devices may help. The true power for building positive attitudes toward reading rests in having children communicate with adults and other children who value reading and who verbalize their true feelings in that regard, giving children reading instruction with materials they can read with reasonable facility, and involving children with materials and reading-related activities that give them pleasure. The remainder of this chapter is devoted to a presentation of specific suggestions to help classroom teachers incorporate these three dimensions into their reading programs.

MODELS

Modeling is an effective approach to attitudinal development. The frequent use of testimonials in commercial advertisements attests to the belief of the advertisers that people want to do what those they admire do. Children have "heroes" in both the adult world and in their peer groups. Elementary school teachers are in a good position to arrange for their students to associate with people who value reading.

The attitudes that classroom teachers project have a significant impact on the direction and the intensity of the attitudes children develop. Teachers should take advantage of their "heroic" stature and make their fondness for reading known to their students. We are advocating more than frequent testimonials which, if they are sincere, are good but not sufficient. We think that teachers should talk with their students about what they are reading and should spend time reading orally to and silently with their students. Teachers should carry reading materials other than those they use in their jobs to school with them and should leave them in conspicuous places so that students see them.

Some teachers give the impression that they are afraid they will be perceived as frivolous if they are not always planning for, teaching, or evaluating students. These teachers present only their work life to their students. The reading these teachers do becomes clearly associated with "work" in the minds of their students. The attitudes these teachers' students form toward reading would almost surely be more positive if the teachers let it be known that they *enjoy* reading in their leisure time.

Parents, too, have a powerful effect on the development of their children's attitudes toward reading, and this effect may be either positive or negative. Parents who try too hard and too soon to shape their children's attitudes may be as detrimental to the achievement of the goal they desire as are parents who are indifferent or who in rare cases actually are openly scornful of people who "waste their time" reading. Parents must be careful to do neither too much nor too little to foster positive attitudes toward reading in their children.

Through home-school association meetings, newsletters, parent-teacher conferences, and other contacts, teachers can stress to parents the importance of not pressuring children or making them overanxious about reading. They can also stress the importance of reading to children, having reading materials in the home, limiting television viewing, and providing quiet times and quiet places for reading. Most important, parents should let their children see them reading and should encourage their children to join in conversations about specific newspaper articles, magazines, or books that someone in the family may be reading. Certainly, as children begin to bring books they can read home, parents should listen carefully to their accomplishments and should praise them sincerely. Children in families that use reading in their daily lives rarely question the value of reading. Children who live in homes where reading is rarely if ever used have much greater difficulty learning that reading can have value for them.

Community Members

Many teachers ask pilots, disc-jockeys, business persons, civil servants, service station operators, and other community members to visit their classes and discuss with students how they use reading in their jobs and what kind of recreational reading they do. Schools might also encourage parents and community members to visit and occasionally use the school library so that students can see that reading is not just something they have to do in order to get through school.

Peers

One reason we are opposed to separating good readers from poor readers for reading instruction is that the students with negative attitudes toward reading are deprived of good peer models. As we pointed out in Chapter 3, we believe that children learn much about how to read and about the value of reading by interacting in small groups formed for the purpose of sharing reading experiences. Teachers should arrange for students with positive attitudes toward reading to communicate in informal settings with students whose attitudes are less positive. In our experience the tendency is for those with the more positive attitudes toward reading to have a greater effect on the others than vice-versa.

Teachers should not expect such tactics as formal book reports, prizes for the best essay on "Why I Like Reading," or bulletin board displays featuring the work of "Eager Readers" to have a positive effect on the attitudes of those students who are not such eager readers. Attitudes are developed slowly through personally satisfying experiences *with* peer models, not at a respectful distance from them. Whether or not displaying the work of eager readers has a laudatory effect on their own attitudes is questionable. Our present position in that regard is that most of these students are ready for the satisfactions to be received from "intrinsic" motivation. The "extrinsic" reinforcements may do more to these students' vanities than they do to maintain their positive attitudes. Obviously, individual differences figure strongly in this matter, as does the age and level of overall reading development of the particular students concerned.

Teachers of Special Subjects

Teachers of special subjects often have opportunities to exert a positive influence on students' attitudes toward reading. Art, music, physical education, foreign language, and any other "special" teachers elementary students may encounter should take every opportunity to encourage students to read interesting material related to their special areas. Often, these teachers are highly regarded by their pupils. For example, the physical education teacher who suggests that a pupil read a book on tennis or an article about Billie Jean King may not only provide the pupil with a good reading experience, but may also lend an air of respectability or a touch of class to the whole business of reading. Most students go through stages in which art, music, or some other special curriculum area is their favorite. Teachers of these areas should have materials at various difficulty levels readily available to pass on to students who are infatuated or truly in love with the subject-matter specialty.

GUIDED SELF-SELECTION OF MATERIALS

One of the best approaches to the development of positive attitudes toward reading is to give students opportunities to both select their own materials and read them in the school setting. Reading should be perceived by students as a natural part of the school day.

We included the word "Guided" in the title of this subsection because we have taught more than a few students who manifested one or more of the following characteristics: (1) they were truly not aware of the array of books, magazines, newspaper sections, or other materials they might be interested in; (2) they truly had no well-defined interests and needed at that point in their lives more help in establishing interests than in satisfying them; and (3) some were "browsers" rather than readers and managed to spend more time looking and exchanging books than in getting into and finishing them. These children need more help than do most others in selecting a good book for themselves.

Interest inventories that ask for students' favorite books, television programs, their hobbies, and other information intended to help teachers identify interests and guide students to materials consistent with their interests are of limited usefulness. Students often respond in terms of what they think teachers would like them to read; or, if they really don't have a favorite book, a hobby, or whatever, they make one up. Besides, a student's hobbies, television favorites, or whatever may or may not reflect reading interests. Tarzan is not on television anymore, nor is the Sears, Roebuck Catalog; yet these materials may be exactly what a particular student is looking for in reading material. Probably, a student's reading interests are identified most clearly in informal conversations about a wide range of topics. The perceptive teacher is always ready to say, "I didn't know you took care of your baby sister. I know where there is a magazine and a newspaper column that tells a lot about how to take care of babies." Or, "I know a story about a girl who had to quit school because she had to take care of her brothers and sisters. Would you like to read it?" This specific kind of guidance may be very helpful to a student's selection of interesting reading material.

In short, students at all academic levels need to feel that they have some say in deciding what to read for themselves, even if what they say is in part the result of teacher guidance. Most children will develop more positive attitudes toward individual selections and reading in general if they choose their own materials. Therefore, teachers should avoid letting children become too dependent on them in regard to materials selection and should gently wean overdependent children. This can often be done gradually, by insisting that a child select from two, then one from three, and so on until the child has learned to trust her or his own judgment in selecting reading materials.

In one school, a paperback book store helped some very reluctant readers develop more positive attitudes toward reading. A local paperback book distributor agreed to keep some specified space in the library stocked with appropriate books. The librarian, with the help of an aide, had the store open at times when the students were able to browse and purchase books. For some reason, students who were extremely reluctant to read a free book, purchased, read, talked about, traded, gave away, and did all kinds of good things with the books they bought. Perhaps some children need to invest something of tangible value to them before they can enjoy a book.

The question always arises as to whether or not students who select or purchase books that seem to be too difficult for them to read with good comprehension should be permitted to do so. Our view is that most children, over a period of time and given materials at a wide range of difficulty to select from, will tend to select those that best match their reading-skills development. For those who don't always find their level, we agree with Hunt (1970, p. 147):

> Every observant teacher has seen the highly motivated reader engrossed in a book which for him is obviously of considerable difficulty. But because interest and involvement are high, he persists in the pursuit of ideas and he gets some. . . . Given the opportunity, then, the reader who finds a really good book for him, the book that has ideas he truly wants to learn about, frequently will outdo his own instructional level of performance. When the criteria of complete comprehension and perfect oral reading are used, then the power of the interest factor is markedly reduced. By constrast, when the classroom atmosphere encourages self-selections, usual reading level performances become less meaningful.*

THE MATERIALS THEMSELVES

For students to learn that reading is a worthwhile activity, it is necessary that they have at their disposal worthwhile materials to read. Teachers, librarians, administrators, and the students should work together to develop collections of materials that include the classics, as well as

---

* Lyman C. Hunt. "The Effect of Self-Selection Interest and Motivation Upon Independent, Instructional, and Frustrational Levels," *Reading Teacher* **24,** 2 (November 1970): 147. Reprinted with permission of Lyman C. Hunt and the International Reading Association.

more recent works, in children's literature. The characters available for children to meet in their reading should range from the true to life to the absurd, but all should be well drawn and representative of all ethnic, racial, and socioeconomic groups. The plots, descriptions, and writing styles available to children in reading matter should also vary, but they too should reflect the work of an imaginative, careful writer. There is so much good literature for children to read that there is no need to resort to materials that seem to be designed more to appeal to the market than to tell good stories. It is difficult, if not impossible, to determine what is "good" in the light of individual preferences in literature. However, it is not difficult to identify books and other materials that are more impressive in their packaging and market appeal than they are in the appeal of their content to children. We urge all teachers to read widely in children's literature before undertaking their teaching responsibilities. We also urge those who select reading materials for children to get some information about the content of the materials either from reading them or by reading reviews of them made by competent authorities on children's literature.

One important consideration in selecting materials for children to read is to include materials that incorporate a wide range of difficulty levels. Although we agree with Hunt (1970) that surprisingly, children are able to read difficult books that they self-select, we also know that a steady diet of difficult books will turn any student away from reading. Publishing companies are becoming more skillful at disguising the "easy" book so that it doesn't embarrass the child who needs an easy book in order to read comfortably. The importance of having unembarrassing, comfortable reading experiences cannot be overemphasized in a discussion about the development of positive attitudes toward reading.

THE CENTRAL LIBRARY

We believe that central libraries or instructional materials centers are important for all elementary schools. However, we also believe that each classroom should have a small, ever-changing collection of materials for students to pick up whenever they have some spare time. The book or article they choose just to kill a few minutes with might result in a very positive reading experience. Besides, some reluctant readers are even more reluctant to visit the central library or the IMC. For these students, a classroom library is essential if they are to overcome their negative attitudes.

A word must be said about the role of the central library or IMC and the people who are in charge there. Attitudes toward reading are influenced by the associations students make with books and other reading materials. Students who are made to feel threatened or unwelcome in a place where reading materials are housed may develop some very negative attitudes toward reading. Fortunately, most librarians realize that they are employed to serve the needs and interests of students. Teachers who are aware of a librarian acting otherwise should feel obliged to report that person's unprofessional conduct to the administration and insist that either the librarian's behavior change or the school change librarians. Too many children have been soured on reading because of a librarian's possessive attitude toward the library and its possessions and an implicit, or at times even explicit, disdain for children's attitudes. A library need not be noisy and disorderly; but in minimizing distractions and preserving order, librarians must be careful not to discourage children from using the materials purchased for them or from visiting the facility in which most of those materials are kept.

CLASSROOM INSTRUCTION

All of the variables we have discussed so far are important contributors to the development of a child's attitude toward reading and can be influenced by the classroom teacher. The remainder of our discussion in this chapter deals with variables that *only* the classroom teacher can affect substantially—the instructional program itself. Indeed, what happens within the context of the instructional program has a profound effect on children's attitudes toward reading.

Reading to Children

Most people, regardless of age, can be captivated by a good story teller. Children are especially susceptible to the charm of a good story being read by a good reader. Therefore, teachers should consider the reading of good stories to children as one of their major responsibilities in the development of positive attitudes toward reading.

Some teachers make the mistake of trying to teach listening skills and reading comprehension while they are reading stories to children. They read, interrupt the progress of the story with questions or other commentary that is more enlightening than entertaining, read some more, and finally quiz their students about the content of the story. The fact is that a good story or other material being read to children for their enjoyment can be destroyed by too much "teaching" in the process. There is a time for teaching listening skills and a time for letting children learn to value the phenomenon by which good ideas from an author are transmitted to themselves via print and through the ability of another person who has learned to use print for transmitting those good ideas. Teachers must be careful that students do not learn to dislike being read to because of the questions that will surely accompany the oral reading. Reading to students from kindergarten through the elementary grades and even through high school is a defensible utilization of teacher time. Justifying the time spent by asking questions is not necessary. Any questions asked or comments made should heighten interest in the material being read, not detract from its charm.

If children are to enjoy an oral reading and thereby develop positive attitudes toward reading, the material that is read must be easy to comprehend. Narrative material is usually easier to follow than is expository material. The fewer characters to keep straight, the better. Also, a fast-moving story line is easier to stay with than long, descriptive passages. In other words, if teachers want children to get caught up in their reading, stories that depend more on plot development and on character interactions are preferable to those with long, descriptive passages and are also preferable to expository material.

Reading a little each day from a whole book may not be as enjoyable for the children as reading shorter selections that can be concluded at one or several reading-listening sessions. Of course, much in this regard depends on the book, the group of students, and other factors that may enter into the picture. However, teachers should guard against reading a story that never seems to end, regardless of how interesting it was when the teacher started it. In our experience, children's interest in long books being read orally begins to wane after a week, even with students in the intermediate grades.

Most publishing companies of instructional materials for children sell audio materials for children to listen to. In addition, a number of schools we have worked in have enlisted the aid of especially good oral readers among the teaching staff and in the community to develop a collection of recordings for students to listen to. Our experience has been that people who are asked to record materials for children are enthusiastic about doing so, especially secondary school students with good oral-reading ability. However, we have found that children enjoy listening to their teacher read more than they do to recordings made by people who may be better oral readers, but who lack the personal touch the reader's presence projects. Perhaps a good procedure would be to utilize both direct teacher reading and recordings to help students from kindergarten upward develop positive attitudes toward reading.

Teaching Reading Skills

One reason for teaching children reading skills is to permit them to read with enough facility to enjoy reading and learn to value it. In other words, we teach cognitive behavior as a means to the achievement of affective behaviors. Krathwohl, *et al.,* have (1964, p. 56) issued a cautionary note in this regard:

There are some instances where the cognitive route to affective achievement has resulted in learning just the opposite of that intended. Thus the infamous example of the careful and detailed study of "good" English classics, which was intended to imbue us with a love of deathless prose, has in many instances alienated us from it instead. Emphasis on very high mastery of one domain may in some instances be gained at the expense of the other.

Teachers must be careful that they do not teach reading skills at the expense of developing positive attitudes toward reading. The key probably lies in gearing the instructional tasks to the child's present ability, not what we wish she or he could do. Children who are always struggling with their books and their skill-development exercises are almost certain to learn to dislike reading. There is a tendency for teachers to push students into more difficult materials the moment they become fluent with the materials they have been working with. Children need time to utilize their fluency and to enjoy their new skills before they start the process of building new ones. They need positive reinforcement from reading tasks they perform with ease, as well as reinforcement while struggling to attain a higher level of skill mastery. Teachers who are interested in fostering positive attitudes will let their students enjoy their "old clothes" before dressing them in new ones.

Evaluating Reading Growth

Evaluation is an important dimension of the reading curriculum. Teachers need to know the effectiveness of their teaching on their students' reading development. However, in making the necessary assessments, it is important to emphasize the positive in the student's reading ability. The teacher can learn much about a student's reading growth by eliciting responses that cannot be judged as correct or incorrect. The "What do you think about . . . ?" kind of question gives the student an opportunity to be evaluated without the intimidation of a "Circle the best answer" or a "Who did what?" solicitation. Teachers typically employ too many right-or-wrong questions for evaluative purposes. Questions that require correct responses should be balanced with open-ended questions that can serve the evaluation purpose as well.

Too many students develop negative attitudes toward reading because they are continually being measured. The anxiety and/or boredom that result from too frequent objective-type evaluations become associated with the act of reading. Students begin to perceive reading as primarily an exercise in responding correctly to questions they are asked by the teacher or that are printed in the book or on a card following every selection they read. This perception is heightened by the practice of having students correct their answers with an answer card or page that is always lurking in the wings, waiting to tell the student how good or how poor a reader she or he has been today.

Silent Reading

Hunt (1967) has presented a strong case for the value of Uninterrupted Sustained Silent Reading (USSR) in the curriculum. In practice, USSR amounts to giving students blocks of school time so that they can read long enough to become personally involved in a reading selection. We believe that this practice is beneficial for the development of positive attitudes, as well as skills. People who value reading know the drawing power a reading selection can have when one is really into the ideas or feelings coming from the lines of print. However, to "get into" a selection requires time and freedom from distractions. Unless the school provides the necessary time and freedom from distractions, many children will never experience the pleasure that comes from being absorbed in an interesting piece of writing. Their out-of-school life is simply too lacking in time or too distracting to allow for quiet time with a book. Television and other activities that are less demanding intellectually are too tempting for some children to resist.

Some schools, secondary and elementary, have adopted the policy of closing the entire school down for everything except silent reading for a specified period of time every day. During this time everyone in the school—the principal, the teachers, all students, teacher aides, and maintenance people—read self-selected material. This policy has profound implications for a technological society with as many nonintellectual distractions as ours presents. The adoption of the library concept by the public schools may be one of the few ways remaining for our society to preserve reading as a cultural characteristic for the majority of the people.

Pupil-Teacher Conferences

Most students like to have the undivided attention of their teacher from time to time. Unfortunately, the pupil-teacher ratio in most classrooms means that individual conferences are more of a luxury than they should be. However, teachers should plan individual reading conferences into the reading curriculum as often as possible. The personal exchanges that occur when a teacher and a student are talking about the feelings a child has toward a book being read can do much to heighten the student's awareness of the value of reading. It is important for a child to know that the teacher takes a personal interest in his or her attitudinal development toward reading.

Group Activities

The students in a fifth-grade class had been divided into small groups to tell one another how they liked the story they had been assigned to read and to explain, if they could, the reasons for their reaction. A boy in one group opened the discussion with the comment, spoken with emphasis, that he hated it. Another person in the group, apparently a bit less emotional asked, "You hated it?" "Well," the first boy said, "I didn't really hate it, but I thought it got boring." Personal interaction with a peer had helped to identify more clearly an attitude toward a particular selection and had probably even modified the attitude. If given opportunities to work together in reading-related activities, students often experience some positive attitudinal development. Of course, the activities must be of suitable difficulty for the students, and they must be carefully planned to coincide with the participating students' interests.

We have found that elementary school students enjoy participating in the following activities and that they learn something about the potential of reading for personal enrichment while participating in them.

Play Reading

Play reading is an activity that teachers use too infrequently for the development of both skills and attitudes. Students enjoy practicing their parts with one another and walking through their lines on a stage that can be fashioned in one corner or on one side of any classroom with movable furniture. If the activity is presented and entered into in a playful spirit, students can take several parts, girls can read boys' parts, and vice-versa, thereby making the problem of fit to numbers and gender of characters unimportant. The idea is to have fun and also give a reasonably good performance. An entire class can be divided into play-reading groups, with the objective of each group presenting readings for the other groups. If the objective of the play-reading activity is to foster positive attitudes toward reading, it is probably better not to critique the performance, certainly not according to professional standards.

Dramatizations

Many short stories or excerpts from longer narrative material, including biographies and autobiographies, are well suited for dramatic adaptations. Students enjoy writing lines of dialogue and acting out scenes from material they have read. They may want to memorize their lines, or they may enjoy engaging in purely creative dramatics, playing the roles of characters they have read about and making up the lines they speak as they move through the scenes. Social studies and other content-area textbooks are often good sources of material that can be adapted for dramatic presentation. As with play reading, the objective for having students dramatize material is for them to have fun and to give a presentation that they can take pride in. Silly, disruptive, or inconsiderate behavior that detracts from the educational value of the activity need not, and indeed should not, be tolerated.

Choral Reading

Choral reading can be fun for students of all ages. The requirements are a good poem or a piece of prose that has a message the students like and a teacher who is uninhibited enough to do some animated directing. Teachers can have part of the group read some parts, the whole group read other parts, and give some students solo parts. Tape recording the product at various stages during its development and when it is finished will help to maintain the students' interest and, hopefully, will give students a sense of pride in their accomplishment.

Debate

Students in the intermediate grades enjoy debating if the rules and procedures are not too tightly structured. Good debate topics can be found in newspapers, magazine articles, stories, and content-area textbooks. For example:

> *Resolved:* All dogs should be required to be on leashes when they are not in the house.

> *Resolved:* The state parks should be reserved for the use of state residents only.

> *Resolved:* Roberto should not have been punished because he only did what Charles told him to do.

> *Resolved:* Smoking cigarettes should be prohibited by law.

In collecting information for their debates, students become aware of the potential of reading material as a source of information. They also enjoy the competitive aspect of developing arguments and counter-arguments to use against opponents.

Focused Discussion

Assigning children to small groups for the purpose of some brain-storming or to arrive at some degree of consensus on a problem or an issue that surfaced during the reading of a particular selection is a good teaching procedure. Teachers may supply each small group with a different focus for discussion; or, each group may focus on the same problem or issue. A spokesperson for each group can be elected by the group or appointed by the teacher to report the "highlights" of the discussion. Students enjoy hearing about how other groups handled the same topic or a topic related to the one they discussed. Illustrative topics that emerge from students' reading are the following:

1. What are the social problems that can be attributed to the automobile? If Henry Ford had been able to foresee these problems, would he have invented the automobile? Should he have?

2. In our story, Karen hid so she wouldn't have to help her family get ready to move. Might you have done what Karen did? Should Karen be punished? What would you tell Karen if you were her mother or her father? What would you say to her if you were her friend and she told you about what she did? Should children Karen's age be expected to help their families? In what ways?

3. What rights, if any, does an animal have? What can be done to

protect the rights of animals? Are zoos good or bad? Should the hunting of animals purely for sport be allowed?

Conversation

Students who are in a curriculum that has reading as a daily activity will generally be eager to share their reading experiences with their teacher and their classmates. Periods of instructional conversation time can be very stimulating to the development of positive attitudes toward reading. Teachers who have succeeded in making recreational reading a regular and enjoyable part of their curricula need to do little more than say, "Who would like to tell us something about a story or article she or he has been reading?" Or, children may be assigned to small groups solely for the purpose of sharing their latest reading experiences with one another.

SUMMARY

The underlying thesis of this chapter is that the development of positive attitudes toward reading rests more heavily on quiet times with books and personal interactions than on exhortations and gimmickry. The child who does not associate with people who truly value reading is unlikely to learn to value reading, regardless of how often the teacher says that reading is wonderful. No publishing company can mass-produce machines, charts, games, pictures, buzzers, buttons, or whatever that are likely to have much potency in attitudinal development. It is easier to mass-produce materials that develop negative attitudes than it is to mass-produce materials that develop positive attitudes. Let the buyer beware!

Furthermore, attitudes are not developed in crash programs or by a kit for reluctant readers or by bulletin board displays of book jackets or the roll call of "eager readers." We agree completely with the following statement by Krathwohl, *et al.* (1964, p. 80):

Some objectives, particularly the complex ones at the top of the affective continuum, are probably obtained as the product of all or at least a major portion, of a student's year in school. Thus measures of a semester's or year's growth would reveal little change. This suggests that an evaluation plan covering at least several grades and involving the coordinated efforts of several teachers is probably a necessity. A plan involving all the grades in a system is likely to be even more effective.

(See Chapter 9 for some specific suggestions for assessing students' attitudinal development toward reading.)

Suggested Activities for the Methods Class

Activity 1

Have each member or selected members of the class tell how he would respond to a fifth-grader's question: "Why should I worry about learning how to read?" Evaluate each response in terms of how convincing it is likely to be to that fifth-grader.

Activity 2

Have each member of the class respond anonymously to the attitude inventory below. Tabulate the responses and construct a class profile. What are the implications that can be gleaned from the profile regarding the likelihood that the members of this class will project an enthusiasm for reading to their students?

Reading Attitude Inventory for Teachers and Prospective Teachers

1. As a leisure-time activity, I value reading highly.
   - _____ Strongly Agree
   - _____ Agree
   - _____ Disagree
   - _____ Strongly Disagree

2. I look forward to doing the reading that I feel is important for a teacher to do.
   - _____ Strongly Agree
   - _____ Agree
   - _____ Disagree
   - _____ Strongly Disagree

3. If someone insisted that I do only what I wanted to do for an entire day, I would spend some part of that day reading.
   - _____ Strongly Agree
   - _____ Agree
   - _____ Disagree
   - _____ Strongly Disagree

4. One reason I value teaching as a profession is that I will have an opportunity to share my love for reading with my students.
   - _____ Strongly Agree
   - _____ Agree

_____ Disagree
_____ Strongly Disagree

5. I think I will be distressed and perhaps a bit angry with my students who clearly do not enjoy reading.
   _____ Strongly Agree
   _____ Agree
   _____ Disagree
   _____ Strongly Disagree

6. People who know me well, know that I enjoy reading.
   _____ Strongly Agree
   _____ Agree
   _____ Disagree
   _____ Strongly Disagree

To construct a class profile, complete the following steps:

1. Assign each "Strongly Agree" response a score of 4; "Agree," 3; "Disagree," 2; and "Strongly Disagree," 1.
2. Have each person submit her or his score for each item.
3. Tabulate a class mean score for each item.

Activity 3

Give yourself a reading attitude score according to the following scale:

4	3	2	1
Avid reader			Reluctant reader

Explain or speculate about the reason for your score. For example, is your fondness for reading probably the result of having parents who read to you a great deal when you were a child? Or, does your reluctance to read probably stem from an unfortunate school experience?

Activity 4

The following responses were elicited from elementary school children while they were reading self-selected books silently in their school library. The question was, "Why did you choose that book?"

Study the responses. What inferences can you draw from them? What implications do they suggest for teachers and/or librarians?

I liked the cover.

It don't have too many big words.

It's about dogs, and I just got one.

We studied about it in class.

Our teacher read it and told us about it.

I just like paperbacks.

It wasn't too thick.

I want to learn about cooking.

It looked like a book for kids in my class.

It's got lots of pictures.

I seen the movie on TV.

It tells how to do tricks and stuff.

I want to be a pro.

My friend read it.

My dad and I go hunting a lot.

We had to have a book to read.

I like mysteries.

The print was big.

It was the smallest one there, and we have to give three reports.

Teaching Suggestions

Suggestion 1

Identify two students who enjoyed a particular reading selection and two who genuinely disliked it. Have them try to explain to you and to each other (and perhaps to the whole class) what they did and did not like about the selection. As a concluding activity, have the students who participated either as speakers or as listeners answer the following question: What makes a story (book, newspaper article, or whatever) "good" to a person?

Suggestion 2

Select a story likely to elicit several emotional responses from your students. Ask them to read the story, paying attention to how they are feeling as they read (e.g., sad, angry, happy, bored, excited). Have them note the different feelings they were aware of as they read and the places in the story where they became aware of those feelings. Have the students compare their notations.

Suggestion 3

Select a novel you think you would enjoy reading and that would not be inappropriate for sharing with your students. Read some of your novel every day and keep your students posted on what's happening in your book.

Suggestion 4

Ask the principal and other teachers in your building to write a short essay entitled "What I like to read best" or "Why I'm glad I Know How to Read." Give the essays to your students to read or read the essays to them and let them guess who wrote each essay. Be sure to include your own essay. Your students may enjoy writing similar essays to see if their friends can identify them from what they wrote.

Suggestion 5

Ask several articulate students to tape record their thoughts and feelings as they read a selection you have chosen for them. Choose a selection you think will stimulate them to want to respond orally. Have them read and record their thoughts and feelings spontaneously in private. Listen to their products; if they are worthwhile in terms of stimulating other students to read the selection, play the recordings for your other students as a prereading motivator.

Suggestion 6

Build a collection of tape-recorded messages from students telling a little bit about reading materials they enjoyed. Have them identify themselves, the particular selection, and where it can be obtained. Let students who don't know what to read next, listen to the recordings for ideas.

Suggestion 7

Have an open and honest discussion with your students about how they think their school could be changed so that they would have more time to read in school (e.g., provide more opportunities to visit the library, have book reports, have more silent-reading time, buy different materials, start a classroom library). Try to implement one or more of their suggestions.

Suggestion 8

Give your students ten minutes to list as many different kinds of reading activities as they can. Have them examine the following list to see how many of their listings are present.

1. Reading a math problem.
2. Reading a history book.

3. Reading the question on a teacher's test.

4. Reading the question on a standardized test.

5. Reading the constitution of a school or neighborhood club.

6. Reading the new cheers for the school team.

7. Reading the words for the school song.

8. Reading the rules for using the tennis courts or the swimming pool.

9. Reading the pamphlets in the school counselor's office.

10. Reading the newspaper.

11. Reading a part in the school play.

12. Reading training rules for athletes.

13. Reading about the contributions of black scientists, athletes, or soldiers.

14. Reading a menu in a restaurant.

15. Reading the directions for assembling or operating a Christmas present.

16. Reading the TV guide.

17. Reading the note left by a friend or family member.

18. Reading advertisements that come in the mail.

19. Reading a recipe.

20. Reading signs for drivers and pedestrians.

21. Reading the questions on the driver's test.

22. Reading the owner's manual for a new car.

23. Reading a map.

24. Reading the instructions for the automatic washer and dryer.

25. Reading a catalogue.

26. Reading the phone book to find a number.

27. Reading hunting or fishing regulations.

28. Reading instructions left by an employer.

29. Reading the labels in supermarkets.

30. Reading directions for taking medicine.

31. Reading magazines in the dentist's or doctor's office.

32. Reading crossword puzzles.

33. Reading programs at plays, concerts, and sports events.

34. Reading billboards.

35. Reading greeting cards.

REFERENCES

Hunt, Lyman C. "The Effect of Self-Selection, Interest and Motivation Upon Independent, Instructional and Frustrational Levels," *The Reading Teacher* **24,** 2 (November 1970): 146–151, 158.

Krathwohl, David B., *et al. Taxonomy of Educational Objectives, Handbook II: Affective Domain.* Pp. 80, 81. Copyright © 1965 by the David McKay Co. Inc.

Stoops, John. "Reading and the Crisis of Values," in *What Is Reading Doing to the Child?* ed. Nancy Larrick and John Stoops, Danville, Ill.: The Interstate Printers and Publishers, 1967, pp. 31–43.

You can upgrade your students' reading comprehension in any classroom where reading is required. You can do this as you go about the everyday activities of the course—as you make the assignment, as you help students master a textbook chapter, as you formulate questions on their reading selections.

ELLEN LAMAR THOMAS
and H. ALAN ROBINSON

11 Teaching Children How to Read Content-Area Materials

A major objective of the elementary school curriculum is the transmission of our culture to each new generation. The efforts of each generation to record and store its accomplishments is testimony to the importance we place on the continuous flow of ideas and information among members of the same generation and between the older and the younger members of our society. One of the major vehicles used by our schools to transmit what we believe or know from one generation to another is printed material. Printed material has become a primary resource for helping teachers pass the funds of knowledge collected and organized in the various content areas on to their students.

The purpose of this chapter is to help teachers to help their students make effective use of textbooks and other printed materials in the content areas, that is, to read them with good comprehension and retention. We believe that the skills learned with materials designed to teach children how to read do not necessarily transfer to materials that children read to learn about their culture. Therefore, the teacher who uses printed material to teach specific content must also be concerned about teaching those children how to read that material. Teachers cannot assume that children who perform well with developmental reading materials and who score high on reading-achievement tests do not need help with the assigned materials in science, social studies, math, and other content areas. Certainly, students must not be forever dependent on their teachers for getting information from print. However, through grade 12 is not forever, and we think that we could build a case for professors helping college students read their textbooks with greater understanding, more appreciation, and better retention.

There are two dimensions to materials used to transmit information: the content itself and the language with which that content is expressed. Either or both of these dimensions can cause problems in comprehension and retention. Therefore, teachers need to prepare students for both the ideational and the linguistic aspects of the material they ask them to read.

A person who reads never stops learning how to read. Every reading experience is different in terms of both the reader's purpose for reading and the content and style of each selection that is read. Even a second reading of the same selection is different from the first reading, because it is probably being read for a different purpose, and certainly it is being read with a different set of background experiences. Therefore, since a reader brings something different to every reading experience and takes something different away from it, every reading experience is unique in more than one sense. A reader who is attentive to the author's craft, as well as to the content of the message, will enlarge his or her vocabulary and will learn how to interpret various types of sentences and larger organizational units (i.e., paragraphs, chapters, units, etc.).

Reading maturity might be defined as a level of achievement at which the reader's reading style is adjusted to satisfy the purpose for reading a selection and to respond to the uniqueness of the content of the selection as it has been expressed by its author. In other words, the mature reader: (1) is flexible in how he or she attacks and responds to different reading selections; (2) knows what to look for; and (3) attends to the vocabulary, sentence structure, and larger organizational patterns the writer has employed. The mature reader learns to think along with all kinds of writers, responding skillfully to the variety of linguistic and organizational devices they use to express themselves.

At this point, we would like to reiterate the difference between teaching reading in the content areas and in information-getting groups (described in Chapter 3). Information-getting groups are a distinct part of the reading curriculum and function within the time alloted for reading instruction. Furthermore, the material the students read is determined by the students' personal interests. By contrast, the material students read as part of a content area is generally prescribed by the objectives of that content-area curriculum. There is no reason why students could not read in groups and make group presentations in the content areas, but the materials they use are carefully written or selected to facilitate the learning of specified content in some kind of logical sequence. For example, a social studies curriculum may be planned so that students study the American Revolution in grade 4, and other topics are sequenced to precede or follow the American Revolution in a logical order. Different curricula might place the American Revolution topic in a different grade. But it would be a rare social studies curriculum that did not include the topic and did not place it in some logical sequence. Therefore, teachers must be prepared to use certain materials to attain certain educational objectives as children proceed through the various content-area curricula.

GENERAL GUIDELINES

Later in this chapter, we will discuss some specific teaching strategies conceived to help students have productive reading experiences with content-area materials. For now, however, we would like to recommend the following general guidelines for elementary teachers in incorporating the teaching of reading into their content-area teaching.

1. *Know which curriculum objectives can be attained best from reading.*

Some knowledge can be learned better by listening, viewing, or manipulating objects than by reading. On the other hand, the rereading, reflections, and other behaviors that reading permits may be very important to a thorough understanding of a concept, memorizing a series of events, learning technical vocabulary, etc. Reading is only one way of learning content-area material. Textbooks and other reading materials should be used selectively and for helping students learn those things that can be learned most efficiently by reading.

2. *Keep reading assignments short.*

Most content-area materials, especially textbooks, are loaded with information and specialized vocabulary. Reading with good comprehension generally requires heavy concentration, pausing to reflect, to produce a mental image, or to put ideas into one's own personal language. Reading content-area materials is vastly different from reading the narrative, poetry, and light expository selections that are preponderant in developmental reading materials. One or two pages of content-area material can often require many minutes of fatiguing thinking.

A major teaching fault is assignment overload of difficult reading material. When too many pages are assigned, students become fatigued and receive little information for their efforts; or, they read too rapidly to comprehend the content and to retain it long enough to do something with it. In time, students develop the habit of reading content-area assignments superficially or not at all. Teachers often assume that students have read the material carefully but have not understood it well enough to discuss it. The fact is that they never read it, at least not carefully enough to master the information presented.

3. *Resist the temptation to "tell" students what they were assigned to read.*

Too often, "discussing" a reading assignment amounts to the teacher's telling the students what they were supposed to learn from their reading. Students soon learn that reading an assignment is not necessary, because their teacher will tell them the "important stuff" anyway. If the teacher plans to give students the information orally, there is really no need to ask the students to read it. A discussion should be just that, not a lecture containing the same information. One sure way to discourage careful reading of assignments in the content areas is to tell students that they won't be held accountable for anything on the test unless it has been "discussed" in class. Students should always be held accountable for learning something from their reading assignments.

4. *Always preview reading assignments carefully before they are made, to discover concepts, vocabulary, sentences, or paragraphs that are likely to cause comprehension problems. Then prepare students for them.*

Smith and Barrett (1974, p. 114) draw the following analogy:

No coach would ever send his team on to the field of play without carefully scouting the opposing players and instructing his team in how best to encounter them. When the players meet, they know their opponents' plays, their own game plan, and the special obstacles to victory presented by each team they play. Unfortunately, too many content area teachers instruct their students after they have been beaten by a selection they were never prepared to encounter. The post-reading activities should be enriching experiences that motivate students to read further in a subject—not replays of a defeat. Unfortunately, too many students lose too many games with content area materials, and they quit trying to win.*

Teachers have a responsibility to preview reading assignments carefully and to give their students the preparation they need to read them with relative ease, confidence, and good comprehension. Students' comprehension is often improved if several guidelines are followed before assigning the reading material:

a) Explaining the overall purpose of the selection, e.g., "The author wants to acquaint readers with the major causes of the American Civil War," or "The author explains the steps to be followed in finding the circumference of a circle."

b) Talking about important concepts that are presented, e.g., "Major historical events can often be traced to specific caused factors—when something happens it is often possible to discover why it happened."

c) Defining vocabulary or phrases likely to be unfamiliar to the students, e.g., osmosis, constituency, sets, metaphor, boondoggle, tempest in a teapot.

d) Citing one or two facts or ideas to look for while the students are reading, e.g., "Pay special attention to the number of men on

---

* Richard J. Smith and Thomas C. Barrett. *Teaching Reading in the Middle Grades*, Reading, Mass.: Addison-Wesley, 1974, p. 114. Reprinted by permission.

each side who were killed at the Battle of Gettysburg," or "Notice how every substance that is combined in a solution must be carefully weighed."

5. *Have materials at various levels of difficulty to use in place of, or in addition to, the textbook.*

The range in reading ability within any group of students increases as the students progress through the grades. Some students are simply unable to read the textbooks that are written for able readers at a particular grade level. Other students are capable of handling material that is more sophisticated than that presented in their textbooks. One approach to the one-textbook-for-a-range-of-reading-abilities problem is to have materials available at various difficulty levels. If teachers organize their courses into units of study, students can be assigned to differing materials relevant to the same topic or unit of study (e.g., the American Civil War, Colonial literature, systems of the body). A teacher using the unit approach might give the entire class some prereading information, perhaps assign the entire class to read a selected passage or selected passages from the textbook, assign other materials to students on the basis of their reading abilities, and ultimately bring the entire class together to share and discuss what they have learned from their reading.

Materials at various difficulty levels that pertain to the different units that are studied can be collected from magazines, newspapers, kits, books designed primarily to teach reading skills, as well as from pamphlets and other sources. Teachers are sometimes concerned when they discover that they are using some of the same material for their content-area teaching that they use for information-getting groups. However, we think that the utilization of the same materials in more than one setting or for different purposes is one sign of a good curriculum; students who do so are manifesting the same behavior that accomplished students use when they consult a source for several purposes and indicate an awareness of the overlapping nature of the various curriculum areas.

TEACHING STRATEGIES

The remainder of this chapter is devoted to specific teaching strategies. We will point out some ideational, organizational, and linguistic aspects of material that we think often cause problems for students.

Then, we will suggest some instructional practices for helping students deal with these aspects so as to improve their comprehension and retention.

Strategy 1

> *Teach students to survey a reading assignment before they read it carefully.*

Reading a content-area assignment without a prereading survey is similar to traveling in unfamiliar territory without a road map. Students should be taught to survey a selection in order to get a general idea of the nature of the content and how it is organized before they embark on a careful reading for details, central thoughts, implications, and other information that can be obtained only by slow, careful reading. Of course, reading selections vary, but for most assignments, reading the first one or two paragraphs and the final, or summary, paragraph slowly and then skimming very rapidly over the material in between will provide a good survey.

Strategy 2

> *Teach students that careful attention to the titles of chapters or subheadings within chapters will help them know what to expect from their reading.*

Students frequently plunge right into a reading assignment and proceed through it without paying any attention to the titles the author has supplied to give them the proper mind set and to direct their reading. Note how careful attention to the following chapter title and the subheadings within the chapter could help students give direction to their reading and organize their thinking about the material in the chapter.

Chapter title:	The United States Immediately After the War
Subhead 1:	A Tired People
Subhead 2:	Industry at Full Production
Subhead 3:	New Political Problems
Subhead 4:	Wartime Inventions and Discoveries
Subhead 5:	A National Urge to Grow and Prosper
Subhead 6:	Summary

Before students began reading this chapter, their attention should be called to the general topic of the chapter and the focus of the divisions within it. Students might be asked the following questions.

1. What do you think the chapter that follows this one might be titled?
2. Look at all of the subheads. Can you suggest any piece of information you think might be included in any one of them?
3. Read the summary right now. Then write down which of the subsections you think will be most interesting to you. When you finish reading the chapter, see if you were right.

Other questions might be asked; or, the teacher might point out the title and subheads in a very straightforward way. The idea is to make students aware of the nature of the content they are to learn and the organizational framework in which it is presented before they begin reading it.

Strategy 3

Discuss with students the precise meaning of key words, key phrases, and figurative language with which they may be unfamiliar.

Authors of textbooks and teachers sometimes forget that elementary school students aren't familiar with terminology that educated adults in our society interpret easily. The following words, phrases, and figures of speech are illustrative of those that are found in textbooks and that are critical to a correct interpretation of an important piece of information.

priority	agent	indicator
organism	castastrophe	set
calculate	systematic	log
rally	heavy heart	appropriated
red herring	pound of flesh	regiment
evolution	infection	pelt
revolution	strange bedfellows	climax
prime	other side of the coin	blacksmith
compound	ratio	vessels
right wing	died in committee	

Some textbooks make obvious attempts to define key words or phrases in context; others define such terminology in a footnote or in parentheses following the term. However, for some texts, teachers must do the defining, and in most texts, teachers must define some of the terms. The point is that nobody knows better than their teachers what terminology students are likely to have trouble with.

Discussing the precise meaning of the terms used in the reading material before having the students read it can prevent many misinterpretations and unproductive reading experiences. We recommend that the terms always be taught to students in sentence contexts. Probably the best approach is to pull the entire sentence in which the term is embedded, out of the context and deal with it that way.

Strategy 4

Teach students to use context clues.

Teaching students to use context clues helps wean them from the kind of teacher assistance described in strategy 3. Most content-area materials are loaded with technical or specialized vocabulary. Many authors and textbook editors are aware of this and embed such terminology in a context that gives clues to the precise meaning they want their readers to get. Teachers should identify opportunities to alert students to the fact that certain terms, which the teacher should specify, can be defined by looking at the words around or near them. This is probably done best by the teacher's having students make a little mark above words that can be defined by using context clues; this mark will remind them to use the clues when they get to those words.

In Chapter 7 our discussion of context clues included the identification and illustration of at least ten different types of context clues, and some of you may want to refer to the subsection entitled "Contextual Analysis." Instead of repeating here all of what we said in that subsection, we will instead present the following illustrations of some of the context clues frequently used by authors of content-area textbooks to help their readers unlock the meaning of unfamiliar terminology. However, context clues are useless unless teachers teach students how to use them and frequently remind them to use what they have learned.

> They bent the *sapling,* a young tree with a lot of spring, to the ground. Then they tied the bait to the topmost branch. The good smell of the fresh meat always *enticed* the hungry animal out of his *lair.*

> The club, which was called a *pestle,* was used to pound the corn into *grist.*

> *Probability,* that is, the chance that something will happen after a certain number of trials . . .

> The pilgrims were not all good sailors. And many of their *shallops,* little sailboats they had brought with them, *foundered* in the high waves and gusty winds.

Forces under the surface of the earth sometime break the rock that forms the earth's crust. The break in the rock is called a *fault.*

An *organism* is made up of *organs* that do special jobs. The human body is an organism and the eye is an organ.

For two weeks Peter had worried and thought about the worst possible results of his telephone call. His *despondent* mood would not allow him to see the one *ray of hope* that might save him.

Gunpowder is also used in the production of *pyrotechnics* for Fourth of July celebrations.

Pachyderms were used to make clearings in the jungle. They pushed over trees with their huge heads and carried them away in their trunks. When one *trumpeted* to express anger or fear, the others in the group joined in. The sound carried through the jungle for miles, sending the smaller animals scurrying into their hiding places.

Molecules are the tiniest pieces into which matter can be broken. They cannot be seen by the human eye without the aid of a *microscope.*

Obviously, context clues cease to be effective if the passage being read contains too many unfamiliar words. However, if the content-area material being read is at a reasonable level of difficulty, using context clues is usually more helpful than phonics analysis is, since many of the words students do not recognize in such materials are irregularly spelled or are not in the students' hearing vocabulary, thereby rendering phonics analysis useless for gaining an accurate definition of the word.

Strategy 5

Teach students to use format aids.

Most content-area textbooks contain format aids to call students' attention to important information or to help them organize their reading. Footnotes, tables, illustrations, bold-face print, underlining, marginal explanations, summary statements, charts, graphs, colored print, glossaries, prefatory statements for chapters and subsections, and other aids are built into textbooks to help students read efficiently and with good comprehension. Often, however, students ignore these aids or use them ineffectively. Teachers should call students' attention to any format aids in each reading assignment they make. It is usually not sufficient to give a lecture on "How to Use This Book" at the beginning of the school year and expect that to suffice. Students need to be instructed and reminded about format clues each time an assignment is made. For example, the teacher might say, "Be sure to study the illustration on page 62, and be sure to read what's printed under it. The footnote on page 63 is important because it refers back to information we studied in Chapter 1. Three words on page 63 are defined in the glossary. Put a little mark above each of them now to remind yourself to look them up when you get to them. The steps in the process being described on page 64 are printed in heavy type. Copy these four steps into your notebooks to help you remember them."

Strategy 6

Teach students to pause periodically in their reading to collect and organize their thoughts.

Too many students take a deep breath, begin reading with the first word of an assignment, and don't stop for another breath until they have read the last word. Consequently, little of the information becomes part of the intellectual framework of the student's mind. To process the many concepts and pieces of information contained on the pages of content-area materials, students must pause occasionally to reflect on the new ideas they are receiving and to fit them into their storehouse of knowledge. Until a reader rethinks the ideas of an author and puts them into his or her own personal language, they are not "owned." This is especially true when the ideas are new or complicated.

A good teaching procedure is to look through the material for logical places for students to pause and reflect. After identifying these places, it is a simple matter to have students place little marks at those places to remind them to pause, think back over what they have read, and make some predictions about what the author will say next. Very often, these "thinking spots" or "pit stops" occur just before a new subsection or just after a summary sentence or paragraph (e.g., "Those were the major reasons for the westward movement" or "The balance of nature is delicate indeed").

Strategy 7

Help students develop the habit of thinking ahead while reading.

As part of Strategy 6, we recommended that after they have thought back over what they have already read, students be taught to make some predictions about what the author will say next. Teaching children to anticipate an author's message is so important to successful content-area reading that we have included it in this chapter as a separate strategy.

In an informal, unpublished study, one of us over a period of years interrupted good and poor readers in his classes and asked them, "What do you think is going to happen next in what you are reading?" Students who were known to be poor in their ability to discuss orally or write about content-area reading assignments were seldom, if ever, giving any thought to what might be coming next in the story, description, exposition, or whatever they were reading. On the other hand, good readers would remark that they thought a particular character was going to get in trouble or that a body system (e.g., circulatory) other than the one they were reading about was going to be described next. In effect, the good readers were preparing their minds for the information they were going to receive next. They were thinking along with, and had "psyched out," the author. The poor readers were being bombarded by ideas they had not prepared themselves for mentally.

Teachers might help students acquire the habit of thinking ahead by having them predict, on the basis of studying a title or after reading one or two paragraphs, what they think the author will probably discuss next, what the author's main point or point of view will be, or what they would logically expect some causes of war to be. For example, given the sentence "War clouds were gathering," the teacher might ask students the following questions:

1. Which of the war clouds will probably be most difficult for the government to blow away?

2. What might the United Nations do to relieve some of the pressure between the two nations?

3. We know that we will read that a small-scale war did occur. How long would you expect it to last? Will other countries get involved? Will air power be used? What measures will be necessary to end the war?

After students have made some predictions and discussed what they think they will read in the next several pages of their assignment, they should be told to read on to discover how insightful they were. Their comprehension will be improved, because they are reading for a purpose and with some personal involvement. If teachers get students engaged in thinking ahead as a regular part of their content-area repertoire of teaching activities, students will develop the habit of anticipating the author's message and will thereby improve their comprehension.

Strategy 8

Teach students how to interpret words that show key relationships between or among ideas.

Content-area materials contain many words that act as signals about the kinds of relationships the reader should form between or among ideas. For example, note the relationships that are signaled by the italicized words in the following sentences:

1. *Although* the metal looks hard, it is in fact very soft. (The reader is signaled to hold an idea tentatively.)
2. They looked forward to a different life, *but* they did not realize the hardships the climate would bring them. (The reader is signaled to change an idea he or she has been forming.)
3. The dogs swim like spaniels; *however,* they will not retrieve birds from the water. (The reader is signaled to negate or change an idea he or she has been forming.)
4. *Somehow,* they survived the first winter. (The reader is signaled to marvel at the accomplishment.)
5. Both substances are necessary. *Therefore,* they must both be present to precipitate the chemical reaction. (The reader is signaled to see the latter statement as essentially a repetition or clarification of the former.)
6. The later settlers disregarded the warnings of those who had gone before them. *Consequently,* they also lost their livestock to the marauding wolves. (The reader is signaled to see a cause-effect relationship.)
7. *Because* percentile ranks are derived scores, they cannot be averaged. (The reader is signaled to see a cause-effect relationship.)

Teachers need not, and indeed should not, call students' attention to every word that signals an important relationship between ideas. However, periodically asking students to explain how one of these words relates to the ideas presented or to simply point out to them the function of one of these words helps them to be alert to function words as important signals in their own thinking.

Strategy 9

Teach students to vocalize sentences that, at first reading, don't communicate.

When authors write, they are aware of the "melody" of each sentence they write. In their minds they "hear" the words they are putting down, as if they were speaking them. To decode those sentences, readers must "tune in" to the "melodies" that are not represented visually, but are in the lines of print nonetheless. In relatively uncomplicated discourse, especially narrative writing, the melodies of the language are easily shared by the reader and the writer. However, in expository writing that may introduce new concepts to the reader, the melodies that carry much of the meaning of a particular sentence may not be immediately apparent. We have all had the experience of reading a sentence and responding with, "Huh?" A second reading, with more subvocalization or even a clearly audible reading, rewards us with the meaning that escaped us the first time. It is not possible to illustrate with a sentence the experience we are describing here, because the experience is a highly individual one which may or may not occur for a given reader with any given sentence. Instead, we must trust that you have had the experience we are describing (probably while reading something from a science or math text) and are cognizant of the "ah, ha!" response that occurs when a more vocalized reading produces the sense of the sentence.

Teachers should explain to students that the vocalization they should suppress when reading materials that are easy to understand should not be suppressed when they require more intonation cues in order to comprehend the sense of a sentence. Students should be told that sometimes reading a sentence aloud to oneself results in a better understanding of the sentence. If students must resort to an oral reading of more than a few sentences in an assignment, the material is obviously too difficult for them, and less difficult material should be assigned. If less difficult material is unavailable, students should be given the information they need orally.

Strategy 10

Teach students to read content-area materials slowly.

The essence of this strategy is contained, in some respect, in all of the other strategies. We have also made it a separate strategy, however, because reading content-area materials slowly is so important for good comprehension and because some students hurry through their reading assignments, thereby learning and retaining very little.

Most students need to be reminded each time an assignment is made that they should allow enough time for a slow, careful reading unless the assignment is an unusually easy one or the purpose is merely to gain an overview or general impression. Of course, it follows that content-area reading assignments should be kept short. Our personal feeling is that students should be given frequent, short, written quizzes on their reading assignments; this will persuade them to develop the habit of reading difficult material slowly and carefully. Teachers must hold students accountable for good comprehension and retention if they expect them to read for those two outcomes.

A FINAL WORD

Teaching reading in the content areas is, in our experience, highly neglected by both elementary and secondary teachers. Teachers at all academic levels are all too likely to make reading assignments without teaching students how to read them. In fact, we think that too many teachers assign material to be read that the teachers themselves have not read carefully. We think that this practice is indefensible. Students have a right to be properly prepared for a reading assignment in the content areas.

We have made a number of specific suggestions for helping students comprehend and retain the information in content-area materials. Certainly, not all of our suggestions should be applied with every assignment that is made; teachers must use their own good judgment. Some of our suggestions are more appropriate for some assignments than for others. Too much instruction in "how" to read an assignment can detract from students' motivation to read it, as well as from their comprehension. However, we think that if teachers were to practice our suggestions regularly and with discretion, students would leave the elementary school with a much better ability to get information from content-area materials than they presently do.

Suggested Activities for the Methods Class

Activity 1

Select the chapter in this book that was the most boring or the most difficult for you to read. Tell how you would introduce that chapter to the next class that reads it, to make it more interesting and more comprehensible.

Activity 2

Have each member of the class obtain an elementary school content-area textbook or a selection that might be used as an elementary school content-area assignment. Each selection should be prepared for presentation to the group of elementary students to whom it might be assigned.

Divide the methods class into groups of four or five for the purpose of sharing what each person has done with the selection he or she chose to help elementary school students read the selection with maximum comprehension.

Activity 3

Have volunteers recall the content-area reading assignments they had the most difficulty with in high school. Have each volunteer tell what the teacher or teachers might have done to make the assignments more productive. Have the volunteers also tell what effect those reading assignments had on their attitudes toward that subject.

Activity 4

Support or refute the following statement:

Students who are spoon-fed every reading assignment will never learn how to read for themselves. Reading should be taught well in the reading class and have it over with.

Teaching Suggestions

Suggestion 1

Randomly assign a class of students to two different treatment groups. Give each group the same reading assignment from a content-area textbook. Tell group 1 only that they should read the assignment carefully because they will be given a comprehension test afterward. Tell group 2 that they will be given a comprehension test, but also prepare them for their reading according to the suggestions in this chapter. Find the mean and the median scores on the comprehension test for both groups. Ask the following as the last two questions on your comprehension test, and analyze the answers to them separately from the rest of the answers on the test.

1. How interesting was this reading assignment?
   Very interesting   Interesting   Boring   Very boring
2. How easy was this assignment to read?
   Very easy   Easy   Hard   Very hard

Suggestion 2

Identify a student whom you consider to be an "average" reader. Choose a selection of about 200 words that might be given as a content-area reading assignment. Ask the student to read the selection orally while you note the number and kinds of errors made. Analyze the errors and decide what kind of prereading preparation might have prevented them.

Suggestion 3

Identify a student whom you consider to be an "average" reader. Ask this student to silently read a selection from a content-area textbook and to give a signal every time he or she is aware of having trouble understanding a word or the information being presented. Don't give the student any help, but record the number of times he or she signals in a ten-minute period. Count the number of words the student read in ten minutes, and divide by ten to get a words-per-minute figure. Then ask the student five comprehension questions. What implications can you draw from your findings?

REFERENCES

Smith, Richard J., and Thomas C. Barrett. *Teaching Reading in the Middle Grades,* Reading, Mass.: Addison-Wesley, 1974.

Thomas, Ellen Lamar, and H. Alan Robinson. *Improving Reading in Every Class,* Boston: Allyn and Bacon, 1972, p. 45.

Since it is true that learning to read a foreign language is a more difficult task than learning to read a native language, it must follow that it is harder for a child to learn to read a dialect which is not his own than to learn to read his own dialect.

KENNETH S. GOODMAN

12 Meeting the Needs of the Linguistically Diverse

There have probably always been advocates of a universal language, a language spoken and understood by all the peoples of the earth. One of the most recent attempts to create a world language was that of Zamenhof, who in the late 1800s devised Esperanto. This artificial language, based on common features of the major European languages, attempts to utilize self-evident grammatical forms (for example, all adjectives end in *a*; all nouns, in *o*). Though thousands of works, including the Bible, are now available in Esperanto, the language has not gained significant acceptance.

Language is certainly one of our most important tools and forms the basis for almost all human relationships. In essence, all language is artificial—babies are not born with the ability to talk. All languages consist of sounds, meaning-bearing units, and grammatical arrangements. The sounds, words, and sentences used to convey a meaning differ greatly from language to language. There is no inherent reason why *chair* should signify "chair" or why *boat* is not *glove*. The sounds, words, and grammatical structures of a language do the jobs that people have, over time, decided they should do.

Nearly 2800 languages are spoken, but a much smaller number have written forms. Certainly, if the users of the nearly three thousand languages could communicate in one language, world understanding would be greater, and the task of developing worldwide literacy would be overwhelmingly simplified. The goal of a common, universal language is, however, precluded by the realities of national traditions, history, cultures, politics, economics, and pride.

Attempts have been made to develop acceptance of multinational regional languages, e.g., Swahili in Kenya, Uganda, and Tanzania, and nearly all countries have adopted an "official" national language. In a number of countries, e.g., England and France, the national language is the native tongue of the majority of the people. In other nations the official language is the native language of practically no one. In Nigeria, for example, more than 200 languages and dialects are spoken, but English is the official language of the country.

Most inhabitants of North America speak English as their native language, regardless of the ethnic origin of their ancestors. But for many North Americans, English is not their native language; for some, it is Spanish, and for others it is Navajo or Menominee or Chinese or French, etc. Yet the key to successful achievement in most American schools is the ability to read English fluently. One of the major responsibilities of elementary teachers is to teach children to read, a task difficult enough when the child's native language *is the same* as the language of instruction and instructional materials, but a task infinitely more difficult when the child's native language is not.

DIALECTS AND LANGUAGES

If all speakers of any of the 2800 languages of the world used the same dialect of the language, teaching children to read the language would probably be less difficult than it is. However, any language used by a large number of people and spoken over a variety of geographical areas exhibits many differences in dialect. A dialect is a form or variety of a spoken language peculiar to a group, community, or region. The basic difference between a *dialect* and a *language* is that the dialects that comprise a given language are to some degree mutually intelligible; languages, on the other hand, are to a large degree mutually unintelligible. The closer a language is to one's own, the more likely one will be to infer fragments of meaning; the closer a dialect is to one's own, the more likely one will be to comprehend. Americans from Boston and Biloxi, for example, can communicate with Britons from Birmingham and with Scots from the Highlands, but with much less efficiency than natives of each of these places can confer with one another.

Every language changes over time and with place, e.g., the "English" of Chaucer, Shakespeare, Twain, and Updike are different. Similarly, just as languages change, so too do the dialects of a language. Dialects differ and change on the basis of geographic distribution and the speakers' ethnic origin, socioeconomic status, age, and occupation. The challenge confronting the teacher of reading is to note the points of linguistic differences between the dialect of the child and that of instruction and to modify the instructional program to accommodate these differences.

In this chapter we will examine ways in which dialects differ and will evaluate some strategies of reading instruction for use with dialectically diverse children. Although the chapter will be addressed mainly to differences in dialect, much of the discussion pertains to language diversity as well. Learning a second dialect differs from learning a second language more in degree than in kind.

Dialect Differences

Dialects differ from one another phonologically (sounds), morphologically (words and affixes), and syntactically (sentences). Phonological differences constitute the different pronunciations speakers use. For example, in some dialects *Don* and *dawn* are pronounced the same, as are *cot* and *caught*. The *o* in *fog* and *log* sounds the same as in *hot* and *lot*. In other dialects *Don, cot, hot,* and *lot* sound alike, but differ in sound from *dawn, caught, fog,* and *log*. In another dialect *tin* and *ten* and *pin* and *pen* have the same vowel pronunciation. In some North American regions no *r* is said in such words as *car, part, heart,* and *butter*; the pronunciations of *a* in *bath, laugh, half, aunt,* and *glass* distinguishes other dialects.

Often, vocabulary is peculiar to regional or social dialects, as can be seen in the following:

Midwest	*Southeast*	*U.S.A.*	*England*
skunk	polecat	trunk	boot
bag	sack	elevator	lift
pit	stone	hood	bonnet
faucet	spigot	line	queue
bubbler	drinking fountain	napkin	serviette

Similarly, the syntactic structures used to convey the same or similar meanings may vary.

Standard dialect	*Nonstandard dialect*
She is happy.	She happy.
How did he fix that?	How he fix that?
Mr. Jones is reading.	Mr. Jones he reading.

No dialect can be considered any better or worse than any other; no dialect is superior or inferior to another. The regional (geographic) varieties of a language are typically viewed as being equal, but unfortunately the social (economic or ethnic) varieties typically are not. Sociolinguists speak of "standard English" and "nonstandard English" as a way of categorizing nonregional dialect differences. Unfortunately, ill-informed (though well-intentioned) teachers and lay people often view nonstandard English as sloppy, incorrect, uneducated, or inferior. Nonstandard dialect is often viewed as poor English that needs to be corrected rather than as a different dialect that needs to be understood if adequate reading instruction is to be provided.

Some teachers may wish to teach their pupils the pronunciation of standard dialect. But to do so is an entirely different task from teaching reading, and if the two are intermixed, considerable confusion for the child can result. Consider the child who is "corrected" for dropping the *l* in the oral reading of *help* (hep), but is later corrected *for* pronouncing the *k* in *knee*. The teacher needs to know the phonological differences (the interference points) of the dialect-speaking pupil so that "different" pronunciations can be accepted.

Children who speak a nonstandard dialect or for whom English is not the native language, present a major instructional concern for teachers of reading. These children may come from one of a number of backgrounds, e.g., Native American, inner city and southern black, rural poor, first-generation American, Spanish-speaking Chicano, Cuban, or Puerto Rican, or large-city Asian or other ethnic groups. Of these groups, perhaps the greatest amount of linguistic research has been done with speakers of black dialects and with Spanish-speaking Americans. In the two lists presented below, the first shows some of the main interference points between standard English and the nonstandard dialect of some black speakers, and the second shows the contrasts between standard dialect and the dialect of some Spanish speakers. The lists are not intended to be complete, only representative. Three types of dialect interference to note in both lists are as follows.

1. *Production of words.* By alternating or omitting sounds (phonemes) new or different words are formed which have entirely different meanings. For example, when the final consonant is dropped (*tool–too, log–law, road–row*), a new word is formed. When some phonemes are substituted for others (/I/ for /ɛ/, /e/ for /i/), new words are also formed: *pin* for *pen* and *pail* for *peel*.

2. *Verb Changes.* Some sound variations change verb tense or agreement and, thus, sentence meaning. For example:

Standard pronunciation	Nonstandard pronunciation	Word change		Grammatical change
/ft/	/f/	*laughed*	*laugh*	tense
/md/	/m/	*aimed*	*aim*	tense
/l/	/#/	*you'll*	*you*	tense
/ts/	/t/	*hits*	*hit*	agreement

3. *Grammatical variations.* An example is the use of subject expression and linking verbs:

Bill and Mike are out playing.   Bill and Mike they out playing.

List 1. Standard English/Nonstandard English Contrasts

Phonological differences causing word changes

Standard English form	Nonstandard form	Word	Child may say
/θr/	/tr/	thread	tread
/θ/	/f/	lath	laugh
/nt/	/n/	meant	men
/oy/	/a/	toil	tall
/ai/	/ah/	find	fond
/l/	/#/	help	hep
/r/	/#/	guard	God
/t/	/#/	suit	Sue
/skt/	/kst/	asked	axed

Phonological differences causing grammatical changes

Standard English form	Nonstandard form	Word	Child may say	Grammatical change
/md/	/m/	timed	time	tense
/nd/	/n/	fined	fine	tense
/st/	/s/	passed	pass	tense
/zd/	/z/	grazed	graze	tense
/l/	/#/	she'll	she	tense
/dz/	/d/	beds	bed	agreement
/lz/	/l/	goals	goal	agreement
/ks/	/k/	kicks	kick	agreement
/nz/	/n/	runs	run	agreement

Grammatical variations*

Variable	Standard English	Negro nonstandard
Linking verb	He is going.	He __ goin'
Possessive marker	John's cousin.	John __ cousin.
Plural marker	I have five cents.	I got five cent__.
Subject expression	John __ lives in New York.	John he live in New York.
Verb form	I drank the milk.	I drunk the milk.
Past marker	Yesterday he walked home.	Yesterday he walk __ home.

* Joan C. Baratz. "Teaching Reading in a Negro School," in *Teaching Black Children to Read*, ed. Joan C. Baratz and Roger W. Shuy, Washington, D.C.: The Center for Applied Linguistics, 1969, pp. 99–100. Reprinted by permission.

Variable	Standard English	Negro nonstandard
Verb agreement	He runs home.	He run _ home.
	She has a bicycle.	She have a bicycle.
Future form	I will go home.	I'ma go home.
"If" construction	I asked if he did it.	I aks did he do it.
Negation	I don't have any.	I don't got none.
	He didn't go.	He ain't go.
Indefinite article	I want an apple.	I want a apple.
Pronoun form	We have to do it.	Us got to do it.
	His book.	He book.
Preposition	He is over at his friend's house.	He over to his friend house.
	He teaches at Francis Pool.	He teach _ Francis Pool.
Be	Statement: He is here all the time.	Statement: He be here.
Do	Contradiction: No he isn't.	Contradiction: No he don't.

List 2. English-Spanish Contrasts
Phonological differences*

English form	Spanish equivalent	Word	Child may say
/i/	/iy/	bit	beet
/æ/	/e/ or /a/	bat	bet
/ə/	/e/ or /a/	but	bet
/ey/	/e/	late	let
/u/	/uw/	full	fool
/b/	/p/	bar	par
/b/	/v/	babies	bavies
/s/	/č/	shoe	chew
/g/	/k/	goat	coat
/ǰ/	/č/	jump	chump
/m/ (final)	/n/	comb	cone
/θ/ (voiceless)	/s, t, or f/	thank	sank
/ð/ (voiced)	/d/	this	dis
/w/	/gw/	way	guay
/z/	/s/	zoo	sue
/ž/	/č/	measure	meachure

* Bonnie S. Schulwitz. "Language and Reading: Problems of the Bilingual Child," paper presented to the Fifth IRA World Congress on Reading, Vienna, Austria, August 13, 1974, pp. 4–5. Reprinted by permission.

Grammatical differences*

Description	English speaker	Spanish-English speaker
A. Use of verb forms		
1. Subject-predicate	The cars run. The car runs.	The cars runs. The car run.
2. Tense	Joe said that he was ready. I needed help yesterday.	Joe said that he is ready. I need help yesterday.
3. Use of be	I am five years old.	I have five years.
4. Negative	Joe isn't here. He didn't go home. Don't come.	Joe is no here. He no go home. He didn't went home. No come.
B. Use of noun and determiner forms		
Plural form	The two cars are big.	The two car are big.
Omission of determiner with noun in certain contexts.	He is a farmer.	He is farmer.
C. Use of pronoun forms		
Omission in question	Is he a farmer?	Is farmer?
Omission in statement	It is ready.	Is ready?
D. Use of adjectives		
Order	The red cap is pretty.	The cap red is pretty.
Ending	The red caps are fine.	The caps red are fine.
Comparison	It is bigger. It is the biggest.	Is more big. Is most big.

* Robert B. Ruddell, *Reading—Language Instruction: Innovative Practices,* Englewood Cliffs, N.J.: Prentice-Hall, 1974, pp. 274–275.

In addition to phonological and grammatical features, dialects often differ in vocabulary. The words *head, heavy, tough,* and *far out,* for example, may trigger entirely different meanings to different people. You may wish to play a game called "generation gap" by writing a one-word association beside each of the following words and comparing your results with those of your classmates.

salt _____   trip _____

pot _____   gay _____

Apollo _____   grass _____

bread _____   plumber _____

fuzz _____   Wallace _____

Dialect, in all its components, represents the culture of its speakers. For example, the idiomatic expressions of a language present great difficulty to the new learner of that language. The Korean child struggling to learn English may find such expressions as "Catch a wink," "Get on the ball," "Take a powder," or "Hit the sack" quite confusing. Similarly, the idioms of a dialect may be accurately intelligible only to the speakers of that dialect; the word *apple,* for example, connotes at least three distinct meanings in this country, i.e., a type of fruit, a local name New Yorkers use to refer to their city (the Big Apple), and the Native American reference to a fellow Indian whose skin is "red," but curries favor from whites.

In the mid-1960s, Adrian Dove created the "Dove Counterbalance Intelligence Test." Its purpose was to demonstrate the discrimination against black students that can result from the use of standard-English intelligence tests. The test was written in the black dialect peculiar to the Watts ghetto in Los Angeles and drew heavily on the vocabulary and idiomatic expressions of its speakers. Since success on most group tests is dependent on one's reading comprehension of the dialect of the test, the match between the language of the test and the test taker is a crucial one. We invite you to take the Adapted Dove Counterbalance Intelligence Test (reprinted at the end of this chapter) as a measure of your dialect IQ.

LEARNING THE DIALECT

Few teachers are, nor are they expected to be, experts in all of the dialects of the English language. It is, though, imperative that new teachers learn as much as possible about the dialects of their pupils so that sensible decisions about appropriate reading instruction can be made. It is not essential for the teacher to *speak* the dialect of the children. In fact, to do so could be very obviously an affectation and could even be insulting. But unless teachers learn the major phonological, syntactic, and lexical (vocabulary) attributes of their pupils, they may create more confusion than they shed light. There are several ways in which the teachers can learn about their pupils' dialects:

1. Requesting in-service training arranged by the school principal or district administrator. Sometimes, school in-service sessions include little more than hearing about someone's trip to Europe, listening to a high-powered book salesperson, or sharing ideas about favorite activities. It seems that a much more important use of in-service time for a teacher new to the district would be to participate in a two- or three-day workshop conducted by speakers of a local dialect, experienced teachers, and consultants. The intent of the workshop would be to foster maximum familiarization with the local dialect and to develop related strategies for reading growth.

2. Conversing with and *listening* to pupils. The pupils might be tape recorded, if they do not find it inhibiting. Later, the tapes can be replayed and analyzed.

3. Listening to each child read orally. Listen to each child's pronunciation of the various sounds, noting the kinds of vocabulary or sentence structure that seem to create problems.

4. Learning about the culture of the children. Through interviews with parents, neighbors, and others, and through reading relevant books, learn as much as possible about the background and culture of the children.

All of the activities above will take time, but as teachers learn the dialect, cultural background, and interests of their pupils, they will be better equipped to select an appropriate reading approach and concomitant reading activities for their students.

READING APPROACHES WITH THE LINGUISTICALLY DIVERSE

In recent decades a number of linguists, teachers, and researchers have concerned themselves with the problems of teaching reading to the linguistically diverse. Countless experiments have been conducted, materials developed, and strategies tried. Essentially, the large number of specific approaches can be placed into eight categories, each of which represents a viewpoint—a philosophy—about language and reading.

1. Teach the children standard English first, then teach them to read.
2. Use conventional reading material, but accept dialect transpositions.
3. Use materials written in nonstandard dialect.
4. Use materials written in standard dialect which minimize dialect/culture differences.
5. Use materials written in standard English which are culturally relevant to the target group.
6. Train teachers properly, for then the materials used will become relatively unimportant.
7. Teach children reading through nonstandard dialect materials, period. Forget about standard English.
8. Use the language-experience approach.

All eight viewpoints recognize the importance of teachers' being knowledgeable about the dialects of the pupils in their class.

Teach Standard English First

We believe that this approach makes more sense for teaching English as a second language than it does for teaching standard English as a second dialect. This viewpoint is based on our knowledge of the way in which language develops in children. People learn to speak and understand spoken language before they learn to read and write. It follows naturally that a Spanish- or Chinese- or Winnebago-speaking child who is to learn to read English should learn to speak and understand the language first. This does not mean that the child must be totally fluent before reading instruction can begin, only that the child must know sufficient oral language to which the printed English can be related.

The most common teaching method stemming from this viewpoint is the oral/aural, or audiolingual, approach, whereby pupils hear a word or phrase spoken by a native speaker and then repeat it until they have learned it. Next, the pupils learn to respond to questions and to substitute new words in the learned pattern. Oral/aural language pattern drills may look like the following.

Lesson 1

Teacher:	This is a book.	Pupil:	This is a book.
	This is a glass.		This is a glass.
	This is a tire.		This is a tire.
	It is a book.		It is a book.
	It is a glass.		It is a glass.
	It is a tire.		It is a tire.
	etc.		etc.

Lesson 2

Teacher:	What is this?	Pupil:	
	It is a book.		It is a book.
	What is this?		It is a glass.
	What is this?		It is a tree.
	etc.		etc.

Lesson 3

Teacher holds up a book.	Pupil:	That is a book.
Teacher holds up a glass.		That is a glass.
Teacher holds up a tire.		That is a tire.
etc.		etc.

Then, the teacher, satisfied that the pupils have orally learned the intended words and patterns, writes the phrases on the chalkboard, on paper strips, or on overhead transparencies. The pupils then follow a listen/speak/read/write sequence to develop mastery of the written patterns and words.

The oral/aural approach is systematic and is built on repetition and drill. It has been used very effectively to teach English as a second language in the United States and elsewhere. However, because the approach is repetitious and can become dull, it has not been used often to teach standard English to speakers of nonstandard dialect. Speakers of nonstandard English come to school with a fully developed English dialect *and* (usually) with a strong desire to learn to read. In addition to possible boredom with the approach, children may become frustrated if required to engage in a period of repetitive oral drill in a new dialect before learning to read.

Accept Dialect Reading of Conventional Materials

This notion acknowledges the pupils' intense interest in learning to read when entering school and, further, recognizes the cost involved in producing separate materials for relatively small groups of children.

The approach is dependent on teacher awareness of the points of difference between the pupils' dialect and the dialect of the printed materials. The approach addresses mainly the phonological differences between dialects, since the syntactic structure and vocabulary are determined by the printed materials. In essence, teachers using this approach are expected to treat pronunciation differences as *differences,* not errors; i.e., if children render a dialect pronunciation, they are not to be "corrected" for making an "error."

Beyond phonological variations, teachers need to know the materials—and the children's dialect—thoroughly enough to anticipate syntactic and vocabulary trouble spots. When unfamiliar sentence patterns or multimeaning words occur in a text, the teacher must be prepared to assist children with the difficult passages. It seems logical that the greater the divergence between the language of the child and the language of learning, the greater the difficulty in learning to read. Thus, this approach is not suitable for helping children who are learning English as a second language, but some teachers use the approach with speakers of nonstandard dialect.

Write Materials in Nonstandard Dialect

This view rests on the assumption that it is easier to learn to read one's own dialect (that spoken by the child and his or her family and friends) than it is to learn to read a different dialect. Several attempts have been made to write and publish books and materials for particular groups of children, using their dialect and drawing on their culture. In recent years, materials have been developed by some Native American groups and in some black communities.

The sequence usually followed is: (1) teach children to read materials written in their own dialect; (2) teach them the oral standard-English forms of the same structures; and then, (3) teach them to read the standard-English forms. This approach is usually addressed to two aspects of language: syntactic structure and vocabulary. Proponents of this approach do not advocate making spelling changes to match the phonology of the children.

An example of materials developed according to this philosophy is the *Chicago Psycholinguistic Reading Series,* published by the Chicago Board of Education. The series consists of eight, small paperback books. The first three books are in two parts: the first is written in "Everyday Talk" (nonstandard dialect); the second, in "School Talk" (standard English). There are two separate editions, Everyday Talk and School Talk, for each of the next four books in the series. The final book is written only in School Talk. Illustrations and story content reflect the southside Chicago neighborhoods of the children for whom the series was written. On a number of pages children make their own illustrations. The examples below show the syntactic differences in the two versions of two of the books. In the series, each of the stories below constitutes an entire book of a dozen or more pages, with illustrations or blank spaces for the child to illustrate.

SCHOOL TALK My Family	EVERYDAY TALK My Family
I have a mama.	I got a mama.
I have a daddy.	I got a daddy.
I have a mama and a daddy.	I got a mama and a daddy.
I have a brother.	I got a brother.
I have a sister.	I got a sister.
I have a brother and a sister.	I got a brother and a sister.
I have a grandmama.	I got a grandmama.

SCHOOL TALK Stop That!	EVERYDAY TALK Stop That!
When I talk, my teacher says, Stop that!	When I be talking, my teacher say, Stop that!
When I run, my teacher says, Stop that!	When I be running, my teacher say, Stop that!
When I fight, my teacher says, Stop that!	When I be fighting, my teacher say, Stop that!
No talking!	No talking!
No running!	No running!
No fighting!	No fighting!
What a school.	What a school.*

The series is intended for beginning readers who typically spend between a half year and two years in the program, and it is accompanied by a strong oral-language program. After completing the series, most children are moved to second-grade materials in a conventional reading series.

Community reaction to nonstandard dialect readers has been mixed. Some parents have accepted the notion of learning to first read materials in one's own dialect, but other parents have rejected these attempts, feeling that their children are not being taught "good English." In general, teachers have been pleased with the materials, which are of high interest to the children for whom they were written.

---

* Mildred R. Gladney, "A Teaching Strategy," in *Language and Learning to Read*, ed. Richard E. Hodges and E. Hugh Rudorf, Boston: Houghton Mifflin, 1972, p. 77. Reprinted by permission.

In summary, the main purpose of dialect materials is to ease initial reading development by creating printed materials that reflect children's speech, while at the same time introducing pupils to an additional dialect—standard English. The emphasis of these materials has been on altering syntactic structure and vocabulary rather than on changing spelling to approximate pronunciation. It is reasonable to expect that local communities and school districts with high enrollments of blacks or Native Americans, for example, will continue to develop such materials. It is unlikely that dialect materials will be written and commercially published for national distribution, however, because of their relatively restricted marketability.

Use Standard Dialect Materials Which Minimize Dialect and Cultural Differences

According to this position, there is much greater commonality of language across dialects than there is differences between them. The major sources of possible dialect interference are known (see pp. 269–272), and materials can be developed that minimize these differences. The viewpoint also contends that materials can be made rather culture-free or neutral to avoid latent ethnic discrimination. For example, one series intended for Spanish-speaking children uses animals and insects, rather than people, as characters in their stories. A number of published reading programs are available that minimize cultural differences, but virtually none have been written that attempt to neutralize dialect.

Use Standard English in Culturally Relevant Materials

In the early 1960s, the first black faces (actually, beige) began to appear in basal-reading series, and gradually story locations moved from the farms and suburbs to the cities. Proponents of cultural relevance held that the major obstacle to successful beginning reading was not dialect deviance, but cultural rejection. Most basal-reading series (see Chapter 5) now recognize the multiethnicity of our society and attempt to include stories pertinent to Native American, Chicano, Asian, and rural poor children, but only in the most recently published books have women been treated realistically. This view contends that "primerese," the language used in many beginning books, is in reality different from everyone's dialect. Many children have obviously learned to read from the "primerese" found in most basal materials. Thus, the major concern of this approach is to increase cultural representativeness and to avoid ethnic discrimination by either commission or omission, so that children do not become alienated by the materials intended to increase their literacy.

Train the Teachers and Don't Worry About the Materials

This approach stems from the belief that the teacher, not the book, is the key to learning to read. Few materials are "teacher-proof." Excellent teachers will teach children to read with the poorest of materials, but poor teachers will fail with the best of materials. This viewpoint argues that teachers must receive proper in-service training about the dialect and culture of the pupils they will teach, so that they can put this knowledge to work, using whatever materials are available.

We support the view that adequate training of teachers—both preservice and in-service—is imperative. But we believe that this factor underlies *all* of the philosophies discussed here and that it is essential to all successful teaching. We do not believe that materials are unimportant, though we feel that they are less important than the teacher. Further, we do not believe that "good teacher training" is in and of itself an approach to teaching reading.

Teach Nonstandard Dialect Only

This belief holds that in a truly multiethnic society, no one should have to worry about learning the dialect of the majority. Rather, children should learn their own dialect and learn to read through it. Contrary to what is usually the case (the minorities learn the dialect of the majority), the majority should learn to understand and accept the nonstandard dialects. If the majority can be rid of its prejudices, and if everyone can be educated in the easiest way (through his or her dialect), no one will be hurt by that dialect. Few could question the moral appropriateness of this view, but it has been rejected largely for being out of touch with the socioeconomic realities of present-day American society. Most upward mobility is still dependent, perhaps unfortunately, on the person's ability to read, spell, and speak standard English.

Use the Language-Experience Approach

Of all the approaches advocated, the language-experience approach is, we believe, the most sensible one to use with linguistically diverse pupils —as with most other children as well. The language-experience approach, as described in Chapter 6, suggests that beginning-reading instruction should involve the language, the culture, the experience, and the interests of the children.

The approach is not cost-prohibitive. Entire series need not be created, edited, and published for only small segments of society. Instead, paper, markers, chalk boards, and chalk form the core of needed materials in the language-experience approach. The approach permits a perfect match between the words and stories the children will initially read and the words and sentence patterns they actually use. Words dictated by children for the individual and group stories should be spelled correctly, we believe, not phonetically as pronounced, so that children are prepared to read the words they will encounter later in print.

Standard English can be taught, much as with the nonstandard printed materials, but must be separated from initial reading so that confusion is kept to a minimum. As indicated earlier, knowing the dialect and culture of the children will be crucial if the teacher is to be of greatest effectiveness. The language-experience approach capitalizes on the natural language of children, their interests, experiences, and enthusiasm. Children experience, dictate, listen, speak, read, and write. Gradually, they learn new vocabulary and alternative ways of saying things. The progression is from dialect communication to reading to learning aspects of a new dialect to reading the new dialect. Once the child is a capable reader, she or he is ready for an individualized reading program, as described in Chapter 3.

SPECIFIC READING ACTIVITIES

In his article, "Reading and the Disadvantaged: Some Psycholinguistic Applications for the Classroom Teacher," Rosen (1973) presents 14 specific suggestions intended to improve the reading abilities of linguistically diverse pupils. Although we find all of the suggestions potentially useful (in fact, we think that the activities would be fun for all types of children), eight of them seem particularly productive.

Active manipulation of print via multisensory input involves a series of activities of highly motivating and reinforcing nature: a) cutting letters for bulletin board captions; b) printing blocks for newspapers and setting printing type for pupil's original stories to be duplicated; c) sign and poster making; d) typing stories; e) writing invisible ink messages; f) diagram and map making; and g) printing captions for timelines, projects, experiments, scrapbooks, and dioramas.

Action directed approaches require active and immediate responses to printed messages. These activities focus attention on the information-bearing nature of print and create opportunities for pupils to eventually produce print by writing their own messages. A wide variety of activities are possible, for example: a) directions on cards, such as, "Open your book to page 12" or "Put your pencil in your desk" or "Let's go out and take a walk"; b) games in print, such as, "Find the note under your red book" (the note says), "Find the key on page 22" (note attached to key), "Open the drawer in back of you" (finds a box with a note), "This Coca Cola is for you!"

Crytography requires a high degree of attention to information processing and has strong motivational influence. Pupils could eventually produce their own codes and pass secret messages to one another involving more and more personally developed and elaborated codes. The teacher herself must first develop and demonstrate to pupils simple cryptograms—printed messages in coded form—either by means of new orthography or by embedding irrelevant and confusing units into message-bearing sentences. The child must break the code and give the message, for example: "Marigold Red is cows dogs the name of cats chickens a dangerous enemy birds pigs spy." (After every third word two plural animate nouns are imbedded.) Pupils would benefit in many areas of reading from this technique. By developing their own graphic symbolization some pupils would be helped to understand the place and use of symbols in messages. Those using standard orthography would have high information-providing experiences, and the technique could provide an interesting modification of the language experience approach.

Grammatical substitutions sensitize children to grammatical relationships while scanning a message. A pupil rapidly scans a sentence and indicates his choice, for example, a) side-by-side verb inflections: My sister (has, have) a boyfriend; b) within sentence substitutions: My mother saw a mouse, or My mother sawing a mouse, or My mother saw a mice; c) orally produced cues: John (ask, asks, asked) a question. The pupil should experiment with changes in intonation and stress to deal with sentences such as these. To avoid influence of phonological differences due to dialect, the activity should not be carried out via oral reading.

Scrambled or distorted order of input requires reconstruction of printed message, sensitizing pupils to information extraction via rapid message recognition and reordering. Consider these examples, a) scrambled words: "Book your close" or "Green was John's bike broken"; b) scrambled syntax: "To walk downtown/it was easier/when the traffic is heavy"; c) jumbled words: "BilliselevenyearsoldandisinthefifthgradeattheArlingtonSchool."

Semantic substitution sensitizes a child to variations in use of vocabulary by requiring him to provide verbally or by sorting cards a synonym or antonym for underlined lexical items in sentences. For example, "The happy boy was hungry." The choices could be cheerful, merry, empty, famished. The child should produce sentences in print for others to manipulate. Specific parts of speech to substitute could be systematically dealt with.

Simple to complex sentences develops the ability to recognize and expand simple concepts, encourages the use of prepositions and conjunctions, and provides experience with complex syntactical units in print. Some examples are a) declarative sentences: "The man who bought the coat liked it; b) exclamatory sentence-to-declarative: "Don't touch that." Expansion: "Mary saw the large spider and yelled 'Don't touch that' "; c) interrogative sentence to declarative: "Where did you go last night?" Expansion: "Father asked Bill, 'Where did you go last night?' "

Sentence interrelationships develop an understanding of how sentences and their interrelations signal meanings. Pupils can produce or search out examples in their texts and from other sources, for example, 1) The man climbed the pole. 2) He fell. 3) His arm was broken. Idea: His arm was broken due to the fall. Through study and manipulation of ideas in sentences and discussion of the relationships, pupils' abilities to extract information from print can be enhanced.*

SUMMARY

Learning to read is a remarkable intellectual accomplishment, and for many children it is a very difficult achievement. Thousands of languages are spoken in the world, and many languages have many dialects. Just as it is easier to learn to read one's native language than it is to read a foreign language, it is easier to read one's own dialect than a different one. Both languages and dialects differ in phonology, syntactic structure, and vocabulary. It is essential for teachers to know the dialect characteristics of their pupils so that potential interferences can be anticipated. Of the major philosophies advanced for teaching reading to the linguistically diverse, we view the language-experience approach as being the most practical and the most sensible for most children in most instructional settings.

Suggested Activities
for the Methods Class

Activity 1

Take the test that follows, and score it, using the key on p. 287. After you finish, discuss the following in small groups.

1. Why did you score as you did?
2. What aspects of dialect used in the test created the greatest difficulty for you?
3. Speculate about speakers of nonstandard dialect who must read books and take tests written in standard English.

---

* Carl L. Rosen. "Reading and the Disadvantaged: Some Psycholinguistic Implications for the Classroom Teacher" in Views on Elementary Reading Instruction, ed. Thomas C. Barrett and Dale D. Johnson, Newark, Delaware: IRA, 1973, pp. 15–19. Reprinted with permission of Carl L. Rosen and the International Reading Association.

ADAPTATION OF DOVE COUNTERBALANCE GENERAL INTELLIGENCE TEST
ADRIAN DOVE AND ALLEN R. SULLIVAN*

Instructions: Circle the letter of the correct answer. Answer each question.

I. Social Customs

1. A "gas head" is a person who has a:

    a. fast moving car
    b. stable of "lace"
    c. "process" or "do"
    d. habit of stealing cars
    e. long jail record for arson

2. Cheap chitlings (not the kind you purchase at a frozen food counter) will taste rubbery unless they are cooked long enough. How soon can you quit cooking them to eat and enjoy them?

    a. 45 minutes
    b. two hours
    c. 24 hours
    d. one week (on a low flame)
    e. one hour

3. If you are thirsty while attending a weekend party, and want an acoholic beverage, you are for a:

    a. slow sip
    b. drink
    c. sip of booze
    d. taste
    e. glass

4. It is said that the first thing a brother does after completing a good meal is:

    a. drink water
    b. exercise
    c. sleep
    d. thank the cook
    e. burp

5. What is a pik used for?

    a. basketball defense
    b. afro hair style
    c. asking a girl to dance
    d. cleaning teeth
    e. turning barbecued meat

II. Personalities

6. Bo Didley is a:

    a. game for children
    b. down home cheap wine

---

* Arthur R. Sullivan. "Counterbalance Intelligence Testing," *Black Academy Review*, March 1971: 9–13, 15.

    c. down home singer

    d. new dance

    e. Moejoe call

7. What are "Dixie Hummingbirds?"

    a. part of the KKK

    b. a swamp disease

    c. a modern gospel group

    d. a Mississippi Negro Parliamentary Group

    e. Deacons

8. Who in this group first said "Black is Beautiful?"

    a. Don L. Lee

    b. Ron Karanga

    c. Malcolm X

    d. Martin Luther King, Jr.

    c. Marcus Garvey

9. What group has for its theme "Freedom Justice and Equality?"

    a. Peace and Freedom Party

    b. Black Panthers

    c. Muslims

    d. NAACP

    e. UNIA

10. Charles Drew is famous for:

    a. inventing the first shoe assembly machine

    b. performing the first open heart surgery

    c. writing "Lift Every Voice and Sing"

    d. perfecting a blood plasma preservative

    e. refining sugar

III. Language Usage

11. Which word is out of place here?

    a. splib

    b. blood

    c. gray

    d. spook

    e. black

12. "Dust" is what you get when

    a. one fusses with you

    b. runs in front of you

    c. a car screeches in front of you

    d. air pollution over the ghetto

    e. when the eagle flies

13. When one chirps he is:

    a. complaining

    b. squealing

    c. singing

    d. cussing

    e. flying the coop

14. When someone is called heavy, he is considered:

    a. handsome and articulate
    b. articulate and intelligent
    c. beautiful and hip
    d. clever and cunning
    e. hip and cool

15. A hog is a:

    a. barbecue
    b. glutton
    c. short
    d. cop
    e. crib

IV. General Knowledge

16. If you throw the dice and seven is showing on the top, was is facing down?

    a. seven
    b. snake eyes
    c. boxcars
    d. little joes
    e. 11

17. "Jet" is:

    a. motorcycle
    b. one of the gangs in West Side Story
    c. a news and gossip magazine
    d. a way of life for the rich
    e. getting something quickly

18. Uhuru means:

    a. justice
    b. loyalty
    c. freedom
    d. peace
    e. equality

19. What are the three basic and fundamental colors of the African flag?

    a. yellow, green and white
    b. red, black and green
    c. brown, black and beige
    d. green, blue and orange
    e. red, white and blue

20. Playing the dozens is the same as playing:

    a. a guitar
    b. house
    c. cribbage
    d. the drums
    e. cards

ANSWER KEY

1. c	6. c	11. c	16. a
2. c	7. c	12. e	17. c
3. d	8. d	13. c	18. c
4. c	9. c	14. b	19. b
5. b	10. d	15. c	20. b

Activity 2

Divide into groups to debate the merits and shortcomings of the eight view-points about teaching reading to the linguistically diverse. After the debates, rank the eight approaches from *most desirable* to *least desirable* and then rank them from *most practical* (realistic) to *least practical*. Is there a close match between your two rankings?

Activity 3

Listen to the two records: (1) *The Dialect of the Black American* (Western Electric, 1970) and (2) *Americans Speaking* (National Council of Teachers of English, 1967). Why is nonstandard dialect viewed as a problem in reading, but regional dialect is not?

Activity 4

List and compare the problems of teaching English as a second language with teaching standard English as a second dialect.

Activity 5

Write one-word associations beside the following words as quickly as you can. Compare your responses with other class members.

acid _____	hangup _____
AFL _____	hawk _____
bag _____	head _____
black _____	joint _____
blitz _____	Sen. McCarthy _____
brother _____	mace _____
busing _____	militant _____
bust _____	Minuteman _____
Camelot _____	moratorium _____
camp _____	pad _____
demonstration _____	panther _____
dove _____	pig _____
drop out _____	pill _____
freak _____	Pueblo _____

rap _____	straight _____
rock _____	topless _____
silo _____	transplant _____
soul _____	tune in _____
split _____	turn on _____
Dr. Spock _____	weatherman _____
stoned _____	

Teaching Suggestions

Suggestion 1

Administer an informal reading inventory (see Chapter 9) to a child who speaks a nonstandard dialect. Note pronunciation differences and problems that seem related to differences in syntactic structure and vocabulary.

Suggestion 2

If there are speakers of nonstandard dialect in your class, tape record a conversation with a group of them. Replay the tape later and record examples of phonological, syntactical, or lexical differences.

Suggestion 3

Play portions of the record *Americans Speaking* or some other dialect record to your class. Generate a discussion on dialect differences and similarities.

Suggestion 4

If you work with a group of very young children who are speakers of a nonstandard dialect, spend time with them daily for two or three weeks, developing individual language-experience stories. Record sentences as used by the children in their dialect. Later, rewrite some of the sentences in standard English. Have the children read both forms of the same sentence. What differences do you note in their oral-reading fluency?

Suggestion 5

Encourage your principal or curriculum coordinator to arrange an in-service workshop on the dialects of the local children.

REFERENCES

Baratz, Joan C. "Teaching Reading in a Negro School," in *Teaching Black Children to Read*, ed. Joan C. Baratz and Roger W. Shuy, Washington, D.C.: The Center for Applied Linguistics, 1969, pp. 99–100.

Gladney, Mildred R. "A Teaching Strategy," in *Language and Learning to Read,* ed. Richard E. Hodges and E. Hugh Rudorf, Boston: Houghton Mifflin, 1972, pp. 73–84.

Goodman, Kenneth S. "Dialect Barriers to Reading Comprehension," in *Contemporary English: Change and Variation,* ed. David L. Shores, Philadelphia: Lippincott, 1972.

Rosen, Carl L. "Reading and the Disadvantaged: Some Psycholinguistic Applications for the Classroom Teacher," in *Views on Elementary Reading Instruction,* ed. Thomas C. Barrett and Dale D. Johnson, Newark, Delaware: International Reading Association, 1973.

Ruddell, Robert B. *Reading—Language Instruction: Innovative Practices,* Englewood Cliffs, N.J.: Prentice-Hall, 1974, pp. 274–275.

Schulwitz, Bonnie Smith. "Language and Reading: Problems of the Bilingual Child," paper presented to the Fifth IRA World Congress on Reading, Vienna, Austria, August 13, 1974, 9 pp.

13 Planning for Grade 1: The First Three Weeks of School

A question beginning teachers frequently ask is, "How do I get started?" Often, they elaborate on that question by saying, "I mean, exactly what do I do the first few weeks of school?" There is no doubt that they are concerned about the day-by-day, hour-by-hour, and even minute-by-minute planning that is required to teach reading. These teachers don't want generalities; they want highly specific suggestions.

We asked Mrs. Sandra Dahl,* whom we have watched teach and for whom we have great respect, to help us respond to this need on the part of beginning teachers for a specific, illustrative plan. We asked Mrs. Dahl if she would record in detail how she organizes and teaches her first-grade students the first three weeks of school during the block of time allotted for reading instruction. We think that you will be as pleased with her contribution to this book as we are. Her illustrative plans provide the specificity we think beginning teachers want.

Mrs. Dahl has organized her plans in a way that allows her readers to see how she and her students are occupied throughout different blocks of time. She specifies a time period and then describes briefly all of the activities that take place within that period.

Mrs. Dahl has, throughout her plans, made notations which we think will be helpful to beginning teachers. She has also indicated clearly which activities she is directly involved with at any given time, so that you can see easily how she moves from student to student or from group to group. Finally, she has specified the objectives, materials, and procedures for each activity she lists.

The plans that comprise this chapter require slow, careful reading. We recommend that they be read at several sittings, so as to avoid information overload. If you will try to visualize the movement and activities that are presented in the plans, we think that your comprehension will be greatly enhanced. In short, the plans require slow, careful reading, but the information that can be obtained from them is well worth the expenditure of time and effort.

A PLAN FOR THE FIRST THREE WEEKS OF GRADE 1—WEEKLY OBJECTIVES

Week 1

Day 1: 1. Begin to assess individual abilities by making general observations.

---

* Sandra Dahl—experienced first-grade teacher and, at the time of this writing, a doctoral candidate at the University of Wisconsin, Madison.

      2. Provide introduction to reading that serves as both a readiness and a reading experience, utilizing group language-experience charts.

Day 2: 1. Assess individual and group readiness for reading.
      2. Introduce manuscript writing and open two special interest centers.

Day 3: 1. Assess ability on specific tasks (printing skill, color words, retention of words on chart story from Day 1).
      2. Note listening skill, attention span, behavior problems today.

Day 4: 1. See how tentative grouping works out and note individual ability more closely.
      2. Note children's use of the activity centers.

Day 5: 1. Introduce IMC and continue to develop positive attitude toward books.
      2. Reserve time to meet individual needs.

Week 2

Day 1: 1. Provide an interesting motivation for experience story.
      2. Allow opportunity for listening, oral expression, and recording of ideas.

Day 2: 1. Build sight vocabulary as base for skill work.
      2. Foster good attitude by praising good work and reading enjoyable prose selection.
      3. Open two additional activity centers.

Day 3: 1. Provide for individualized attention and special assessment.
      2. Continue to develop skills and attitude.

Day 4: 1. Introduce pantomime as a form of expression.
      2. Recording, reading, and skill building are continued.

Day 5: 1. Introduce various equipment in the IMC in preparation for individual use.
      2. Build reading skill and work on phoneme-grapheme relationship.

Week 3

Day 1: 1. Encourage oral expression through sharing time and puppetry.
      2. Continue to work on building reading skills.

Day 2: 1. Practice and present puppet show to class (this will motivate other groups to request similar activities).
      2. Continue to build developmental reading skill.

Day 3: 1. Provide group and individual instruction in reading skills.
2. Encourage interest in self-directed reading by allowing time to listen to child read page in self-selected book.

Day 4: 1. Provide group instruction in reading skill.
2. Give specific help to individuals according to demonstrated needs.

Day 5: 1. Increase appreciation of literature through trip to IMC and check individuals on careful and correct use of equipment.
2. Continued guidance in reading-skill development.

DAILY PLANS

Week 1—Day 1

Time	Objectives, Materials, Motivation, Procedures, and Followup		Notes
8:50–9:00 (10 min.)	*Opening:*	Welcome children, help them find places, note calendar and weather	Name cards in manuscript-writing are taped on desk tops
9:00–9:20 (20 min.)	(Whole class) *Objective:*	Welcome and introduction	
	Materials:	Name tags to pin on children	Cutouts of leaves, animals, etc.
	Procedures:	Call names, child tells something of self, family, pet	Note shy child and do not force speaking
9:20–9:30 (10 min.)	(Whole class) *Objective:*	Chance for listening and oral expression	
	Procedure:	Discuss expectations for school year—need for cooperation, good listening habits, room rules	Teacher guides discussion, rather than lectures
			Children may state that they *expect* to learn how to read
9:30–9:40 (10 min.)	(Whole class) *Objective:*	Provide motivation for experience story	
	Materials:	Classroom pet, food, name card, felt-tip pen	
	Procedure:	Gather class around pet cage, encourage comments,	Make note of verbal children, watch for

Week 1—Day 1 (cont.)

Time	Objectives, Materials, Motivation, Procedures, and Followup		Notes
		choose name and print name on tag, attach to cage	child who appears disinterested
9:40–10:00 (20 min.)	(Whole class) *Objectives:*	Record group chart story in manner outlined in Chapter 6	Teacher needs to prod class with leading questions if children are hesitant to contribute
	Materials:	Chart tablet, felt-tip pen, pet cage on table near chart	Place chart tablet at level visible to everyone
	Procedure:	Explain task, encourage free expression, record comments	Teacher comments on a few letters and words while recording; remind children to watch carefully
10:00–10:10 (10 min.)	(Whole class) *Objective:*	Reread story, note individual abilities	Let the children get up and stretch a bit; rhymes and songs can be found to use at times such as this and are good to have in "bag of tricks"
	Procedure:	Teacher reads story, using normal intonation, and sweeps hand along lines; volunteers read story with teacher's help, identify a word or letter they know	
10:10–10:30 (20 min.)	(Whole class) *Objective:*	Draw pictures to reinforce theme of story; provide something for children to carry home to show parents	This activity provides a worthwhile project to show parents
	Materials:	9" × 18" manila paper folded in half, crayons	Provide extra boxes of crayons, as children do not bring all supplies on the first day
	Procedure:	Discuss what may appear in picture related to chart	Some children will finish in a couple min-

Week 1—Day 1

Time	Objectives, Materials, Motivation, Procedures, and Followup	Notes
	story, demonstrate how to use top half of paper for picture, instruct children to put name on top of paper, collect papers	utes and do not want to work on picture any more; circulate and talk to these and other children, print any words child requests on picture
	Followup: Use any time remaining for children to show their pictures and tell about them	Some may still be working
Later in day	Pass out pictures with story stapled to lower half of manila paper, reread story as group, suggest that children show story to parents, and tell them about class pet	Teacher or aide will have used the break time to type and mimeograph the chart story
		Solves dilemma in many households when anxious parent asks about the school day and child has little to say

Comments

First-grade children come into the classroom expecting to learn how to read. You have provided them with a positive step in that direction on the first day of school. Children want to carry something along home with them to show to their families. The illustrated chart story satisfies this need in a meaningful way. You may wish to send a brief note (pinned to each child's collar) which explains to the parents that the child is not expected to be able to "read" the story in total. It may be worthwhile to explain this program to the parents during a PTA meeting or parents' visiting night.

After thinking about the day's activities, make note of children who seemed especially interested in the story development or who seemed to know a few words or letters. Note those who were easily distracted and the ones who were unable to contribute to the activities. Divide the class into two groups (A and B) for tomorrow's work. Include a few "contributors" in each of the groups.

Week 1—Day 2

Time	Objectives, Materials, Motivation, Procedures, and Followup		Notes
8:50–9:00 (10 min.)	*Opening:*	Date, weather, announcements, sharing	Child may have special news or item to show
9:00–9:20 (20 min.)	(Whole class) *Objective:*	Introduction to manuscript writing	Want child to develop facility and good habits in printing, so is free to devote effort to creative expression in written exercises
	Materials:	Prepare lines on chalkboard, manuscript paper with child's name on top lines, lower-case 1 on next sets of lines	
	Procedure:	Demonstrate on chalkboard, noting lines and spaces, check position of paper and assign letter 1, move around room, giving individual help	Note left-handed child and aid paper position; i.e., slant paper to left
			Teach child to insert index and pointer fingers after a letter to leave space
			Do not give up! This may be the most frustrating day of the school year. Take heart, they will learn to print *and* to stay on "the top line."
9:20–9:35 (15 min.)	(Whole class) *Objective:*	Introduction of activity centers	Children may not be expected to use free time productively unless they are guided into situation
	Procedure:	Explain library corner and art center, noting rules for use and cleanup (refer to Chapter 6 for hints on procedures)	Work out a system limiting number in center; could fashion
9:35–9:40 (5 min.)	Call names for Group A and direct them to chart story developed on Day 1; direct Group		yarn ties to signify area: 4 red ties =

Week 1—Day 2 (cont.)

Time	Objectives, Materials, Motivation, Procedures, and Followup	Notes
	B to activity center. (Groups were determined at end of Day 1's activities)	library; 4 blue ties = art. Hang in central place in room
		In early days, help child select activity
9:40–9:55 (15 min.)	(Group A)	
	Objective: Assessment of readiness; reading of story; sight vocabulary	Teacher provides illustration for chart story; later, child may volunteer to draw one
	Materials: Chart story, pointer	
	Motivation: Choose child to retell story in own words	
	Procedures: Reread story, read story as a group, volunteer reads story with teacher help; children locate words, letters they recognize, letter in own name, etc.	Insure all can view chart
		Note children who recall words, recognize several letters, seem interested
9:55–10:10 (15 min.)	Group A chooses activity	If child does not volunteer, find word that begins like child's name and print both word and name on board, note beginning letter and sound
	Group B same lesson as Group A; provide alternative strategies in line with individual children's abilities	
10:10–10:30 (20 min.)	(Whole class)	
	Objective: Appreciation of prose	Children love to sit on the floor around the teacher during storyime. An old log provides an interesting chair for the teacher
	Materials: Picture book	
	Motivation: Show cover, encourage speculation as to characters, theme, etc.	
	Procedure: Read story, making sure to move the book so all can view the illustrations	

Comments

Do not be discouraged by your first day at teaching manuscript writing. Some children have no concept of lines and spaces on the manuscript paper, so they will need additional guidance. Perhaps it will help to seat a struggling child near one who is catching on to the task. One word of caution is needed with regard to scheduling. You may find that the 20-minute allottment is not sufficient in these early lessons. Children may need much individual help on this difficult task; therefore, as in all other sections of a lesson plan, the teacher must remain flexible. This flexibility extends to procedures as well as to the timing factor.

Today's work on the chart story should have given you some very general notions about individual abilities. As the week moves on, individual readinesses will become more apparent.

Catch potential behavior problems and begin to guide actions. You may consider various seating arrangements as one solution. The success of your individualized program lies, in part, on guiding children into useful, independent free-time activities.

Week 1—Day 3

Time	Objectives, Materials, Motivation, Procedures, and Followup		Notes
8:50–9:00 (10 min.)	*Opening:*	Date, weather, attendance	Children answer roll call with favorite color, letter, rhyming word, animal, etc.
9:00–9:20 (20 min.)	(Whole class) *Objective:*	Teach letter forms: l, o, h	
	Materials:	Manuscript paper with child's name and example of l, o, h on individual lines on chalkboard and on papers	Music staff liner is useful in drawing lines on chalkboard
			If child has trouble, make dots for child to trace in forming the letters
	Procedures:	Review lines and spaces, supervise copying of name, demonstrate and supervise line of each letter	
			Save time by having papers on desks before school starts
9:20–9:35 (15 min.)	(Whole class) *Objective:*	Evaluate listening ability; provide creative activity	

Week 1—Day 3 (cont.)

Time	Objectives, Materials, Motivation, Procedures, and Followup		Notes
	Materials:	Prepare sentences for children to act out	Sometimes, "props" (old hats, a mask, etc.) encourage a shy child
	Procedure:	Teacher reads sentence, child acts as directed	
9:35–9:45 (15 min.)	(Whole class) *Objective:*	Introduction of color words and color chart	Color words are useful addition to sight vocabulary
	Materials:	Chart or bulletin board display of colors and color words, two worksheets	
	Motivation:	Need to know colors and words to do much of our work	
	Procedure:	Volunteers name colors as teacher points, children "read" color words on chart, discuss how class may refer to chart in completing work	Quickly run through flash cards of color words if some indicate recognition
	Followup:	Worksheet 1 to those who seem to recognize color words; worksheet 2 to those not recognizing words	Worksheet 1 = several colors; worksheet 2 = red, blue
9:45–10:05 (20 min.)	(Group A)	Color worksheets and choose activity center	
	(Group B) *Objective:*	Work on sentences and words on chart story	
	Materials:	Chart story, pointer, sentence strips, copies of story	
	Motivation:	Question specific details of story as aid to recall	

Week 1—Day 3 (cont.)

Time	Objectives, Materials, Motivation, Procedures, and Followup		Notes
	Procedure:	Read story as group, teacher reads sentence strips, and children locate and read same sentence in story. Cut strips into words and help children match and read the words.	Teacher is offering opportunity to read, but is not making demands on child; if plans prove too challenging, rescue lesson by checking phoneme-grapheme relationships, letter names, etc.
	Followup:	Provide individual copies of story, instruct class to read story silently, underline known words, illustrate story (leave space for picture when typing story)	
10:05–10:25 (20 min.)	(Group B)	Followup assignment and color worksheet	
	(Group A)	Same plan as Group B above, except followup	Be prepared to use the time to the best purposes. Teacher is evaluating the child's ability to deal with the various components of reading, so alter activities that are not reaching that goal
	Followup:	Provide individual copies of story; children read silently and underline known words. Can illustrate during free time later same day.	
10:25–10:30 (5 min.)	Check Group A's work quickly, just to see if children have completed assignments		Teacher must be aware of children who fail to carry out their work or who complete work in an unacceptable manner

Comments

On the basis of the past three days' observations, along with readiness-test scores, the teacher may wish to form three tentative instructional groups. Differences in abilities are becoming evident by this time; however, as the days pass, it may be necessary to make adjustments.

In the hypothetical groups used in this plan, Group A is composed of children who seem ready to begin the developmental reading program and will soon move into individual dictation; Group B children vary in knowledge of phoneme-grapheme relationships, letter recognition, and other skills, so will continue the group chart story approach with more reinforcement than needed in Group A; Group C will need more readiness activities, and these will be offered in conjunction with the reading of words chosen by individual children.

Week 1—Day 4

Time	Objectives, Materials, Motivation, Procedures, and Followup		Notes
8:50–9:00 (10 min.)	*Opening:*	Date, weather, news, attendance	Ask if volunteer can name days of the week
9:00–9:10 (10 min.)	(Whole class) *Objective:*	Appreciation of poetry	
	Materials:	Copy of poem on wall chart, illustrate with picture or drawing	
	Motivation:	Elicit rhyming words, ask class to listen for rhyming words in poem	
	Procedure:	Read poem through, read again if children seem to enjoy it, ask volunteers for rhyming words	Main purpose is pleasure, so do not overemphasize the rhyming unless class seems to enjoy the activity
9:10–9:25 (15 min.)	(Whole class) *Objective:*	Auditory discrimination, rhyming words	
	Materials:	Filmstrip and projector	Alternative: wall chart or game
	Procedure:	Teacher reads frame, and volunteer chooses rhyming picture to complete jingle	
	Followup:	Assign workbook page on matching pictures whose names rhyme	Be sure to name each picture prior to sending children to work

Week 1—Day 4 (cont.)

Time	Objectives, Materials, Motivation, Procedures, and Followup	Notes
9:25–9:45 (20 min.)	Group B and C followup on rhyming (workbook page)	
	Group B Modeling clay (free activity)	
	Group C Free time to work in activity center	
	(Group A, highest interest ability)	
	Objective: Begin to build word banks	
	Materials: Word banks, cards (¾" × 1½"), felt-tip pen, individual story notebooks, vocabulary books	Word banks = file boxes of any type; notebooks = folder to keep stories in; vocabulary books = alphabetized notebook
	Motivation: Each will keep own record of known words, can use these to write own stories	
	Procedure: Volunteers read from individual copies, teacher points to underlined word and notes it on card if child recognizes it, continue around table until all words are recorded, demonstrate how to alphabetize word cards	Help children place stories in notebook before returning to desks
	Followup: Children return to desks and record words in vocabulary books, file word cards, worksheet on color	
9:45–10:05 (20 min.)·	Group A Follow-up activities given in group	
	Group B Free time to work in activity center	
	(Group C)	
	Objective: Assess knowledge of letter names	Attempt to schedule lowest group second, as these students find it most difficult to find worthwhile activities if left to their
	Materials: Alphabet flash cards, letter game	
	Motivation: Tell how to play game	

Week 1—Day 4 (cont.)

Time	Objectives, Materials, Motivation, Procedures, and Followup		Notes
	Procedure:	Run through flash cards as a check; play game, giving help when needed	own direction for extended period
	Followup:	Assign worksheet on matching upper- and lower-case letters, demonstrate	Suggest children make use of wall alphabet chart
10:05–10:25 (20 min.)	Group A Activity center Group C Followup activity		
	(Group B) *Objective:*	Build sight vocabulary, assess knowledge of letter names	
	Materials:	Individual stories, alphabet flash cards	Teacher or aide has mimeographed copies of the chart story, and each child receives a copy
	Motivation:	Read story together and see if anyone can read alone (teacher gives support), children read underlined words to teacher, play identification game with alphabet cards	
10:25–10:30 (5 min.)	Use time to check a child on a skill you are questioning		Perhaps you wonder about a child who did not name any letters correctly

Comments

Think about the lessons you have taught today and decide whether or not you made good judgments about grouping. It may be a good idea to begin to make some general notes on each child, using any form you favor. It is important to watch for children who do poorly on their individual assignments and then rush to the activity centers. Taking action on these problems at an early stage will help prevent serious problems later in the year.

Week 1—Day 5

Time	Objectives, Materials, Motivation, Procedures, and Followup		Notes
8:50–9:00 (10 min.)	*Opening:*	Date, weather, attendance	Weather charts note daily changes in weather or can record weather for entire month
9:00–9:15 (15 min.)	(Whole class) *Objective:*	Increase awareness of words and build sight vocabulary	
	Materials:	Tagboard strips (3″ × 9″), pen	Items may include door, windows, globe, books, chairs, easel, etc. (note opportunity to casually mention plural nouns)
	Motivation:	Class discusses items that can be labeled	
	Procedure:	Teacher spells and prints labels and attaches to objects	
	Followup:	Children point to and "read" chosen item, may print words into vocabulary books during free time	
9:15–9:45 (30 min.)	(Whole class) *Objective:*	Introduction to IMC	IMC = instructional materials center
	Materials:	Pencil	
	Motivation:	Discuss librarian's role as a friend and helper	Teacher may choose books to read to the class
	Procedure:	Librarian reads selection to class, shows picture book and easy-reader section, demonstrates check-out procedures, care of books, and due dates	Teacher may need to aid child having difficulty finding a book; watch for behavior problems and talk to child (effective use of IMC depends on self-control)
9:45–9:55 (10 min.)	(Whole class) *Objective:*	Develop positive attitude	Teacher may tell children of a favorite author and show
	Materials:	Children's and teacher's selections	

Week 1—Day 5 (cont.)

Time	Objectives, Materials, Motivation, Procedures, and Followup		Notes
	Procedure:	Teacher shows selections, children show own selection if they so desire	where author's name is printed. Experience has shown that this sends a few children to the librarian requesting other books by same author
9:55–10:10 (15 min.)	Group A	View books, record classroom labels	Arrange for members of Group A or a second-grade child to supervise game
	Group C	Assign game to increase ability to recognize letters (form two subgroups)	
	(Group B) *Objective:*	Sight-vocabulary recording	
	Materials:	Word banks, blank cards, pen, individual stories, notebook	
	Procedure:	Reread story as review, teacher circulates and prints underlined words on card if child recognizes it, demonstrate filing of words, enter story into notebook	
	Followup:	Record words in vocabulary books, file word cards in word bank	
10:10–10:30 (20 min.)	Group A	Explain and assign page in phonics book as check on phoneme-grapheme relationship	
	Group B	Followup lesson	
	Group C	Activity center (two children listen to cassette/filmstrip or rhyming)	Teacher starts machines (has organized materials prior to beginning of school day)

Week 1—Day 5 (cont.)

Time	Objectives, Materials, Motivation, Procedures, and Followup	Notes
	(Special help)	
	Objective: Work with individual children	
	Procedure: Two children seem to be reading, so check, using informal measure, e.g., basic word list, couple levels in basal textbook, read in chosen library book, oral-reading paragraphs from test	Alternative: if a few children cannot seem to work on their own, discuss need for co-operation, may give each special responsibility, e.g., taking notes to office, etc.

Comments

After one complete week of activities, the children have demonstrated class and individual strengths and weaknesses. You may find that several children are familiar with such skills as color words, some phoneme-grapheme relationships, rhyming words, or use of paper-and-pencil-type activities. Others seem oblivious to most reading/language-related activities. The teacher will need to vary assignments and to give individual guidance to meet the variety of needs. Thus, the introductory reading program progresses along with a continuing readiness program.

It is important to note the real task at hand and to keep that task in mind while building and carrying out the lesson plans. We are trying to help children discover "how to read." Students are ready to learn in some ways, but not in others. The task of the teacher, then, is to make use of every opportunity to open the way to that discovery process.

Week 2—Day 1

Time	Objectives, Materials, Motivation, Procedures, and Followup	Notes
8:50–9:00 (10 min.)	*Opening:* Date, weather, attendance	
9:00–9:10 (10 min.)	(Whole class) Read note on board announcing guest who	Some classrooms

Week 2—Day 1 (cont.)

Time	Objectives, Materials, Motivation, Procedures, and Followup	Notes
	will arrive soon, discuss questions class may ask, rules of politeness, etc.	have a mascot (puppet or stuffed animal) who holds all notes, receives letters from children, wears hearing aid or glasses (if causing problem to individual)
9:10–9:30 (20 min.)	Teacher has arranged for high school quarterback to come in and talk to the children; teacher and guest have met to discuss format earlier in month; guest arrives in uniform	Alternative guests: policeman, plumber, nurse, cheerleader, bus driver Quarterback chosen because observer may view a primary playground in September and find it full of minicheerleaders and minifootball players
9:30–9:50 (20 min.)	Groups B and C paint picture of guest (need water colors, water cups, paper, and art smocks)	Most will include jersey number in painting!

	(Group A)		Choose one child to fill water cups (use a "long-nosed" pitcher to help prevent spilling)
	Objective:	Record group story	
	Materials:	Chart tablet, pen	
	Motivation:	Children discuss speaker	
	Procedure:	Record comments, read story to group, volunteers read story	Provide space for completed paintings
	Followup:	Paint water color picture	

Time			Notes
9:50–10:10 (20 min.)	Group A	Painting	
	Group B	Assign specific task in activity center (printing for one who needs practice, tape/worksheet on auditory discrimination, etc.)	On days when exciting things occur, it is best to plan more structured activities to do in centers

Week 2—Day 1 (cont.)

Time	Objectives, Materials, Motivation, Procedures, and Followup		Notes
	(Group C)		
	Objective:	Develop sight vocabulary	
	Materials:	Blank cards (3″ × 9″), pen, envelopes to hold sight words	
	Motivation:	Discuss guest	
	Procedure:	Each chooses word for day, teacher records word on card, child reads word and names any letter she or he can	Teacher may list two of chosen words on board if they begin with same letter, note relationship
	Followup:	Trace word with finger and print word on paper	
10:10–10:30 (20 min.)	Group A	Activity center with specific purpose	
	Group C	Play "fishing game" teacher has set up in activity center	Place plastic magnet-backed letters in pail behind a small screen, attach another magnet to a string (the fishpole); child keeps all letters named correctly.
	(Group B)		
	Objective:	Record story (same plan as given for Group A above)	

Comments

Students in group C will choose a new word each day as a means of building a personal sight vocabulary. These words can be used in readiness activities, thus lending an individual touch to the lessons. For example, a child low on recognition of letters may increase this awareness by tracing and printing the letters of new words.

Children enjoy the novelty of classroom guests. Moreover, guests are able to supply first-hand information and experiences to the children. Guests provide another opportunity for listening and oral expression, vital components of the language-arts program. In order to ensure success, the teacher must meet with the guest before the presentation and discuss appropriate content and format.

Week 2—Day 2

Time	Objectives, Materials, Motivation, Procedures, and Followup		Notes
8:50–9:00 (10 min.)	*Opening:*	Date, weather, attendance	Note weather conditions one week ago
9:00–9:15 (15 min.)	(Whole class) *Objective:*	Teach letter forms b, m, and review l, o, h	Tape plastic alphabet cards to each desk as guide
	Materials:	Paper, pencils, lines on board	Remind children to space between letters or words
	Procedure:	Each places own name on paper	Having paper on desks before school starts saves time
9:15–9:35 (20 min.)	Group A	Practice words in word bank with friend	
	Group C	Worksheet puzzle of football player: Sheet #1 = puzzle pieces to cut and color according to directions Sheet #2 = form of player	
	(Group B) *Objective:*	Reread chart story, build phoneme-grapheme relationship	
	Materials:	Individual copies of story, letter/picture cards, card holder, pencils	
	Motivation:	Volunteer summarizes story and another reads from own copy	

Week 2—Day 2 (cont.)

Time	Objectives, Materials, Motivation, Procedures, and Followup		Notes
	Procedure:	Teacher displays letters b, m, l, and corresponding picture depicting initial consonant sound, prints picture word on board; volunteers find words in story that have same beginning; teacher prints words on board under cue word	Letters depend on words found in story
	Followup:	Read story orally to friend, go to desk and underline known words, enter words into vocabulary book	May need to review use of vocabulary book
9:35–9:45 (10 min.)	Introduce two new centers—science and creative writing		
9:45–10:05 (20 min.)	Group A	Centers	
	Group B	Followup activity	
	(Group C) *Objective:*	Record sight word, review known words	
	Materials:	Pen, cards, individual envelopes	
	Motivation:	Recall football topic, discuss other fall activities; suggest that children may wish to choose to learn word concerning these activities	May be a good idea to have a fall filmstrip ready in case the discussion is not successful
	Procedure:	Review word in envelope; teacher shows label and color words and child keeps any she or he knows; choose new word and teacher records word, each reads own word and shows class	
	Followup:	Trace new word(s) and enter them into vocabulary book	

Week 2—Day 2 (cont.)

Time	Objectives, Materials, Motivation, Procedures, and Followup		Notes
10:05–10:25 (20 min.)	Group B	Centers or play	
	Group C	Followup activity	
	(Group A) *Objective:*	Build sight vocabulary	
	Materials:	Cards, pen word banks, sentence strips, copies of story, notebooks	
	Motivation:	Recall content of story, words children recognize	Many will remember the word *football* and the player's name with no trouble
	Procedure:	Volunteer reads story from own copy, teacher shows sentence strips, and child locates sentence in story and reads; children find words they know and underline; teacher notes common words and lists them on board	Common words will appear on a bulletin board soon (football, quarterback, goal post, tackle are almost certain choices)
10:25–10:40 (15 min.)	(Whole class) *Objective:*	Appreciation of prose	When reading story at snack time, it is necessary to make rules about disposal of cartons and straws
	Materials:	Book a child has brought to show	
	Procedure:	Since it is time for snacks, the children gather around teacher with milk and crackers	

Comments

Schools vary in the type of manuscript-writing program for children. Some make use of workbook-type lessons; others combine a printing-phonics program. The lessons described here relate to the total reading-language concept. Children will soon be encouraged to create individual stories on their own; thus, helping them become familiar with manuscript paper makes that task a bit simpler. The goal of teaching printing in this format is to present the skill in as natural a manner as possible.

Week 2—Day 3

Time	Objectives, Materials, Motivation, Procedures, and Followup		Notes
8:50–9:00 (10 min.)	*Opening*	Date, weather, attendance, announcements	
9:00–9:15 (15 min.)	(Whole class) *Objective:*	Three new manuscript forms (e, m, i)	It is a good idea to set a time for sharpening pencils prior to the opening exercises
	Materials:	Paper, pencils, lines on board	
	Procedure:	Demonstrate and assign printing of letters	Watch for child who continues to demonstrate problems in printing
9:15–9:25 (10 min.)	(Whole class) *Objective:*	Appreciation of poetry	
	Materials:	Print and illustrate poem on chart tablet	Although the object is not forced memoriza- tion, children like to learn a few poems to use on special days (loss of tooth, new shoes, rainy day, etc.)
	Procedure:	Read poem for enjoyment, children may give rhyming words if desired, see if any- one can say last week's poem with the teacher	
9:25–9:40 (15 min.)	Small-group skill activity; teacher has formed several small groups based on need (letter recognition, color words, auditory discrim- ination) and has prepared modes of learning. Teacher time is used to check skill or give an individual special help		Have materials and A-V aids set up with list of children's names
9:40–10:00 (20 min.)	Groups A and B illustrate individual copies of chart story, read story silently, review underlined words		
	(Group C) *Objective:*	Build sight vocabulary	To make a tachis- toscope, cut out a tag- board shape (animal, etc.), with three slits
	Materials:	Cards, pen, individual tachistoscopes	

Week 2—Day 3 (cont.)

Time	Objectives, Materials, Motivation, Procedures, and Followup		Notes
	Motivation:	Free choice of topic, so each child may chose any type of word	cut out in the center. Print sight words on a tagboard strip the same width as the slits. Insert the strip so that words can be exposed one at a time.
	Procedure:	Teacher records child's daily word and also adds it to list prepared for tachistoscopes; teacher guides children in forming phrases on table with own cards, e.g., a blue football	
			Function words can be the teacher's daily word choice. Choose from word list found in this textbook.
	Followup:	Explain how to pull tab and expose words in tachistoscope window; children read through words, record new word in vocabulary book, choose partner to play the phonics games teacher has arranged in library center	
10:00–10:20 (20 min.)	Group C	Follow-up activities	
	Group B	Worksheet: Football helmets, with space to print favorite words from story	
	(Group A) *Objective:*	Record slight vocabulary and work on plural formation, intonation	
	Materials:	Cards, stories, pen, word banks	
	Procedure:	Volunteers read story while others listen; children tell who they like to listen to (focus on intonation); teacher records all words recognized; children dump all words on table and inductively arrive at plural formation	Teacher can list words on board or just line words up on the table

Week 2—Day 3 (cont.)

Time	Objectives, Materials, Motivation, Procedures, and Followup	Notes
	Followup: Enter all words into word bank	
10:20–10:30 (20 min.)	Group B brings worksheet to reading table, and each student reads favorite words. Popular words are listed by teacher on bulletin board	

Comments

Children are involved in building sight vocabularies that will increasingly be used to teach word-recognition skills. Although not much group time is spent on specific and sequential drill, the children are certainly making some good observations about the unlocking of words. They are watching the teacher use letters to print words, filing words with the same beginning letter (and usually the same sound) behind the common file card, playing many letter-sound-rhyming-type games in the learning centers, and are engaged in specific activities as the need presents itself in the work on the chart story.

The teacher is reminded to make short notes about each child as situations occur. This makes it easier to form the little "reinforcement" groups as described in today's lesson (9:25–9:40).

Week 2—Day 4

Time	Objectives, Materials, Motivation, Procedures, Followup	Notes
8:50–9:00 (10 min.)	*Opening:* Date, weather, attendence	
9:00–9:20 (20 min.)	(Whole class) *Objective:* Expression through pantomime	
	Motivation: Teacher presents various characters and children guess	
	Procedure: Assign groups of two to three children to chose characters to present later in day	May practice during free time

Week 2—Day 4 (cont.)

Time	Objectives, Materials, Motivation, Procedures, Followup	Notes
9:20–9:40 (20 min.)	**Group B** Worksheet on phoneme-grapheme relationship	
	Group C Cassette and corresponding worksheet on following directions	
	(Group A)	
	Objective: Recording of experience story	
	Materials: Caterpillars, tablet, pen, art supplies	Science corner equipped with books, filmstrips, pictures, chart depicting life cycle
	Motivation: (Have viewed life cycle of butterfly on film in science recently), let caterpillars move around while children recall film	
	Procedure: Record contributions on chart, reread as group, then individuals read; have child locate sentence giving specific information	
	Followup: Children use water-crayons to make caterpillars and butterflies to display in room	
9:40–10:00 (20 min.)	**Group A** Water-crayon picture	
	Group B Centers, work on pantomime	
	(Group C)	
	Objective: Sight vocabulary, phoneme-grapheme relationship	
	Materials: Blank sentence strips, pen, strip holder, word banks	As children collect several words, discard envelopes and begin to use word banks
	Procedure: Teacher prints any word child wants to learn; dump	Many will choose words from Group A's

Week 2—Day 4 (cont.)

Time	Objectives, Materials, Motivation, Procedures, Followup		Notes
		all words on table; teacher places consonant letter on board, children identify it and show any word they have that begins with that letter, note same sound; teacher helps each child arrange word cards in phrase or sentence form, if child can read it teacher prints line on sentence strip for child to keep	story! (butterfly, chrysalis, etc.) Can arrange words on desk as "seat-work" assignment and even copy these on paper
	Followup:	File cards in word bank, work on pantomime	
10:00–10:15 (15 min.)	Group A	Pantomime assignment	
	Group C	Follow-up activities	
	Group B Record on word cards all recognized words from football story		
10:15–10:30 (15 min.)	Begin to allow children to present pantomime, teacher encourages and praises children's effort, children guess characters		

Week 2—Day 5

Time	Objectives, Materials, Motivation, Procedures, Followup		Notes
8:50–9:00 (10 min.)	*Opening:*	Date, weather, attendance	Show copy of newspaper and forecast section, encourage those interested to look at this at home
9:00–9:15 (15 min.)	(Whole class) *Objective:*	Introduce two new letter forms—(t. a); review others	Children have been using most of the letters in their work: however, you are calling attention to an ac-
	Materials:	Paper, pencils, lines on board	

Week 2—Day 5 (cont.)

Time	Objectives, Materials, Motivation, Procedures, Followup		Notes
	Procedure:	Demonstrate and supervise lesson, use words to review known forms, e.g., *bat*	ceptable manner of printing these letters Praise neat work and the children will strive for good papers
9:15–9:45 (30 min.)	(Whole class, in IMC) *Objective:*	Appreciation of literature, introduction to equipment	
	Procedure:	Librarian reads or tells story; children are instructed in use of equipment (small groups aided by teacher, librarian, aids); choose and check out books	Children have used some items in the classroom and perhaps in the kindergarten
9:45–9:50 (5 min.)	Teacher reviews filmstrip viewer and recorder, shows children the set of filmstrip and cassette stories they can use		Remind children to be careful when using items and to report damage right away
9:50–10:00 (10 min.)	Group C	Worksheet to review color words	
	Group B	Workbook on phoneme-grapheme relationship	
	(Group A) *Objective:*	Oral/silent reading of story, building of sight vocabulary	
	Materials:	Individual copies of story, large caterpillar on chalk ledge (segments hold sight words)	
	Procedure:	Review main theme of story; couple read story from own copy; teacher names words that many may recognize (caterpillar, fuzzy, etc.), and children locate these on own copy; these words are recorded on caterpillar	As children learn more common words, caterpillar grows

Week 2—Day 5 (cont.)

Time	Objectives, Materials, Motivation, Procedures, Followup	Notes
	Followup: Reread story silently, underline known words and enter in vocabulary book, illustrate personal copies of story	
10:00–10:20 (20 min.)	Group A Follow-up activities	
	Group C Subgroups (two view stories with filmstrip projector/cassette, three play rhyming game, etc.)	
	(Group B) *Objective:* Record story	Using a variety of topics increases common vocabulary (Group A children will most likely watch and learn words like *zoo, zebra,* etc.; others will have learned to recognize *caterpillar* by noting Group A's work!)
	Materials: Film-loop projector, tablet, pen, zoo picture, manila paper (9″ × 11″)	
	Motivation Show film loop (two minutes), discuss film and zoo picture	
	Procedure: Record story, read to children, volunteers read	
	Followup: Give each child a piece of manila paper; child chooses specific zoo animal to draw and cut out for the zoo word chart	The zoo words, football words, caterpillar words, etc., can be placed in large notebook as a type of classroom dictionary
10:20–10:30 (10 min.)	Group A Activity center or look at new books	
	Group B Follow-up activity	
	(Group C) *Objective:* Review of sight vocabulary, matching phonics game	Following today's lesson, teacher may wish to provide each child with blank strips for tachistoscope. The
	Materials: Personal tachistoscopes, letter/picture phonics cards	

Week 2—Day 5 (cont.)

Time	Objectives, Materials, Motivation, Procedures, Followup		Notes
	Procedure:	Child reads words on tachistoscope, teacher displays letter/picture card, and children contribute personal word with same beginning sound; teacher prints words on board in line	children may take them home and share them with parents. Extra strips can be used to play letter or word games with the parents.

Comments

It is an exciting and rewarding experience to see children respond to lessons the teacher prepares and presents so carefully. The response seems to encourage greater effort on the teacher's part. However, not all children progress at the same rate; in fact, many move very slowly. Lesson plans for this latter group often lack the spark and creative vent exhibited in activities offered the "higher" groups. To avoid this common trap, it will be necessary for the teacher to extend additional efforts. Remember, these children are responding in line with their individual abilities. Helping these children to develop a positive attitude and interest in reading may be one of your greatest challenges. Meeting challenges requires well-developed plans.

Week 3—Day 1

Time	Objectives, Materials, Motivation, Procedures, and Followup		Notes
8:50–9:00 (10 min.)	*Opening:*	Date, weather, attendance	Note week-end dates and weather conditions
9:00–9:15 (15 min.)	(Whole class) *Objective:*	Encourage oral expression	Tell children that on Friday, they should come prepared to share a thought or special item
	Procedure:	Volunteers share any topics with class; teacher limits time for each individual	
9:15–9:35 (20 min.)	Group A	Phonics book: individualized assignments according to need	Child who has shown knowledge of beginning sounds and

Week 3—Day 1 (cont.)

Time	Objectives, Materials, Motivation, Procedures, and Followup		Notes
	Group C	Subgroups (one works with tape and rhyming words, other has filmstrip/tape on beginning sounds)	rhyming can try page on ending sounds
	(Group B) *Objective:*	Review chart story	
	Materials:	Chart story, sentence strips, individual copies of story	
	Motivation:	Teacher makes comments about story; children tell if comments are true or false	
	Procedure:	Teacher reads story, individuals read sentences shown on strips (find identical sentence on own copy), teacher cuts strips into phrases and repeats procedure	
	Followup:	Read story silently at desk, illustrate in space left at top of page, add desired words to vocabulary book	
9:35–9:55 (20 min.)	Group B	Follow-up activities	
	Group C	Special art project aimed at following specific directions and increasing small motor ability	Teacher will learn much from this assignment: child may not be able to recall directing, may have no idea how to use supplies such as glue, etc.

Group A
Teacher has taped fairytale chosen by children on Friday (is on file in IMC now); as group, children will present puppet show based on that taped story, discuss materials available for puppets and scenery or stage

Week 3—Day 1 (cont.)

Time	Objectives, Materials, Motivation, Procedures, and Followup		Notes
9:55–10:15 (20 min.)	Group A	IMC to listen to tape of fairytale	Teacher has made necessary arrangements with librarian
	Group B (Group C)	Activity centers	
	Objective:	Increasing and reviewing sight vocabulary, building personal sentences	
	Materials:	Word banks, sentence strips	
	Motivation:	Children may keep any sentence strips they can read and can take them home to show parents	
	Procedure:	Children select word to learn, teacher records word, each dumps words on table and tries to form sentences (teacher aids), teacher records on sentence strip any sentence child can read	Children have function words teacher has chosen as soon as they can recognize them
	Followup:	Teacher has prepared worksheet for each child, with words child is to illustrate: a red pencil, the black and white zebra, etc., according to personal sight vocabulary	
10:15–10:30 (15 min.)	Group B	Give each child a picture dictionary with marker in section showing zoo animals; child chooses favorite animal and prints sentence about animal (child uses vocabulary book as spelling aid if necessary and may sit at creative writing table if desired)	Teacher accepts any "sentences" produced and gives encouragement when these are turned in
	Group C	Follow-up activity	

Week 3—Day 1 (cont.)

Time	Objectives, Materials, Motivation, Procedures, and Followup	Notes
	Group A Have returned from IMC, class choses one member to be head of puppet show, decide on needed characters and list on board; chairperson and teacher distribute materials needed for puppets and stage scenery according to group decisions on needed items	Children may use any free time to work on their project

Comments

This is the first group project the children are engaged in that requires them to make many decisions without the teacher. Choosing an able child as chairperson makes a big difference in the success of the project. The puppet show encourages the children to work together toward a definite goal, to compromise in decision making, to realize the steps involved in developing the project, and to practice in order to present a worthwhile performance. Although the teacher serves as an overseer, children should be allowed to make the major decisions and to learn through their successes and mistakes.

In the near future, try to plan for similiar experiences for the other children in the classroom. For instance, next week Group C may enjoy constructing some finger puppets, which could be used in presenting a couple of favorite nursery rhymes the children have learned to recite. The puppets should be kept in a special place for further use—they provide a novel way to encourage children to practice sight words and other skills.

Week 3—Day 2

Time	Objectives, Materials, Motivation, Procedures, Followup		Notes
8:50–9:00 (10 min.)	*Opening:*	Date, weather, attendance, read announcement on board	Teacher has printed a note to class telling about puppet show—title, time, names of characters
9:00–9:15 (15 min.)	(Whole class) *Objective:*	Practice in manuscript writing	

Week 3—Day 2 (cont.)

Time	Objectives, Materials, Motivation, Procedures, Followup		Notes
	Materials:	Paper, pen, lines on board	
	Procedure:	Demonstrate and supervise printing of new and former letters	
9:15–9:25 (10 min.)	Group B	Read chart story from own copy with partner and underline known sight words	
	Group C	Worksheet on color words	
	Group A	Teacher and children review sequence of fairy tale and important lines specific characters need to include	
9:25–9:55 (20 min.)	Group A	Practices puppet show	
	Group B	Specific skill work, using materials in IMC	Teacher has arranged for specific skill work prior to beginning of school day
	(Group C) *Objective:*	Work on phoneme-grapheme relationship, build sight vocabulary	
	Materials:	Blank cards, word banks, bag of items (objects to demonstrate beginning sounds)	
	Procedure:	Children choose word and teacher records it on card; children reach into bag and remove item (pencil, bird, dime, etc.) and name it; teacher records item's name on board, children look in word bank for any words with same beginning letter and sound	If children are unable to come up with a word, teacher suggests topic (not word)

Week 3—Day 2 (cont.)

Time	Objectives, Materials, Motivation, Procedures, Followup		Notes
	Followup:	Children print new word in vocabulary book and file new word in bank	
9:55–10:10 (15 min.)	Group A gives puppet show to rest of class; following show, they may wish to show how they made puppets and what they liked and disliked about the project		
10:10–10:30 (20 min.)	Group A	Creative-writing assignment in form of letter to parents telling about the puppet show	Teacher may print format for letter on board, along with needed words (puppet, dear, Mom, Dad, etc.)
	Group C	Give each child an envelope containing five pictures; children paste these to manila paper in sequence (can find these in workbooks that have been partially used or ones teacher keeps for individual skill reinforcement)	
	(Group B) *Objective:*	Review story, build word banks	
	Materials:	Word banks, blank cards, individual stories, pen	
	Motivation:	Each child shows how he or she illustrated personal copy of story	
	Procedure:	Volunteer reads story orally; record sight words on blank cards; read names of zoo animals on chart; each child reads sentence about favorite animal (written yesterday); file new sight words	Teacher should rotate daily, so all children get turn reading to group

Week 3—Day 3

Time	Objectives, Materials, Motivation, Procedures, Followup		Notes
8:50–9:00 (10 min.)	*Opening:*	Date, weather, attendance	
9:00–9:15 (15 min.)	(Whole class) *Objective:*	Appreciation of poetry; follow procedure given earlier in plans (see Week 1— Day 4)	
9:30–9:50 (20 min.)	Group A	Find easy reader in library corner and attempt to read (child may work with partner)	Teacher must take time during day to listen to children read their selected page (use odd minutes before recesses, etc.)
	Group C	Worksheet: letters (Bb, Tt, etc.) printed across top; child finds and prints words from word bank in appropriate column	
	(Group B) *Objective:*	Review of stories; special attention given to intonation (encourage children to read stories with normal expression)	
	Materials:	Tape recorder, individual notebooks containing stories	
	Procedure:	Children choose one of the stories and practice silently; children take turns reading into tape recorder (teacher exphasizes good oral-reading expression); listen to tape	
	Followup:	Children form sentences at desk with words from word bank and print sentences on manuscript paper	
9:50–10:10 (20 min.)	Group A	Distribute picture dictionaries and locate area of inter-	

Week 3—Day 3 (cont.)

Time	Objectives, Materials, Motivation, Procedures, Followup	Notes
	est; assign children creative-writing exercise, using topic chosen	
	Group B	Follow-up activities	
	(Group C)		
	Objective:	Stimulate awareness of reading as a useful activity	
	Materials:	Prepare a chart that shows a simple cookie recipe—ingredients for cookies labeled with words, utensils	
	Motivation:	Discuss ingredients children think may be included in cookies, show need for recipe (ingredient, amount needed, etc.)	Do not be surprised if the flour is called "powder," shortening is called "paste," etc. You will learn much about the children's experiences through activities such as the one described here.
	Procedure:	Read the recipe and allow each child a turn to *find* an ingredient, "read" the label, and add the ingredient; give each a chance to stir, form, and decorate the cookies	It is a good idea to invite a parent to come in and help with the baking of the cookies. This frees the teacher to work with the next group.
			Don't forget to allow Group C to treat their classmates to cookies at milktime!
10:10–10:40 (30 min.)	Group C	Children and aide or parent bake cookies	Remember to reserve the kitchen well in advance
	Group B	Free choice in activity center (two children assigned needed skill work)	

Week 3—Day 3 (cont.)

Time	Objectives, Materials, Motivation, Procedures, Followup		Notes
	(Group A)		
	Objective:	Begin recording of individual stories	
	Materials:	Manuscript paper with space at top for picture, pen, picture of family engaged in interesting activity	Many social studies units begin with study of the family, so children may already be familiar with topic
	Motivation:	Discuss family activities children enjoy	
	Procedure:	Children are asked to think about activity they would like to discuss in their own story; while teacher records story for one child, others are illustrating story they will record; teacher records story, reads it to child, and child then reads complete story	Group A may drink milk while working on pictures
	Followup:	Child reads story silently and underlines words recognized, then enters story in notebook	

Week 3—Day 4

Time	Objectives, Materials, Motivation, Procedures, Followup		Notes
8:50–9:00 (10 min.)	*Opening:*	Date, weather, attendance	
9:00–9:20 (20 min.)	(Whole class)		
	Objective:	Appreciation of literature	Teacher may select other combinations and place them in library center for next two days
	Materials:	Record/book combination of good quality	
	Procedure:	Play record and show pictures	

Week 3—Day 4 (cont.)

Time	Objectives, Materials, Motivation, Procedures, Followup		Notes
	Followup:	Children tell favorite part of story and tell how they would like to change story	
9:20–9:40 (20 min.)	Group A	Each child reads individual story to partner, underlines additional words	
	Group C	Go to IMC and work on specific assignments teacher has arranged	
	(Group B) *Objective:*	Record group chart story	
	Materials:	Picture book used in exercise above, chart tablet, pen	
	Motivation:	Recall plot and characters contained in story; suggest that children write chart story that changes ending of story in the book; discuss	
	Procedure:	Record story as children comment; teacher and children read story together; individuals read story while others watch and listen	
	Followup:	Children design book cover on folded construction paper on which teacher has printed title of story (copies of story will be inserted) and children can take these home	
9:40–10:00 (20 min.)	Group A	Creative-writing assignment topic: family member	
	Group B	Follow-up activity	
	(Group C) *Objective:*	Begin to record individual sentences	

Week 3—Day 4 (cont.)

Time	Objectives, Materials, Motivation, Procedures, Followup	Notes
	Materials: Mount motivating picture on construction paper, with manuscript paper attached below	
	Motivation: Children show and discuss own picture	
	Procedure: Children comment on picture and teacher records one sentence; read sentence to child, child reads to teacher and group	
10:00–10:30 (30 minutes)	Meet with individual members of Group A and check retention of sight vocabulary (underlined words)	Assign a group art project to be completed at own desks
	Use remaining time to work with individual demonstrating special need	

Week 3—Day 5

Time	Objectives, Materials, Motivation, Procedures, Followup	Notes
8:50–9:00 (10 min.)	*Opening:* Date, weather, attendance	Continue to use attendance as means of oral expression or thinking experience (i.e., name the largest animal you have seen)
9:00–9:15 (15 min.)	(Whole class) *Objective:* Manuscript-writing practice	
	Materials: Paper, pencils, sentence printed on chalkboard	
	Motivation: Ask volunteer to read sentence	
	Procedure: Call attention to space left between words, small mark used for period; supervise while children print	Children often run words together and make many punctuation marks gigantic

Week 3—Day 5 (cont.)

Time	Objectives, Materials, Motivation, Procedures, Followup	Notes
9:15–9:45 (30 min.)	(Whole class, in IMC) *Objective:* Appreciation of literature, use of equipment *Procedure:* Librarian reads from anthology of children's poetry and shows pictures; teacher and librarian help children discover new items in IMC and help those who have trouble with equipment; children return old books and find new ones	
9:45–9:55 (10 min.)	Teacher and children share new books: show special picture or word that is recognized	
9:55–10:15 (20 min.)	Group A Activity centers Group C Worksheet on phonics skill (Group B) *Objective:* Work on group chart story *Materials:* Copies of story, sentence strips, strip holder *Procedure:* Children reread story, teacher displays sentence strips at random along chalk ledge, volunteers read sentences and place in correct order in strip holder, child who reads strip well can keep it	
10:15–10:30 (15 min.)	Teacher assigns members of class to specific games designed to increase reading-skill development Teacher uses time to work with small group of children on specific skill need	Members of different instructional groups are working together

Suggested Activities for the Methods Class

Activity 1

Read the lesson plan for Week 1—Day 2. Write an alternative plan, using different activities to achieve the same broad assessment objective.

Activity 2

Break into small groups to discuss Week 2—Day 5. In particular, discuss the following:

1. Are the objectives legitimate?
2. Are there better ways of attaining these objectives?
3. Do you anticipate a "classroom management problem" today?

Activity 3

In class discussion, consider Week 3—Day 2. Is the top group receiving preferential treatment? What are the all-class benefits of assigning this activity to the top group? What are the pro's and con's of doing puppet work with the bottom group first? The full class?

Activity 4

Read the lesson plan for Week 3—Day 4. Write an alternative plan, using different activities to achieve the same goal for Group C.

A FINAL COMMENT

For most parents and children, beginning first grade means "learning to read." Considerable excitement and anxiety about learning to read are very much a part of the children's first three weeks of first grade. Teachers should realize that this is a critical time in each child's life insofar as learning to read and enjoying reading are concerned. It is also a critical time in most parents' lives insofar as supporting the school program, motivating their children, and setting a good emotional climate at home for their children's school activities are concerned.

Good advice for first-grade teachers for the first three weeks of school is to be well prepared and to project a feeling of confidence. Both children and parents need to feel that the first-grade teacher has the ability to do the job. Being prepared leads to a feeling of confidence within the teacher, which in turn generates others' confidence in the teacher.

Beginning first-grade teachers should plan to spend at least several days of quiet planning before the children arrive. Schedules and activities should be thought through carefully, children's and parent's needs anticipated, and materials identified and organized. Activities for at least three days should be thoroughly prepared before the children arrive. Some changes may be called for after the children arrive, but the plan should be ready. The following are three concerns for the first three weeks of school:

1. Parents should receive some information to assure them that reading (or reading readiness) is being taught (e.g., a work sheet brought home, a note about the story that was read to the class).

2. All children should have several successful experiences related to reading (e.g., described what was in a picture, answered a question about a story, drew a picture that received praise, sat still and listened to a story).

3. All children should be kept busy with activities appropriate for their abilities and keyed to their interests. Great care should be taken to ensure that children are neither bored nor frustrated with reading during the first several weeks of school.

14 Planning
for Grade 4:
The First
Three Weeks
of School

In keeping with our concern for making this a highly practical textbook for beginning teachers, we have enlisted the aid of another practicing teacher to help us write this chapter. Mrs. Dixie Lee Spiegel * has prepared a plan showing in detail how she groups and teaches her fourth-grade students during the first three weeks of school in the block of time allotted for reading instruction. We think that you will be pleased with the specificity of her illustrative plans and her informative notations regarding very practical concerns.

Mrs. Spiegel's plans focus on the different groups of children she forms in her classroom and carefully delineate the activities each group participates in during specified time periods. The format of Mrs. Spiegel's planning is, therefore, somewhat different from that illustrated by Mrs. Dahl in Chapter 13. The two formats illustrate two alternatives for the writing of lesson plans. We believe that the only difference is one of personal preference, and we think that you will profit from seeing both approaches and will, in your own planning, use whichever suits you best.

Like Mrs. Dahl, Mrs. Spiegel has indicated clearly which activities she is directly involved with at any given time, so that you can see how she moves from group to group. She also has specified objectives, materials, and procedures for each activity.

We urge you to read Chapter 14 slowly. The greatest benefit will come from visualizing the movement and activities that are described in the plans. There is much information in the plans that needs thinking through. Like Chapter 13, Chapter 14 will take some time to digest. But we think that the time will be well spent by prospective teachers who are uncertain about "how to get started."

A PLAN FOR THE FIRST THREE WEEKS OF GRADE 4— WEEKLY OBJECTIVES

Week 1

1. Assess individuals' reading strengths and weaknesses by administering an informal reading inventory to each student
2. Provide for reading for enjoyment through the formation of recreational-reading groups
3. Promote interest in reading by introducing learning centers, reading

---

* Dixie Lee Spiegel—experienced fourth-grade teacher and at the time of this writing, a doctoral candidate at the University of Wisconsin, Madison.

games, and other materials related to reading housed within the classroom

4. Increase students' comprehension of written materials by beginning work on two skills that all students will probably need to have developed more fully: identifying the main idea and developing the ability to create mental pictures of conditions described in a passage

5. Begin assessing and improving dictionary skills.

Week 2

1. Provide for individualization in skill development by developing tentative groupings for skill instruction; confirm these by oral reading in the assigned basal readers

2. Continue developing dictionary skills

3. Develop proper intonational patterns for oral reading

4. Continue developing the ability to identify the main idea

5. Continue developing the ability to construct mental pictures and to attend to important details

6. Begin assessing and improving word-attack skills, e.g., vowel sounds

7. Promote interest in reading to gather information by introducing the better readers in the class to the concept of information-getting groups

8. Begin developing higher-level comprehension skills

9. Reevaluate initial groupings.

Week 3

1. Provide for further individualization in skill development through the formation of temporary, small, skills groups (the needs are to be assessed through formal and informal assessments and through the evaluation of students' performance on their workbook assignments)

2. Continue work on the development of higher-level comprehension skills

3. Provide opportunities for the better readers to use reading for getting information through the formation of information-getting groups.

DAILY PLANS

Week 1—Day 1

Time	Objectives, Materials, and Procedures	Notes
		All activities are done on a whole-group basis the first day.
		No informal reading inventories (IRIs) are given on the first day. This gives the students a chance to settle down and become accustomed to a new room, new classmates, and a new teacher.
9–9:10 (10 min.)	**(Activity 1)** *Objectives:* Familiarize class with reading-class format and expectations; instill enthusiasm for reading	
	Materials: None	
	Procedure: Explain the operation of the three basic reading groups: skill development, recreational, and information-getting (see Chapter 3)	
9:10–9:35 (20 min.)	**(Activity 2)** *Objectives:* Familiarize the students with classroom reading materials; instill enthusiasm for reading these materials	
	Materials: Materials that are housed in the classroom (basal series, newspapers, kits, paperback collections, workbooks, tapes, magazines, reference books)	

Week 1—Day 1 (cont.)

Time	Objectives, Materials, and Procedures		Notes
	Procedure:	Explore with the children the many different purposes for reading the materials and the many reading-related activities the class will engage in (e.g., debates, silent reading, plays, tape recordings, discussions)	
		Informally examine the materials, commenting on the use of pictures, special packaging, and formats. Provide a demonstration of how to use a particular kit, book, game, paperback library, or machine. Give students opportunities to ask questions and to make suggestions about the materials and how they might be used within the context of the three different groups each student will participate in.	
9:35–9:40 (5 min.)	(Activity 3) *Objectives:*	Familiarize the class with the record-keeping necessary for maintaining a circulating library (if the classroom has one)	A chart may be useful for this. The chart should be displayed near the check-out file until all children are familiar with procedures.
	Materials:	Check-out materials (chart)	
	Procedures:	Demonstrate the check-out procedure (if any) for classroom reading materials	
9:40–10 (20 min.)	(Activity 4) *Objectives:*	Provide a pleasurable listening experience	Don't ask factual questions. Ask higher-level questions that ask for predic-
	Materials:	Book or other reading material	

Week 1—Day 1 (cont.)

Time	Objectives, Materials, and Procedures		Notes
	Procedures:	Read to the class the first chapter of a short novel or a complete short story or interesting poem. If time permits, discuss the story with the class, stressing the students' personal reactions to the story.	tions, emotional reactions, inferences, etc.

Week 1—Day 2

Time	Objectives, Materials, and Procedures		Notes
9–9:15 (15 min.)	*Objective:*	Familiarize class with another reading kit or audio-visual aid	Be sure to choose a sample lesson that even the poorest reader can successfully complete without guidance. Demonstrate difficult materials to more capable students in small groups at a later time.
	Materials:	Whatever is being demonstrated	
	Procedure:	Demonstrate the use of the material to the whole class. Then choose two or three volunteers to exhibit their understanding of the procedure, if an audio-visual aid is used. If a kit is used, do a whole-class sample lesson.	
9:15–9:20 (5 min.)	*Objective:*	Review check-out procedures for reading materials	
	Materials:	Chart	
	Procedure:	Review procedures and appoint a temporary librarian	
9:20–9:30 (10 min.)	*Objective:*	Establish procedures to be used during recreational-reading time	
	Materials:	None	

Week 1—Day 2 (cont.)

Time	Objectives, Materials, and Procedures	Notes
	Procedure: (See Chapter 3) Discuss the purpose of recreational-reading groups. Permit small groups to find reading materials *of their choice.* Those who are waiting to choose materials may:	

    a) Work on assignments for other subjects, such as spelling, arithmetic, or social studies

    b) Draw a picture illustrating some part of the story that was read to the class on Day 1

    c) Write short descriptions of the kinds of materials they most enjoy reading and books they have enjoyed

    d) Complete a just-for-fun cloze exercise (see Chapter 9)

Time	Objectives, Materials, and Procedures	Notes
9:30–9:55 (25 min.)	*Objectives:* Assess reading strengths and weaknesses; establish rapport with students as individuals	Give IRIs today only to the more confident students
	Materials: IRIs	An IRI so early in the week may be threatening to a poor reader and give an inaccurate picture of that child's reading ability.
	Procedure: While the class is choosing reading materials and after they are engaged in recreational reading, administer IRIs. Plan on at least 5–10 minutes with each student.	Be relaxed and encouraging. Work in a quiet area. Insist that those involved in recreational reading not disturb you.

Week 1—Day 2 (cont.)

Time	Objectives, Materials, and Procedures		Notes
9:55–10 (5 min.)	*Objective:*	Establish procedures to be used at the end of recreational-reading time	Don't be discouraged if this activity doesn't go well this first time.
	Materials:	None	
	Procedure:	Begin with a discussion of something you have read recently. Then invite individual students to discuss what they have just read.	
			Whenever time permits, continue reading the story that was begun on Day 1.

Week 1—Day 3

Time	Objectives, Materials, and Procedures		Notes
9–9:10 (10 min.)	*Objectives, etc.:*	Same as Day 2, activity 1 (familiarizing students with reading materials)	
		or	
	Procedure:	Demonstrate a reading game or the use of a learning center	
9:10–9:35 (25 min.)	*Objectives, etc.:*	Same as Day 2, activity 4 (administering IRIs)	Choose some poor readers as well as superior and average today for IRIs to avoid feelings about labels. ("The teacher is testing all the good kids today, so I must be stupid.") Administer IRIs *throughout the day,* whenever time permits.
	Procedure:	Students will engage in recreational reading if not being tested.	

Week 1—Day 3 (cont.)

Time	Objectives, Materials, and Procedures		Notes
9:35–9:40 (5 min.)	*Objectives, etc.:*	Same as Day 2, activity 5 (sharing recreational reading)	
9:40–10 (20 min.)	*Objectives:*	Develop the concept of main idea; practice finding main ideas in short selections	Science and social studies materials are excellent for discussing main ideas. In addition, many reading kits are made up of cards with short selections that are good for this activity. Be sure to choose selections that do have main ideas. Also, be sure to use selections that all students can read.
	Materials:	Several short paragraphs, all with main ideas. Some of the paragraphs should have the main idea stated at the beginning; some at the end; one or two should have the main idea only implied. Either use overhead transparencies or give each student a copy of each paragraph.	
	Procedure:	As a group, discuss the concept of a main idea. Give practice with a few oral examples. Then have the first paragraph read aloud. Ask for identification of the main idea and have that sentence underlined. Follow this procedure with all of the paragraphs, beginning with those in which the main idea is stated at the beginning of the paragraph. Then move to those paragraphs in which the main idea is stated last. Point out that main ideas are sometimes (but not always) given in the first or last sentence. Then discuss the concept of the *implied* main idea and work on the paragraph(s) that follow this format.	

Week 1—Day 4

Time	Objectives, Materials, and Procedures		Notes
9–9:15 (15 min.)	*Objective:*	Review and practice finding the main idea	Telling them the exact number of paragraphs with implied main ideas will give the students confidence and may keep them from just underlining any sentence in those paragraphs.
	Materials:	Five or six short paragraphs, as described in Day 3, activity 4. Each child should have a copy of each paragraph.	
	Procedure:	Instruct children to underline the main idea *if* the paragraph has one. Warn them that one paragraph will have only an implied main idea. The students should write that implied main idea after the paragraph. After all children are finished, discuss why certain answers are correct.	
9:15–9:25 (10 min.)	*Objective:*	Assess dictionary skills	
	Materials:	Worksheet which assesses abilities to: (1) use guide words, (2) alphabetize, (3) choose the correct meaning when a word has multiple meanings, and (4) recognize and use dictionary respellings	
	Procedure:	Administer the test, stressing that this is just a way of finding out which skills will need to be taught. Do not discuss the skills, except to give students the information they will need to complete the worksheet.	
9:25–9:50 (25 min.)	Recreational reading and administration of IRIs		From this point forward in this illustrative plan, an activity

Week 1—Day 4 (cont.)

Time	Objectives, Materials, and Procedures	Notes
		which has already been fully described as to objectives and procedures will just be identified by a phrase that names the activity.
9:50–10 (10 min.)	Reading to the class	

Week 1—Day 5

Time	Objectives, Materials, and Procedures		Notes
9–9:30 (30 min.)	*Objective:*	Develop the ability to hear important details and therefore create a clear mental picture	
	Materials:	A descriptive passage—either teacher-written or from a trade book—paper, and crayons	(Introductory paragraphs in literature often use much description in order to set a mood and place the action in the reader's mind)
	Procedure:	Discuss what kinds of details one would want to remember in order to get a clear mental picture of what an author has written (e.g., what time of day or year it was, what the weather was like, where the story took place, what the people looked like, what kinds of clothing the people wore). Then read the passage, instructing the children to take notes about important details. Then, each child may draw a mental picture of what was described.	

Week 1—Day 5 (cont.)

Time	Objectives, Materials, and Procedures		Notes
		After completion, compare the drawings and discuss different interpretations.	
		And at the same time	
		Administer IRIs.	
9:30–9:40 (10 min.)	*Objectives:*	Develop dictionary skills; recreational reading	Continue sharing recreational reading as often as possible.
	Materials:	Examples needed to illustrate the skills being discussed; dictionaries	
9:40–10:00 (20 min.)	*Procedure:*	Meet with three small groups that have been identified according to the dictionary skills needed. Some groups may work on more than one skill. Discuss and practice these skills as a group, using dictionaries when appropriate. While one small group is meeting, the rest of the class should be engaged in recreational reading or completion of their pictures.	

Week 2—Day 1

Time	Objectives, Materials, and Procedures		Notes
9–9:20 (20 min.)	*Objectives:*	Review and practice dictionary skills; recreational reading	
	Materials:	Examples needed to illustrate each skill; dictionaries; worksheets for independent practice	

Week 2—Day 1 (cont.)

Time	Objectives, Materials, and Procedures		Notes
	Procedure:	Give each group five minutes of review; then have each child do a worksheet reinforcing the skill(s) taught. Those who are waiting for instruction or who have finished their assignment are to do recreational reading.	
9:20–9:35 (15 min.)	Objective:	Develop proper intonational patterns for oral reading	Be sure the passage is easy, so that the students can devote their attention to intonation and not just to decoding words.
	Materials:	One copy for each student of a short passage appropriate for oral reading (e.g., a section of an easy play, a page from a familiar basal reader, a short descriptive passage, or a dialogue)	
	Procedure:	Discuss the importance of reading in phrase units and with proper expression. Point out the importance of punctuation clues. Practice as a group and as individuals reading the selected passage aloud, *following the teacher's model.*	
9:35–9:50 (15 min.)	Objectives, etc.:	Same as Week 1—Day 4, activity 1 (reviewing and practicing identifying the main idea)	
9:50–10 (10 min.)	Objective:	Practice reacting to important details and developing a mental picture	
	Materials:	Several teacher-written passages about animals, with general information given	

Week 2—Day 1 (cont.)

Time	Objectives, Materials, and Procedures	Notes
	first and more specific information given last; a list of animals on the board for each paragraph.	

a) *Example:* List A (on the board): giraffe, lion, zebra, cow, snake, cheetah, bear, horse, rhinoceros, tiger, dog, leopard, whale, sheep, elephant

   1) Paragraph A: (1) This animal has four legs. (2) It is not usually found on a farm. (3) It is a member of the cat family, and (4) its fur is spotted. (5) It can run as fast as 70 mph.

Time	Objectives, Materials, and Procedures	Notes
Sometime during the rest of the day	Finish administering IRIs	Develop three tentative ability groups for skills instruction. Select basal materials for each group, based on the reading level and skill strengths and weaknesses of the members of the group.

Week 2—Day 2

Time	Objectives, Materials, and Procedures	Notes
9–9:20 9:20–9:40 9:40–10 (20 min. each)	*Objectives:* Introduce each reading group to basal reader; affirm your judgment of each child's group placement	By this time the class should have been divided into three groups: superior readers, average readers, and poor readers. In an actual classroom, of course, these labels may not be ap-
	Materials: Basal readers, manual	
	Procedure: Meet with each group for 20 minutes. Follow the manual suggestions for introducing the story, background con-	

Week 2—Day 2 (cont.)

Time	Objectives, Materials, and Procedures		Notes

cepts, and vocabulary. Then have the story read *aloud,* in order to judge each child's ability to handle the text. Be sure to discuss the story with the group as the story is read and after it has been completed. The manual will give suggestions for questions, but do not limit discussion to just these questions.

(Those students not meeting with the teacher will work on activities 2–4 described below.)

plicable to a specific group. For the sake of simplicity, *within the lesson plans,* the following labels will be attached to the groups: Group A—superior readers; Group B—average readers; and Group C—poor readers. Within the classroom, it is usually easier just to call groups by the names of their basal texts (e.g., the *More Fun with Words* group) rather than to give them "cute" names, as "Packers," or "Pythons."

Time	Objectives, Materials, and Procedures		Notes
(10 min.)	*Objective:*	Practice dictionary skills	If workbooks are to be used, it would be best *not* to use them until you are convinced that each child has been placed in the right group.
	Materials:	Three sets of worksheets for independent practice	
	Procedure:	Each child will do one or more worksheets reinforcing the skill(s) he or she has been reviewing.	
(15 min.)	*Objective:*	Practice reading a passage with proper intonation	
	Materials:	One copy for each student of an easy passage suitable for oral reading (see suggestions for Week 2—Day 1, activity 2)	
	Procedure:	Pair students, trying to place a poor reader with a better reader. Ask the students to	

Week 2—Day 2 (cont.)

Time	Objectives, Materials, and Procedures	Notes
	practice reading the selection to each other with proper intonation	
(15 min.)	Recreational reading	After meeting with each basal-skills-development group, make any adjustments in grouping needed, based on information obtained during these meetings. If a student seems to be struggling with the reading in Group B, for example, it might be wise to move that student to Group C, where he or she will be more likely to meet with success. Conversely, if a student seems to be more advanced than the rest of the group, moving the student to the next higher group might present a needed challenge, prevent boredom, and enhance the student's self-esteem.

Week 2—Day 3

Time	Objectives, Materials, and Procedures		Notes
9–9:10 (10 min.)	(Group A) *Objectives:*	Have the students become familiar with the background and vocabulary necessary for understanding the	When a group is meeting with the teacher, that time span has been put within a

Week 2—Day 3 (cont.)

Time	Objectives, Materials, and Procedures		Notes
		story; have the students become interested in the story in order to promote careful reading; introduce the pattern of much independent work to these superior students	box in the plans. This will help in preventing the scheduling of two teacher-directed activities at the same time.
	Materials:	Basals, workbooks, manual	
	Procedure:	Follow manual's suggestions for introducing story and motivating students; assign silent reading of the story; assign skill work from workbooks	
9:10–9:40 (30 min.)	Assign independent silent reading of basal-reader story and work on skills in workbooks		Until you have "your feet on the ground," it is inevitable that you will make assign-ments that are not necessary for certain students as individ-uals. That is, because you are not familiar with the children and their individual strengths and weak-nesses, you will occa-sionally assign work to a *group* which *in-dividuals* within that group do not need to do. You can get around this to some extent if you tell these students that if they complete the first half of the worksheet per-fectly, they don't have to do the second half. Assign a capable stu-dent to do the check-
9:40–9:55 (15 min.)	Recreational reading		
9:55–10 (5 min.)	*Objective:*	Practice oral reading with proper intonation and fluency	
	Materials:	Worksheet from Week 2—Day 2, activity 3	
	Procedure:	Meeting with the *whole class,* have the students read the passage orally, modeling the teacher's oral reading. Practice until a reasonably good performance is attained by the group.	

Week 2—Day 3 (cont.)

Time	Objectives, Materials, and Procedures	Notes

ing as each student finishes the first half of a page. (Not every assignment lends itself to such division, of course.)

9–9:10
(10 min.)

(Group C)

Objective: Assess vowel knowledge (Part I)

Materials: Worksheet (described below)

Procedure: Students are to work independently on a worksheet on which they are to mark the real word which has the same vowel sound as a given nonsense word. The following format should be used:

Directions: In each line below, draw a line under the real word that has the same vowel sound as the "made-up" word that is given first. Look at this example:

fash	cake	hat	car

If the made-up word "fash" has the same vowel sound as "cake," you should draw a line under "cake"; if it has the same vowel sound as "hat," you should draw a line under "hat," and so on.

1. chay	cake	hat	car
2. naim	hat	cake	car
3. parp	car	cake	hat
4. maje	hat	car	cake
5. shap	cake	car	hat
6. weach	see	bed	her
7. berk	bed	her	see
8. cleej	her	bed	see
9. pes	see	bed	her
10. de	her	see	bed

To avoid student fatigue or boredom, test only the vowel sounds of *a* and *e* at this time. Note that only major vowel combinations are tested. Less common combinations can be tested later.

The use of nonsense words to test mastery of phonics skills is encouraged because if real words are used, one can never really tell if the child used the *rules* he or she has learned or if the child is familiar with the real word (i.e., it is in the child's sight-word vocabulary).

Week 2—Day 3 (cont.)

Time	Objectives, Materials, and Procedures	Notes

9:10–9:30 (20 min.)

Objectives: Have the students become familiar with the background and vocabulary necessary for understanding the story; have the students become interested in the story in order to promote careful reading; provide for directed silent reading of the story; provide for skill development

Materials: Basal texts, workbooks, manual

Procedure: Follow the manual's suggestions for introducing the story background and vocabulary, for motivating the students through prereading exercises, and for directing silent reading. Assign skills work from the workbook.

Notes: Because poor readers often need much guidance in silent reading, it would be wise to direct their silent reading for at least the first several days. For example, ask them to read to find specific information or to be able to discuss certain ideas when they are finished reading. Break the reading assignment into several parts, each preceded by such prereading activities.

9:30–9:45 (15 min.) Independent work on skills in workbook.

9:45–9:55 (10 min.) Recreational reading

9:55–10 (5 min.) See whole-class activity under Group A, activity 4.

9–9:10 (10 min.) (Group B)

Objective: Assess vowel knowledge

Materials: Worksheet (described below)

Procedure: The worksheet should follow the format described in Week 2—Day 3, Group C, activity 1. Knowledge of the following vowel clusters might be tested: *oil, cause, out, good, moon.*

Notes: The vowel sounds tested for Group B are "harder" than the ones assessed for Group C.

| 1. joip | cow boy put |
| 2. laum | cake hat saw |

Week 2—Day 3 (cont.)

Time	Objectives, Materials, and Procedures	Notes

	3. touk boy cow go	
	4. moob go top put	
	5. woog do go top	
9:10:–9:30 (20 min.)	Recreational reading	
9:30–9:50 (20 min.)	*Objectives:* Have the students become familiar with the background and vocabulary necessary for understanding the story; have the students become interested in the story in order to promote careful reading; provide for directed silent reading of the story; provide for skill development	Directed silent reading which divides the selection into sections for the average group should be discontinued as soon as you feel the students no longer need this aid on a regular basis. Do continue to give prereading guides and set purposes for all groups.
	Materials: Basal texts, workbooks, manual	
	Procedure: Follow manual's suggestions for introducing the story, motivating the students, and directing silent reading. Assign skill work from the workbook.	
9:50–9:55 (5 min.)	Begin independent work on skills in workbook.	
9:55–10 (5 min.)	See whole-class activity under Group A, activity 4.	

Week 2—Day 4

Time	Objectives, Materials, and Procedures	Notes
9–9:15 (15 min.)	(Group B) *Objectives:* Develop literal and inferential comprehension of the story; enhance enjoyment of	Some teachers feel that it is best to meet with the poorest read-

Week 2—Day 4 (cont.)

Time	Objectives, Materials, and Procedures		Notes
		the story; provide for further skill development (through assignments in the workbook)	ers second rather than first or last, thus not challenging their attention span for independent work too much.
	Materials:	Basal texts, workbooks, and manual	
	Procedure:	Follow the manual suggestions; be sure to ask more than just factual questions	
9:15–9:40 (25 min.)		Independent work on skills in workbook (including completing assignment given on Week 2—Day 3).	Most workbooks have more than just one page of skill work allotted to each story in the text. Plan your pacing of these assignments carefully. Remember, as you become more familiar with the children, you will not want to assign *every* page to *every* child.
9:40–9:50 (10 min.)	*Objective:*	Assess dictionary skills studied on Week 1—Day 5 through Week 2—Day 2.	
	Materials:	Four sets of independent worksheets (one for each skill)	
	Procedure:	Each student is to complete a worksheet for each dictionary skill studied, as a final test of mastery of these skills. This work is to be done independently by each student.	
9:50–10 (10 min.)		Recreational reading	
9–9:15 (15 min.)	(Group C) *Objective:*	Assess vowel knowledge	
	(Part II) *Materials:*	Worksheet (described below)	
	Procedure:	Worksheet should follow the format described in Week 2—Day 3, Group C, activity 1. Use the following nonsense words and key words.	

Week 2—Day 4 (cont.)

Time	Objectives, Materials, and Procedures	Notes

1. pite	time	pig	bird
2. rist	pig	bird	time
3. cly	bird	time	pig
4. mie	pig	time	bird
5. tirm	time	bird	pig
6. coab	go	or	top
7. crob	or	go	top
8. borm	top	go	or
9. loje	go	top	or
10. lo	or	go	top
11. mupe	rule	duck	turn
12. burm	duck	turn	rule
13. cum	turn	duck	rule

9:15–9:35
(20 min.)   *Objectives:*   Develop literal and inferential comprehension of the story; enhance enjoyment of the story; provide for further skill development (through assignments in the workbook)

Materials: Basal texts, workbooks, and manual

Procedure: Follow manual suggestions. Be sure to ask more than just factual questions. If the manual does not suggest inferential or evaluative questions for the story, prepare such questions before meeting with the class. In addition, be ready to make use of the students' own questions in relation to the story.

9:35–9:50
(15 min.)   Independent work on skills in workbooks.

9:50–10
(10 min.)   See Group B, activity 3

Week 2—Day 4 (cont.)

Time	Objectives, Materials, and Procedures	Notes
9–9:10 (10 min.)	**(Group A)** See Group B, activity 3	
9:10–9:35 (25 min.)	Recreational reading	
9:35–9:50 (15 min.)	*Objectives:* Develop literal and inferential comprehension of the story; enhance the enjoyment of the story; provide for further skill development (through assignments in the workbook) *Materials:* Basal texts, workbooks, and manual Procedure Follow manual suggestions. Be sure to ask more than just factual suggestions. (See suggestions under Group C, activity 2, Week 2—Day 4)	
9:50–10 (10 min.)	*Objectives:* Introduce concept of information-getting groups; informally demonstrate the utility of the newspaper for getting information (see discussion of this technique in Chapter 3). *Materials:* Newspaper *Procedure:* Discuss information-getting groups, as described in Chapter 3. Discuss a newspaper article you have read, and invite the students to comment about interesting information that they have found in the newspaper. Ask each student to bring an interesting newspaper article to class the next day.	

Week 2—Day 5

Time	Objectives, Materials, and Procedures	Notes
9–9:15 (15 min.)	(Group A) *Objectives:* Identify common interests of students through newspaper articles brought to class; develop concept of the newspaper as a source of information	
	Materials: Newspaper articles brought by the students	
	Procedure: Each student is to present an article and tell what interesting information she or he received from it. Other students should be encouraged to add comments.	
9:15–9:40 (25 min.)	Independent work on skills in workbook (assigned on Week 2—Day 4)	
9:40–10 (20 min.)	Recreational reading	
9–9:15 (15 min.)	(Group C) Recreational reading	
9:15–9:35 (20 min.)	*Objectives:* Have the students become familiar with the background and vocabulary necessary for understanding the story; have the students become interested in the story in order to promote careful reading; provide for directed silent reading of the story; provide for skill development	
	Materials and Procedure: See Week 2—Day 3, Group C, activity 2	
9:35–9:50 (15 min.)	Independent work on skills in workbooks	

Week 2—Day 5 (cont.)

Time	Objectives, Materials, and Procedures		Notes
9:50–10 (10 min.)	Small-group skills work with teacher for students who need work on specific vowel sounds, as assessed on Days 3 and 4 of Week 2		
	or		
	Recreational reading		
9–9:20 (20 min.)	(Group B)		
	Objective:	Develop higher-level comprehension skills	
	Materials:	Worksheet with inferential and evaluative questions based on story read in basal reader	
	Procedure:	Students are to answer these questions. Be sure to stress that many of these questions do not have a "right" answer, but answers should be defensible.	
9:20–9:35 (15 min.)	Recreational reading		
9:35–9:50 (15 min.)	*Objectives:*	Have the students become familiar with the background and vocabulary necessary for understanding the story; have the students become interested in the story in order to promote careful reading of the story; provide for skill development	
	Materials and Procedures:	See Week 2—Day 3, Group B, activity 3	
9:50–10 (10 min.)	Silent reading from basal texts		

Week 3—Day 1

Time	Objectives, Materials, and Procedures	Notes
9–9:10 (10 min.)	(Group B) Small-group skills work based on needs assessed through performance on workbook exercises or vowel assessment (assessed on Week 2—Day 4) *or* Independent work in workbooks (assigned on Week 2—Day 5)	
9:10–9:20 (10 min.)	Independent work in workbooks (assigned on Week 2—Day 5) *or* Recreational reading	
9:20–9:35 (15 min.)	*Objectives:* Develop literal and inferential comprehension of the story; enhance enjoyment of the story; provide for further skill development (through assignments in the workbook) *Materials and Procedures:* See Week 2—Day 4, Group B, activity 3.	
9:35–10 (25 min.)	Independent skills work in workbooks	
9–9:15 (15 min.)	(Group C) Finish independent work on skills in workbooks (assigned on Week 2—Day 5); do independent follow-up exercises for small-group skills work	
9:15–9:35 (20 min.)	*Objective:* Develop higher-level comprehension skills *Materials and Procedures:* See Week 2—Day 5, Group B, activity 1.	
9:35–9:50 (15 min.)	*Objectives:* Develop literal and inferential comprehension of the	

Week 3—Day 1 (cont.)

Time	Objectives, Materials, and Procedures		Notes
		story; enhance enjoyment of the story; provide for further skill development (through assignments in the workbook)	
	Materials and Procedures:	See Week 2—Day 4, Group B, activity 3.	
9:50–10 (10 min.)	Independent work on skills in workbook		
9–9:10; 9:10–9:20 (20 min.)	(Group A) *Objectives:*	Identify common interest of students; form information-getting groups	
	Materials:	Newspaper articles brought by the students	
	Procedure:	Students should continue discussing articles without teacher guidance. After ten minutes, the teacher should join the group, ask the students to suggest possible topics for interest groups, and list these on the board. Have the students choose which topics they would like to gather information about, and divide the class into small interest groups (as described in Chapter 3).	
9:20–9:50 (30 min.)	Recreational reading		
9:50–10 (10 min.)	*Objectives:*	Have the students become familiar with the background and vocabulary necessary for understanding the story; have the students become interested in the story in order to promote	

Week 3—Day 1 (cont.)

Time	Objectives, Materials, and Procedures	Notes
	careful reading of the story; provide for skill development	
	Materials and Procedures: See Week 2—Day 3, Group A, activity 1.	

Week 3—Day 2

Time	Objectives, Materials, and Procedures	Notes
9–9:10 (10 min.)	(Group C) Small-group skills work based on needs assessed through evaluation of performance with workbook exercises	
	or	
	Independent work on skills in workbooks (assigned on Week 3—Day 1)	
9:10–9:20 (10 min.)	Same as activity 1 above, but with a different skills group	
9:20–9:30 (10 min.)	*Objective:* Develop higher-level comprehension skills	
	Materials: Worksheets with inferential and evaluative questions based on story read in basal reader. This assignment was to have been completed on Week 3—Day 1.	
	Procedure: Students present and explain reasons for answers.	
9:30–9:40 (10 min.)	Follow-up work on small-group skills	
9:40–9:50 (10 min.)	Recreational reading	
9:50–10 (10 min.)	*Objectives:* Have the students become familiar with the back-	

Week 3—Day 2 (cont.)

Time	Objectives, Materials, and Procedures	Notes

ground and vocabulary necessary for understanding the story; have the students become interested in the story in order to promote careful reading; provide for skill development

Materials and Procedures: See Week 2—Day 3, Group B, activity 3.

9–9:10 (10 min.) (Group B)
Follow-up work on small-group skills

or

Recreational reading

9:10–9:30 (20 min.) Recreational reading

9:30–9:40 (10 min.)

Objective: Development of higher-level comprehension skills

Materials: Worksheets with inferential and evaluative questions based on story read in the basal reader. This assignment was to have been completed on Week 2—Day 5.

Procedure: Students present and explain reasons for answers.

9:40–9:50 (10 min.)

Objectives: Have the students become familiar with the background and vocabulary necessary for understanding the story; have the students become interested in the story in order to promote careful reading; provide for skill development

Materials and Procedures: See Week 2—Day 3, Group B, activity 3.

Week 3—Day 2 (cont.)

Time	Objectives, Materials, and Procedures		Notes
9:50–10 (10 min.)	Silent reading of assigned story in basal text		
9–9:30 (30 min.)	(Group A) Silent reading of assigned story in basal text and skills work in workbooks		
9:30–10 (30 min.)	*Objective:*	Development of a bibliography by each information-getting group	
	Materials:	None	
	Procedure:	Students are to investigate classroom and IMC materials. Each interest group is to compile a reading list comprised of at least one selection per group member.	

Week 3—Day 3

Time	Objectives, Materials, and Procedures		Notes
9–9:15 (15 min.)	(Group A) *Objectives:*	Develop literal and inferential comprehension of the story, enhance enjoyment of the story; provide for further skill development (through assignments in the workbooks)	
	Materials and Procedures:	See Week 2—Day 4, Group A, activity 3.	
9:15–9:25 (10 min.)	*Objective:*	Development of a bibliography by each information-getting group	Individual students who are really interested in a topic will be able to read materials at a more diffi-cult level than those they usually can deal with. Do not make
	Materials:	None	
	Procedure:	Students are to continue work begun on Week 3—Day 2. Before students begin work independently, the	

Week 3—Day 3 (cont.)

Time	Objectives, Materials, and Procedures		Notes
	teacher should check these bibliographies in order to see if the materials are appropriate for the topic and for the individiual readers.		quick judgments about a book being too hard for a student; have the student read silently a portion of the book in question and then report what he or she has learned from the passage. In this way a fairly accurate judgment can be made.
9:25–9:45 (20 min.)	Independent work on skills in workbook		
9:45–10 (15 min.)	*Objectives:*	Begin work in information-getting groups	
	Materials:	Reading materials on group bibliographies	
	Procedure:	Independent reading and group discussion, as described in Chapter 3.	
9–9:10 (10 min.)	(Group C) Independent follow-up work on small-group skills (introduced on Week 3—Day 2)		
	or		
	Recreational reading		
9:10–9:25 (15 min.)	Silent reading of assigned story in basal text (introduced on Week 3—Day 2)		
9:25–9:45 (20 min.)	*Objectives:*	Develop literal and inferential comprehension of the story; enhance enjoyment of the story; provide for further skill development (through assignments in the workbook)	
	Materials and Procedure:	See Week 2—Day 4, Group A, activity 3.	

Week 3—Day 3 (cont.)

Time	Objectives, Materials, and Procedures	Notes
9:45–10 (15 min.)	Independent work on skills in workbook	
9–9:20 (20 min.)	(Group B) Independent work on skills in workbook (assigned on Week 3—Day 2)	
9:20–9:30 (10 min.)	Independent follow-up work on small-group skills (introduced on Week 3—Day 1 and developed on Week 3—Day 2) *or* Recreational reading	
9:30–9:45 (15 min.)	Recreational reading	
9:45–10 (15 min.)	*Objectives:* Develop literal and inferential comprehension of the story; enhance enjoyment of the story; provide for further skill development (through assignments in the workbook) *Materials and Procedures:* See Week 2—Day 4, Group A, activity 3.	

Week 3—Day 4

Time	Objectives, Materials, and Procedures	Notes
9–9:15 (15 min.)	(Group B) *Objectives:* Have the students become familiar with the background and vocabulary necessary for understanding the story; have the students become interested in the story in order to promote careful reading; provide for skill development *Materials and Procedures:* See Week 2—Day 3, Group B, activity 3.	

Week 3—Day 4 (cont.)

Time	Objectives, Materials, and Procedures	Notes
9:15–9:45 (30 min.)	Silent reading of assigned story in basal text and independent skills work in workbooks (assigned on Days 3 and 4 of Week 3)	
9:45–10 (15 min.)	Recreational reading	
9–9:15 (15 min.)	(Group C) Independent skills work in workbooks (assigned on Week 3—Day 3)	
9:15–9:35 (20 min.)	*Objectives:* Have the students become familiar with the background and vocabulary necessary for understanding the story; have the students become interested in the story in order to promote careful reading; provide for skill development *Materials and Procedure:* See Week 2—Day 3, Group B, activity 3.	
9:35–9:45 (10 min.)	New small-group skills work based on needs assessed through evaluation of performance with workbook exercises *or* Independent skills work in workbooks	
9:45–10 (15 min.)	Same as activity 3 above, but a different group and skill	
9–9:30 (30 min.)	(Group A) Continue reading and discussing in information-getting groups	
9:30–10 (30 min.)	Recreational reading	

Week 3—Day 5

Time	Objectives, Materials, and Procedures	Notes

9–9:10
(10 min.)

(Group B)
Small-group skills work (introduced on
Week 3—Day 4)

or

Recreational reading

9:10–9:20
(10 min.)

Same as activity 1 above, but with a different group and a different skill

9:20–9:35
(15 min.)

Objectives: Develop literal and inferential comprehension; en-
hance enjoyment of the
story; provide for further
skill development (through
assignments in the work-
book)

Materials and   See Week 2—Day 4, Group
Procedure: A, activity 3.

9:35–10
(25 min.)

Independent skills work in workbooks and
independent follow-up work for small-group
skills

9–9:10
(10 min.)

(Group C)
Independent follow-up work on small-group
skills

9:10–9:25
(15 min.)

Independent work on skills in workbooks
(assigned on Week 3—Day 4)

9:25–9:35
(10 min.)

Recreational reading

9:35–9:50
(15 min.)

Objectives: Develop literal and inferential comprehension of the
story; enhance the enjoy-
ment of the story; provide
for further skill development through assignments
in the workbook

Week 3—Day 5 (cont.)

Time	Objectives, Materials, and Procedures	Notes
	Materials and Procedure: See Week 2—Day 4, Group A, activity 3.	
9:50–10 (10 min.)	Independent work on skills in workbooks	
9–9:50 (50 min.)	(Group A) Continue reading and discussing in information-getting groups. Students should begin comparing information and organizing it for some sort of class presentation, e.g., a panel discussion, an illustrated lecture, or a model exhibit.	
9:50–10 (10 min.)	*Objective:* Development of higher-level comprehension skills	
	Materials: Worksheets assigned on Week 3—Day 4, with inferential and evaluative questions based on the story read in the basal reader.	
	Procedure: Students present and explain reasons for answers.	

Suggested Activities for the Methods Class

Activity 1

Compare the methods of lesson-plan organization presented in Chapters 13 and 14. You will note that in Chapter 13, the plans are organized by blocks of time. We can note the activities of the teacher and all the groups during any specific time period. In Chapter 14 the plans are organized by groups of children. For each group we can note the activities across different time periods. Consider these two alternative formats. Through class discussion, try to determine which method of organizing lesson plans would be most helpful to you.

Activity 2

Read the lesson plan for Week 2—Day 3. Compare the assessment procedure with the discussion of phonics generalizations presented in Chapter 7. Are they compatible? What is being tested—decoding or encoding of letter-sound correspondences?

Activity 3

Select a lesson plan for any of the 15 days. Prepare an alternative plan which will achieve the same objectives, but through different activities.

Index